An Executive's Guide
To
Econometric Forecasting

Edited by
Al Migliaro
Institute of Business Forecasting

C.L. Jain
St. John's University

 **Graceway Publishing Company, Inc.**

An Executive's Guide To
Econometric Forecasting: 2nd Edition

Manufactured in the United States of America

Library of Congress Catalog Card No. 86-082818
ISBN 0-932126-14-6   Softcover

Published by:
Graceway Publishing Company, Inc.
P.O. Box 159, Station "C"
Flushing, New York 11367
(718) 261-0759

TABLE OF CONTENTS

PREFACE

Econometric models are in many ways different from time series and judgmental models. What they can do, the other models cannot. They can provide not only forecasts but also insights to interrelationships—how price is related to the sales, how GNP is related to the sales, and so on. They allow the technician to play "what if game"—what will happen if advertising outlay is raised by "X" amount, how the introduction of a new product by the competitor will impact the company. Econometric models let you react quickly to environmental changes. If price is raised due to the increase in the price of raw material, forecast can be quickly revised by plugging the new price in the model. Turning points are most difficult to forecast. Econometric models do not guarantee good forecasts of turning points, but they generally give better results than many other models.

While econometric models can do all that, they are highly sophisticated and thus are difficult to understand. The objective of this revised edition, like the one before it, is to make the subject of econometric modeling understandable to business executives who don't have advanced degrees in economics, mathematics or statistics but need to grasp the subject matter to make decisions. With that objective in mind, the material is written practically jargon free. Every word and phrase of jargon so beloved by technicians is translated into common business English.

Reading this entire volume will not make you an expert in econometrics unless you already know how to build an econometric model. What it will do for you, it will help you to evaluate forecasts prepared by econometricians and/or give enough information to ask sensible questions. Also, if you are in the process of evaluating a forecast service bureau it can provide you the information you need to make the right choice for your company, as well as to evaluate and use their advice. The editors in their own previous experience as business managers have operated on the theory that "it takes one to know one." If you are not "one," then do the next best thing: learn everything you can about what "one" knows so that you can be a better judge of "one's" performance.

Econometric models were originally developed to prepare forecasts of macro variables such as GNP, disposable income, interest rates, inflation, etc. Now, with increasing sophistication in forecasting, they are finding their way into a company level forecasting and their use is increasing. Macro forecasts, provided by service bureaus or obtained from published sources, are used as an input to a company level forecasting model.

The use of econometric models in a company environment is growing because of the increasing awareness of what such models can do. The models are becoming larger and larger. The computer power is growing larger and getting less expensive.

Companies and forecasting service bureaus are pouring more and more money into developing larger, more complex, and more disaggregated models, which would result in greater forecasting accuracy.

Efforts are being made to mechanize forecasting models so that anyone with the same information can replicate forecasts. Although econometric models are highly sophisticated, a lot of judgment (anywhere from 20 to 30%) goes into preparing forecasts. As a result, the day will never come when an econometric model will become a "black box."

In this revised volume we added a number of new topics as well as articles to make it as complete as possible. We added topics on how to detect and deal with structural changes (shifts in the direction and the size of a trend), ways to improve regression based models, how to prepare regional forecasts, the process of simulation to determine the impact of various scenarios, and what economists are thinking about leading economic indicators. The number of articles are increased from 18 to 33.

This volume includes eleven parts, Part 1 explains what econometric models are all about. How econometric models are prepared. What you need to prepare such a model. Part II describes structural problems, and suggests ways to detect and deal with them. Part III outlines various ways to improve regression based models. In the past, we received a number of calls (mostly from Fortune 500) asking for help in evaluating econometric service bureau services. Part IV is the response to their inquiries. We interviewed three major service bureaus (Chase Econometric, DRI and Wharton Econometric) to get information about their models, underlying assumptions, the kinds of services they offer and their cost. (As this volume goes to the press, Chase Econometrics has been acquired by Wharton Econometric.) We also sought answers from Dr. Vladimir Simunek about the Kent Model. We were surprised what we learned from him.

Part V discusses what econometric models can and cannot do, and how to evaluate and use such models. Part VI discusses how simulation can be used to determine the impact of different policy scenarios, as well as how accurately an econometric model forecasts interest rates. Part VII gives a guide to select an econometric service bureau. Part VIII shows how to prepare regional forecasts. In recent years there has been a controversy on the subject whether leading economic indicators are really leading. Part IX looks into that controversy. If there are long wave cycles (40-60 years) and they can be detected and measured, the job of a forecaster to forecast the state of the economy would become somewhat easier. Part X investigates the presence of such cycles.

The effectiveness of a model, whether it is econometric or of any other kind, depends upon how it uses the information. The overuse of statistical relations among variables and underuse of information available from written and mental sources can weaken the reliability of a model. System dynamic models tend to overcome these shortcomings. Part XI explains the system dynamic model and how it can be used in national and corporate strategies.

Thanks to the contributing writers who made this volume possible. Also, thanks to Jean-Ednar Nelson, graduate assistant, who prepared the index. Mr. Al Migliaro, co-editor of this volume, who is no longer in this world, played a key role in the preparation of the first edition. In every step of the way he wanted to make sure that the material covered is not only useful but also understandable to business executives who are not well versed with statistics and/or mathematics. I tried to follow his footsteps in revising this edition. Whether or not I succeeded I leave it to the judgment of readers.

C.L. Jain
St. John's University

PART I

The Basics

Chapter 1
Basic Elements of Econometric Forecasting

Jack Malehorn
United Telephone System—Eastern Group

Econometric forecasting is not a magical function devoid of management input, but instead provides an excellent opportunity for management's insight and direction into the model building process as a way to quantify decision making processes. Forecasting should not be a part-time but a full-time activity, given the complete support of management. Ideally, econometric forecasting involves a cooperative effort between the analyst-technician and the supervisor/manager. This paper emphasizes the proper usage of econometric forecasting as a management tool and focuses on several pertinent issues for both the manager and the technician.

Role of Econometrics

Econometrics can best be defined as a combination of mathematics, statistics and economic theory. By accepting this definition, we encounter the first problem. Inherently, at almost any level of management, mathematics and statistics are generally assumed to be complex and confusing subjects, while economic theory is considered to be an equally difficult subject, full of theoretical pitfalls and questionable assumptions, seemingly without direct application. Nevertheless, the dynamic marketplace which impacts decision making can be placed into better perspective with the proper use of econometrics. Econometric modeling should be an essential component of a manager's portfolio of quantitative and analytical tools. Undoubtedly, its acceptance as a forecasting and planning tool will gain in prominence over time as decision making capabilities are realigned toward more quantitative methods, as opposed to subjective, "seat of the pants" techniques.

Econometrics is often viewed solely as a forecasting device. However, emphasis should be placed upon the use of econometrics as a management tool to describe the marketplace in which a business functions. In other words, the main thrust of econometrics should be the specification of behavioral relationships which influence a product or marketplace. Done properly, forecast accuracy will be forthcoming. As an example, suppose a demand model for widgets is hypothesized. At this point, management's insight is extremely valuable. Management expertise would help to draw inferences—as to the direction and extent of causality—regarding such factors as the price of widgets, the influence of income, age or other socio-demographic variables which could impact the demand for widgets.

Why is this property of econometrics important? One reason is that any time a forecast or a point estimate is made, it is more often wrong than not. The most likely response to this problem is that forecasts should be couched in what practitioners refer to as confidence intervals or probability statements which surround the average forecast value. But how are these probability estimates derived? The main problem is that forecasts should not be the end product. What is often overlooked are several important stages which precede the ultimate forecast. Managers interested in only the end result, i.e. forecast accuracy, and not truly committed to the actual process of forecasting, jeopardize the efficacy of the forecast process itself. That is, even though a forecast may be correct this instance, what about the next time? Or, suppose a forecast is reasonably accurate but for all the wrong reasons. In either case, the likelihood of not being surprised sometime in the future is slim.

Detailed Analysis

Econometric model building should not be construed as a cookbook approach of selecting among a host of variables to develop a forecast model. Proper modeling includes detailed analysis, an understanding of the theoretical structure of the marketplace, and practical intuition. For example, suppose that we are not sure of how price will influence the demand for our product. Through the use of econometric modeling we can first test the significance of price. Is it a meaningful variable or not, which in itself conveys an important amount of knowledge. Next, we can ascertain the price elasticity of our product. Is the demand for our product responsive to price changes or not? Again, a very important managerial inference. This simple example describes the benefits which can result through management inference in combination with econometric model building techniques. The specification of behavioral relationships and supporting market analysis provides a capsule summary of the competitive environment.

Sensitivity Analysis

Econometrics also has the capability of enhancing sensitivity analysis, better known as the "what if" game. After the historical relationships between the subject matter being investigated and the explanatory variables are specified, questions regarding, for example, the influence of an increase or decrease in price and/or advertising on product demand can be entertained. In this way, econometrics has become a viable tool for management by enabling specific questions to be addressed. Of course, these questions and the subsequent response can only be supported in their fullest by the concurrent analytical work. In other words, before, during and after the forecast process, analysis is a necessary component. Analysis provides a timely reminder of the environment which encompasses the marketplace. Analysis allows us to keep abreast of changing events within the marketplace—especially important in the 1980's—and, finally, analysis provides a learning tool so that we are able to know with some certainty what effect the marketplace is having on our particular product. Through the implementation of econometric techniques and supporting research and analysis, management ideas or recommendations can be tested and subsequent changes incorporated into the decision making process.

Basic Ingredients

Econometric forecasting is destined to play an increasing role in the evolution of formal forecasting systems. Correct or appropriate application of econometric techniques requires decisions regarding personnel, data, and software.

Personnel: In today's business environment there clearly exists a need for an individual—a business economist—with the ability to analyze market forces in an attempt to understand and keep abreast of the changing marketplace. An excellent example of the necessity of a business economist is indicated by an event which occurred early in the 1980's. At that time, the U.S. economy was hit by two successive recessions of a degree of severity not equalled since the Great Depression. At the same time, several new products

were introduced which did extremely well. These products were characterized as being high priced items aimed at the upper end of the consumer market. Why should products like these do well when economic theory would suggest otherwise? Sociologists have suggested that given the successive periods of poor economic performance by the U.S. economy, those individuals with a fairly affluent lifestyle (or with credit limits which could afford to mirror such lifestyles) wanted to separate themselves from the masses through a type of escape mechanism. Therefore, those entrepreneurs willing to take a gamble introduced products which were high priced, luxury items and, in retrospect, did extremely well. Now, it is not known in this particular example whether an analytical approach using econometric models was used or not. However, in today's economy, an uneducated gamble is certainly not worth the risk when sound econometric techniques are available. Given the ubiquitous degree of uncertainty which envelopes the domestic marketplace due to foreign competition, tax reform and debt-burdened consumers, today's business decisions require professionals with the ability to foresee and address these problems.

Data: Without a doubt, an essential component of econometric model building is data. The lack of data or poor data will distort even the best model. Three sources of data which have proven to be very worthwhile include: 1) state government, 2) Federal Reserve System, and 3) university systems.

Beyond a national-macroeconomic perspective (where major econometric firms such as Chase Econometrics, DRI, and Wharton provide ample support), the disaggregation of markets on a regional, state, or local level can be enhanced through contact with the state government. Most state governments, through their respective administrations or departments of labor, have the ability to collect data and to disseminate information concerning the state's economy. At a

minimum, this would include employment, unemployment, income and retail sales. In both Pennsylvania and New Jersey, the state government and labor department provide data and supporting insight into the condition of the state and local economies in an astute, professional manner.

The branches of the Federal Reserve System also provide both data and research materials. Their publications are an excellent example of applied economic research.

Across the country, many universities extend research capabilities and data collection to the surrounding business community. As an example, the Center for Regional Busines Analysis at Pennsylvania State University provides a detailed analysis of the commonwealth's economy and regions within Pennsylvania, and has proven to be a worthwhile resource.

Software: For a minimum investment, a complete economic forecasting system can be set up within an office. Two packages, affordable and user friendly, with which I have had experience are MicroTSP and Forecast Master. Micro-TSP is an excellent software package especially designed for econometric forecasting, although it also provides other time series techniques. Forecast Master is an excellent software package especially designed for time series forecasting. The two in combination provide an excellent statistical forecasting library. You may ask, "Why more than one software package?" From my own personal experiences, each forecasting problem is unique and therefore requires a wide array of tools in order to deal with the forecasting problem effectively. In today's environment, it is very doubtful that there exists one comprehensive software package to handle every conceivable forecasting situation.

Practical Suggestions

Clearly, econometric modeling is as much an art as a science. A few practical aspects of econometric forecasting for both the manager and technician/business economist follow:

(1) *A Clearly Defined Objective Function:* Often, the poor performance of a model is due to a poorly defined or misunderstood dependent variable. One technique to enhance the objective function is to discuss firsthand the data with those individuals in charge of data collection, e.g. a firm's accountants. In essence, the technician should understand how the data are collected, how they are processed and any unusual quirks which may be hidden from initial view of the subject at hand. If anything, undertaking this effort should enhance the technician's insight into the matter being investigated.

(2) *Choice of Independent (Explanatory) Variables:* The importance of the analyst in knowing the intricacies of the data incorporated into the modeling efforts cannot be stressed enough. A model of local economic activity faces the dual difficulty of the general paucity of data, as well as the fact that state and local data are subject to interpretation. For example, the United Telephone System—Eastern Group Service Area covers sections of Pennsylvania and New Jersey and is predominantly rural in nature. An analysis of the Pennsylvania economy suggests that by most measures of economic performance, it is performing near or at the national average. Analyzing the state data more closely, it becomes apparent that the Philadelphia area carries the state. Therefore, an upward biasness would be introduced if the state data are used to proxy other portions of the state.

(3) Data Methodologies: Employment data provide one of the best measures of state and local economic activity. However, employment data (as outlined in a recent article by David Avery from the Federal Reserve Bank of Atlanta) consist of two different measures: the household survey measure, and the establishment or payroll survey method. The differences are signficant between the two measures and the results emanating from an uninformed choice can be

TABLE 1
CHARACTERISTICS OF EMPLOYMENT DATA BASED ON DIFFERENT SURVEY MEASURES

Household/Resident Survey	Non-Farm-Establishment Payroll Survey
•Does not classify individuals according to the type of industry (by SIC codes)	•Classifies individuals according to the type of industry (by SIC codes)
• indicates employment status for those individuals 16 years of age or older.	•Indicates employment status for those individuals 16 years of age or older
•Includes virtually all types of employed, e.g. business establishments, family operated, government, non-profit, armed forces, domestic workers, self-employed, foreigners, etc.	•Does not include virtually all types of employed, e.g. business establishments, family operated, government, non-profit, armed forces, domestic workers, self-employed, foreigners, etc.
•Not estimated from a large statistical reliability sample.	•Estimated from a large statistical reliability sample.
•Does not count dual job holders.	•Counts dual job holders.
•Does not include hours and earnings data.	•Includes hours and earnings data.
•Includes other socioeconomic information such as age, marital status, sex, race.	•Does not include other socioeconomic information such as age, marital status, sex, race.

misleading. The main characteristics of each measure are shown in Table 1.

These characteristics are important in selecting which employment measure to use. For example, in New Jersey, approximately 440,000 nonfarm payroll jobs have been added since 1979. However, the vast majority of jobs have been in the service sector where dual job holding is common. Therefore, the residence employment series, if used, may not accurately reflect economic conditions in New Jersey, since it does not recognize dual job holding.

Another example of the difference between the two mesures is the treatment of agricultural employment. Most farm workers are missed using the establishment payroll technique, since the majority are not on formal payrolls. Therefore, in an agricultural based economy, the residence series may better represent local economic conditions.

(4) *Diversity Among Explanatory Variables:* "Don't put all of your eggs in one basket" is good advice for individuals involved in building econometric models. For example, suppose that you were concerned with the sale of refrigerators or other household appliances. The housing market would be expected to be strongly and positively correlated with the demand for such items. However, an econometric model based only on housing type variables creates a certain amount of inherent risk, if housing is not clearly defined for your particular product or if the demand for refrigerators is influenced by other factors beside new housing, e.g. energy efficiency. In addition, housing variables sometimes exhibit significant variability resulting in subsequent forecast error.

(5) *An Eclectic Blend:* Whether local, state, regional, or national, econometric models should exhibit a balanced blend among the independent variables. Whenever possible, an eclectic balance among the major schools of thought, e.g. Keynesian (demand based), Monetarist,

6

and Supply Side, should be employed. By selecting carefully among the independent variables, the analyst can often minimize forecast error and guard against the pro-

blem of inherent structural instability within the model●

References

Avery, David. "Two Measures of Employment: What Can They Tell Us?" **Economic Review: The Federal Reserve Bank of Atlanta.** August/September, 1986.

Chapter 2
The National Econometric Model— A Layman's Guide

A. Migliaro
Institute of Business Forecasting

Macro econometric models were originally designed to help Government policy makers devise fiscal and monetary policies that would promote stability and growth for the nation. They are supposed to tell policy makers how their decisions will affect the various sectors of the economy, and supposedly prevent action that would lead to recession or depression.

It is only in recent years that the models have been used as business forecasting tools. This development was a natural extension of the original use by policy makers: if the models can forecast the outcomes of various government policy actions, the reasoning went, then business should be able to develop strategies in keeping with those outcomes.

Central to the use of the models as policy-making tools is that they are based on economic theories on which there is no concensus among economists or the politicians they serve.

Demand Model

The controversy surrounds not only the theories upon which the models are built, but also around the methods used to derive the data. Indeed, even the simple model we propose to use in this article as an example will draw fire from some economists, because it is "demand" oriented, i.e., it says that the entire economy can be explained by "demand prices" and "demand quantities." We shall use it as an example, nevertheless, because it is a good point of departure for explaining the basics. ("Demand prices" refers to the prices *buyers,* representing the "demand side," are willing to pay; "demand quantities" refers to the quantities the demand side is willing to consume at demand prices.)

The model we shall use in this article is: GNP = C + I + G where, C = personal consumption expenditures, I = business investment, and G = Government purchases. Despite its size and simplicity, the model does describe the total economic activity of a "closed" economy, i.e., an economy without imports and exports. We could expand it to an "open" economy model by adding a net export (NE − exports minus imports) and thus: GNP = C + I + G + NE.

For the sake of simplicity, the closed economy model will be used. Such an economy consists of three major groups ("economic agents") (1) households, (2) businesses, (3) Government. Each plays a role in creating GNP, and GNP plays a role in creating the level of activity that takes place in each of the sectors; it's a simultaneous, feedback system in which everything affects everything else.

Since the model says that the value of GNP *depends on* (is a function of) the items on the right-hand side of the equation, GNP is called the "dependent" variable, and the others the "independent" variables; and since the independent variables *explain* the dependent variable, the equation is an "explanatory" model. It is also a "causal" model, because it shows the cause and effect relationships between the dependent and independent variables.

Finding the value of GNP (model solution) requires that values be assigned to or determined or computed for each of the independent variables: consumption (C), business investment (I), and Government purchases (G).

To accomplish that, it is necessary to define the functions of each of the components of the economy: household, business, and government. Defining the functions leads to the construction of equations used in the model to find the values of each of the independent variables, C, I, and G. When this is accomplished, the "structure" of the model is "specified."

Sector Functions

The household sector performs four functions: earns income ($Y), spends money ($C), pays taxes ($T), saves money ($S). We will deal with only Y and C for our purpose. The business sector performs two functions: invests money in plant, equipment, and inventories ($I) and produces goods and services ($Y). It may seem strange that the symbol $Y is used to denote both the income of households and goods and services produced by the business sector. But the economic theory (demand) under which the National Income and Product Accounts (NIPA) are set up holds that the total value of goods produced is exactly equal to total expenditures of all sectors, i.e., everything that is *demanded* is produced. Such an accounting system avoids double counting; only the expenditures by the final user of the good is counted.

The Government sector establishes fiscal policy by: spending money ($G), collecting taxes ($T). We deal only with Government spending in our model.

It is well to recognize at this point that the value of each variable represents the total of all activities that occur as part of the variable, i.e. they are "aggregates." Income, for example, includes all income sources: wages, interest, rent and profits; personal consumption expenditures (C) is the total of all expenditures by final users of all goods and services, durables and non-durables. If we wanted to we could break down each variable into its component parts ("disaggregate" the data). The result would be that we would have a much larger model containing an almost infinite number of independent variables, and an even larger number of equations—which is how most macro-econometric models in use today are built. But the basic procedures followed in building and solving the model would be essentially the same as outlined in relation to our small model.

As has already been pointed out, numerical values must be assigned to or determined or computed for each independent variable. This brings us to one of the most confusing aspects of model building: the determination of which of the variables are external (eXogenous) to the system and which are internal (eNdogenous). The confusion attending these two terms is not totally due to their similarity in spelling; the major source of confusion stems from the fact that the words take their specific meaning from the context in which they are used, and from the point of view of the model builder.

Generally, an eXogenous variable is one whose numerical value is predetermined (the value is assumed or computed outside of the model) or established by a person or group empowered to do so: the Congress of the U.S. in the case of the defense budget, the company president or board of directors in the case of the advertising budget are examples. When we determine the values outside of the model either judgmentally or by a method of calculation, we have produced a "given," or an "input assumption."

In the same general terms, eNdogenous variables are those whose value is calculated by the internal workings of the model based upon the interrelationships and interactions of the structure of the model. In this instance, we can treat the nation's defense budget and the company's advertising budget as endogenous by changing the point of view: the policy-making body (Congress) wishes to limit the amount of the defense budget to a figure that will not contribute more than two percentage points to the inflation rate, for example. The defense budget in such a case is eNdogenous, because its value will be determined by the model through interaction with other variables. Similarly, the company advertising budget would be eNdogenous when the forecaster changes the point of view from a given to a question: how much should be spent on advertising to meet a sales quota of X units of product?

When a variable is determined to be endogenous, the model must contain a structural equation that specifies the particular relationship that exists between that variable on the one hand and the exogenous variables and the other endogenous variables on the other.

Political Savvy

Armed with this information, let's return to the three variables (C, I and G) defined earlier to determine which of them are exogenous and which endogenous. Since the problem is being approached from the viewpoint of an econometric service bureau—a private forecaster—(in contrast to a government policy maker)—we can say that one of the three variables, Government spending, is eXogenous, because it is set by Congress. We are assuming here that two things are true: (1) the Congress has adopted a spending program at the time when the forecast is made (2) it will not be changed over the period covered by the forecast ("forecast horizon"). Should the first not be true, the forecaster must exercise political judgment and gather information to arrive at a best guess about which of a number of proposals being considered is the most likely to be adopted (the "scenario"), and incorporate the resul-

tant values into the model. Since consumption (C) and investment (I) will be determined by the interrelationships between variables (internal workings of the model), they will be treated as endogenous variables in our model.

In this respect, it should be pointed out that the company forecaster, using a similar model to forecast sales, for example, may treat the values of all three of the variables as exogenous, because their values are provided by an outside private forecasting service .

Having determined that one of the three variables is exogenous, leaves two for which values need to be determined.

The Coefficients

The value of each variable is found through structural equations. The equation for personal consumption is $C = bY$, i.e. consumption is equal to total income multiplied by a factor (b) which represents the proportion of income used on personal consumption expenditures. The proportion, denoted by the symbol b, is the "coefficient" of the equation; its value is "estimated" using certain techniques based on past behavior. This equation is called a "behavioral equation," because it comes from what is believed to be the patterns of past economic behavior of members of a sector(s) represented in the model; consumers in this case.

The amount of money people invest is influenced, in part, by the interest rate. But regardless of the rate, they will invest a certain sum. Given these hypotheses, we can say that the amount of money invested (I) will be some fixed amount at any interest rate (the "intercept"—"a") plus a proportional amount (b, the "coefficient") which is influenced by the interest rate (r). Since the proportion invested is influenced by the interest rate, and we estimate the proportion on the basis of historical behavior ("regression analysis"), we have the *behavioral* equation: $I = a + br$. In this equation a is the "intercept" and b the coefficient. The coefficient is "estimated" on the basis of the past data that best measures historical behavior; hence, a behavioral equation. The intercept is estimated by regression analysis.

The value of G in this case is given by an act of Congress, an exogenous variable.

The simple model we are using specifies only two behavioral equations—$C = bY$ and $I = a + br$. Absent from it are "identity" equations, an equation that states a structural relationship which is "true by definition," and the variables of which do not depend on coefficients for their values, as for example: $D \equiv G-T$, ($\equiv$ denotes identity), that the Government deficit is the difference between Government purchases and taxes collected is a self-evident truth. Most macro

models include identity equations. Ours doesn't.

The forecaster's decisions about the relationships between variables, the choice of endogenous and exogenous variables, and the design of the equations to show the structural relationships constitute the "specification" of the "structure" of the model, or, to put it another way, a description of how the economy operates as perceived by the model builder. This is the point in model building at which economic theory plays an important role.

Computing the values of the coefficients on the basis of historical data constitutes "estimation" of the model. One of a number of statistical methods available to compute the coefficient is "regression analysis," another is exponential least squares regression .

In any equation, time is denoted by appending the subscript t to a symbol, thus X_t to indicate the current period; X_{t+1}, the next period, and X_{t-1}, the previous period. When no subscript appears, the time period is current.

Since we are forecasting future values in our two behavioral equations, and those values are a function of current values, the consumption equation is written $C_{t+1} = b(Y_t)$, and the investment equation is written $I_{t+1} = a + br_t$. And, the model itself would be $GNP_{t+1} = C_{t+1} + I_{t+1} + G_{t+1}$ Read $C_{t+1} = b(Y_t)$ as consumption in the next period will be equal to that portion (b) of *current* income that economic agents (consumers) have spent on average in the past; $I_{t+1} = a + br_t$ as investment in the *next* period will be equal to the average amount invested at any interest rate (a) plus (or minus) an average portion (b) that was invested in the past at the *current* interest rate. Thus, GNP in the next period will be equal to consumption expenditures in the next period plus investment in the next period, plus Government spending in the next period. Plug in the values of C_{t+1}, I_{t+1}, and G_{t+1} into the model to forecast GNP_{t+1}.

The reader may have discerned throughout the discussion that all values (save for Government spending) are based on historical relationships. As a consequence, when historical patterns change as the result of a shock to the economy as, for example, the sharp rise in energy prices, the model will miss the turning point. (More on this subject below.)

Not So Simple

The relative simplicity of our explanation could mislead the uninitiated into a belief that making an economic forecast with an econometric model is a mechanical process. It is not. A great deal of judgment and creative thought enter the process.

Regression Analysis

Regression analysis in one of a number of statistical methods used to find the values of coefficients. In this particular application it can also be referred to as "ordinary least squares," or simply "least squares" method.

The two behavioral equations mentioned in Article 1 are: $C_{t+1} = bY_{t+1}$ and $I_{t+1} = a + br_t$. We need to find the value of a (the intercept) and b (the coefficent) of each equation; we will illustrate the method using the second equation $(I_{t+1} =)$ as an example. The equation for a is:

$$a = \frac{\Sigma y}{n} - b\left(\frac{\Sigma r}{n}\right)$$

The equation for b is:

$$b = \frac{n \Sigma ry - \Sigma r \Sigma y}{n \Sigma r^2 - (\Sigma r)^2}$$

The equation for b is solved first, because we need it to solve for a. $\Sigma =$ sum of; n = number of prior years for which data are available, and which are being used to represent history, 5 in this case; y = the actual amount of business investment in each of the prior years; r = the actual interest rate in each of the prior years (see Table 1).

Using the data from Table 1, we solve for b:

$$b = \frac{(5)(372) - (57)(34)}{(5)(687) - (57)^2}$$

(Some confusion may arise between Σr^2 and $(\Sigma r)^2$. In the first case we are taking the sum of all of the r squareds which appears at the foot of Col, 4 in Table 1; in the other we are taking the sum of all of the rs (foot of Col. 2) and squaring it, which equals 3249. Hence,

$$b = \frac{1860 - 1938}{3435 - 3249} = \frac{-78}{186}$$

$$= -.419$$

We now solve for a:

$$a = \frac{34}{5} - (-.419)\frac{57}{5}$$

$$= 6.8 + 4.776 = 11.576$$

These two solutions mean:
1. The amount invested by business at any interest rate based on historical data is $11.576 Billion
2. For each unit of change in r (the interest rate) businesses will change the amount invested by —.419 (the coefficient), showing an inverse relationship between investment and interest rates, i.e. as rates go up, investment declines.

We can now solve the behavioral equation for predicting business investment during the forecast period, if we have a forecast of the interest rate. Assuming an interest rate of 10%:

$$I_{t+1} = a + br_t$$

$$I_{t+1} = 11.576 + (-.419)(10)$$

$$I_{t+1} = 11.576 - 4.19$$

$$I_{t+1} = \$7.386$$

That means that at an interest rate of 10%, investment will probably total $7.386 Billion.

A realization, for example, that not all industries and all companies within an industry are affected by the same economic factors, led to the development of larger models in which each of the major components of demand—C, I, and G—are broken down (disaggregated) into their various parts. We are all aware that some industries are capital intensive, some labor intensive some are interest sensitive, some raw-material-price sensitive, etc. While GNP is a useful barometer of total economic activity, industry and company forecasters need more detailed information about the variables that affect their businesses, and their own function within a company: the finance officer will want a forecast of interest rates and stock prices to help him devise a financing strategy; the marketing manager will want forecasts of personal disposable income, housing starts of single-family dwelling units, and unemployment to help forecast sales and prepare a marketing strategy; the purchasing agent will want forecasts of availability and prices of raw materials to develop a purchasing and inventory program, etc.

Forecasters have kept up with the demand for forecasts of these various components by building larger models. This development led to greater complexity with one model currently forecasting 1,699 macroeconomic variables and 42,236 inter-industry variables (the Kent model).

Hundreds, even thousands, of equations are involved in forecasting so many variables. In addition, many different forecasting methods are used, one for each variable with economists choosing the one they consider most suitable to the variable—time series, multiple regression, input/output, etc.

It would seem that with such a variety and number of methods and equations available to make forecasts, there should be no need for human judgment, and certainly no reason for error: we could treat a model as a "black box." Yet judgment plays an important role, and errors have given rise to a new cottage industry in error analysis .

In discussing the role of judgment, we must keep in mind that the forecasters employed by forecasting services are economists. Many of them, like physicians, lawyers, and other professionals who specialize in one area of their profession, specialize in one sector of the economy or one industry. In addition, they have a certain view of the world which is based on their training, and frequently their social and political viewpoints. Do not make the mistake of viewing economics as a hard science, such as physics, for example, just because both use mathematical formulations. While two physicists working independently in two widely sepa-

	Business Investment Billions of $	Interest Rate (%)	TABLE 1		
Year	1	2	3	4	5
	y	r	ry	r²	y²
1978	8	8	64	64	64
1979	8	9	72	81	64
1980	7	11	77	121	49
1981	6	14	84	196	36
1882	5	15	75	225	25
Σ Sums	34	57	372	687	238

rated parts of the world can prove that e = mc^2, two economists working in the same room cannot even agree on how the economy operates .

Besides interjecting his/her view on how the economy functions, there is another dimension to the judgment factor. Being a specialist in the operations of an industry, the economist develops a model of how the industry operates, including in it the various components that affect the particular industry being studied. Just as a securities analyst keeps in touch with the industry for which he/she is responsible, so does the economist. This is done by contacts with knowledgeable people in the industry, reading the business and trade press, etc. The object is to keep well informed about trends and developments in the industry that may affect input assumptions to the industry model. This model—call it a model within a model—can take one of a number of forms; input/output, regression, etc. The industry model makes a forecast for the industry, which serves as input to the big model. In this respect, recall that it was pointed out earlier that the economy is a simultaneous feedback system in which everything affects everything else—no component is an island. This means that the industry model is influenced by all other components in the large model, and it is having an effect on all other components. That's one of the reasons powerful computers are required to run the model.

When the industry forecast comes off the computer, the economist/analyst, on the basis of his knowledge and belief of how the industry and the economy work, may reject the forecast as unreasonable. He/she will ·then analyze the input assumptions and data, and make changes. He might also consult people in the industry before making changes. Richard M. Young, of Chase Econometrics, told us a story of how he discovered airplanes on an airfield which were distorting the inventory component in a model.

Turning Points

One of the major problems facing a forecaster is accuracy, the measurement of which is itself a point of controversy (there are some who believe that the models may be right; it is the Government's statistics of actual outcomes against which forecast accuracy is judged that are wrong). An issue that is closely related to accuracy is the ability of the models to anticipate turning points in the economy. Those who say that the models fail on this point, place the blame on their reliance on historical relationships in estimating the coefficients.

An example of this phenomenom was an experiment by economists at the Federal Reserve Bank of Minneapolis in 1970. Using a modified version of the Wharton model (since changed) to examine the forecasted economic impact of alternative money-growth rates, the experimenters found that if the Fed increased the rate from the then current 5% per year to as much as 20%, output and employment would rise significantly, but the effect on inflation would be negligible, amounting to no more than what it would be with a money-stock growth rate of 3%. Even a Keynesian who, until recently, had little regard for the effect of monetary policy on the economic variables, would not accept such a conclusion.

The experimenters imply that the inflation outcome predicted by the model was probably wrong, because a 20% growth-rate policy "is very different from the historical norm." It is when a model makes predictions such as the one in this experiment that the forecaster's judgment enters the equation. ●

Chapter 3
A Company Level Econometric Model— A Layman's Guide

A. Migliaro
Institute of Business Forecasting

A company uses the output of a macro model in two ways:
1. As input to models used within the company to prepare company forecasts and business strategies.

company to prepare company forecasts and business strategies

2. As the starting point to the preparation of a macro economic forecast of its own on the basis of a scenario reflecting management's view of the economy rather than that of the forecasting service bureau

Implicit in each of these uses is the notion that before committing the company to any one service bureau, management ascertain (1) which variables have a significant relationship to its business, (2) how well each service bureau has forecasted those variables in the past, (3) how knowledgeable the forecaster responsible for the industry is about how the industry operates, and (4) the economic theory underlying the macro model. The last-mentioned item is important, because it allows management to make better judgments about the assumptions made by the forecaster in preparing the forecast ·

Tentative selection of the macro variables whose values are believed to have a significant impact on the company's business is accomplished by expert judgment, i.e., members of management representing various activities—finance, marketing, purchasing, inventory management, production, etc. They participate in the selection, because each has different needs. The finance officer would be interested in those variables affecting money supply and costs—interest rates—for example; marketing may zero in on disposable income, unemployment and housing starts; purchasing on raw materials supplies and prices, etc. Selection of the significant macro variables by these experts is tentative at this point, because it's based only on their collective judgment and their needs as they perceive them.

These experts will not help only in selecting the significant variables, but also in judging the extent of a service bureau's knowledge of the industry, the accuracy of past forecasts, and the input assumptions and judgment of the forecaster. Some companies use more than one service bureau, either because they want a second opinion or because they find that one bureau gives better forecasts of some variables and another is better on others.

What If?

Upon receipt of the macro and industry forecasts from the bureau, a company may do either one of two things: (1) reject the conclusions of the macro model, because management disagrees with the underlying assumptions concerning the choice of the most likely scenario, and prepare its own forecast based on its choice of a scenario, or (2) accept the conclusions, and prepare a company forecast. If the first procedure is followed, the company forecast will be based on its own macro forecast. Service bureaus sell access to their massive data bases to allow clients to play "what if" games, a procedure in which a client uses its own input assumptions, e.g., "what if the budget deficit amounts to $180 billion?" The bureau's computer will run the model and produce new values for those variables affected by the budget deficit.

Minimize Risk

Some service bureaus obviate the need for the "what if" procedure by producing a number of scenarios, e.g., best case, intermediate case, worst case, applying probabilities to each. Whether a company accepts the views of its service bureau or its own, the result is the same: it helps the company minimize its risk exposure and optimize its opportunities. The finance officer can, for example, develop a financing strategy that exploits advantageous money market conditions as indicated in the forecast.

Since almost all other functions in a company are based on expected sales volume, we will use the sales forecast as a basis for showing how the output of the macro model is used to prepare a company forecast.

Either one of two procedures can be used to make the company forecast. The simplest is to take the industry sales forecast produced by the macro model, and assume a share of market based on historical patterns; any adjustments to the share-of-market figure would be based on management judgment about any competitive strategies it plans during the forecast period, and other factors of which it has knowledge—new outlets or territories, additions to the sales force, product improvements, etc. The other is to construct a company ("micro") model, using those variables from the macro model that have been selected for their impact on company sales, and certain internal variables unique to the company.

There are three major steps in constructing either a company or a macro model:
1. Specification
2. Estimation
3. Validation

We shall construct a model to demonstrate these steps. To keep the example within manageable limits, we shall use only four independent variables, and multiple regression to make the forecast. The model we'll work with says ("Specifies") that Sales volume (S) is a function of advertising expenditures (X_1), price of product (X_2), personal disposable income (X_3), and unemployment rate (X_4), or $S = f(X_1, X_2, X_3, X_4)$. Read: Sales is a function of Advertising expenditures, etc. This "function" is converted into a multiple regression, thus:

$$S = a + b_1X_1 + b_2X_2 + b_3X_3 + b_4X_4$$

where S = sales volume either in dollars or units

a = the constant (or intercept) a figure which expresses the sales volume that would be obtained regardless of the values of the independent variables; its value is determined internally by multiple regression analysis.

b = the estimated coefficient of regression

$X_1 \ldots X_4$ = the value of each independent variable

Note that the model is made up of four independent variables; X_1, X_2, X_3, and X_4, and that each has a b in front of it, the coefficient. Hence, the value of each X is multiplied by the value of the related coefficient. What is meant by b_1X_1 is that some portion of the dependent variable (Sales, in this case) is "explained," or "caused by," the amount spent on advertising. The portion is measured by the value of b_1 (in the case of advertising), the regression coefficient.

Without the jargon, what we've said is that over some specific period in the past sales have gone up (down) by a certain amount on average when we increased (decreased) advertising expenditures by a certain amount (b_1X_1).

Saying this about each regression coefficient ($b_1 \ldots b_4$) and each independent variable, we have "specified" the structure of the model.

Correlation

Before moving on to "estimation," we must make sure that the variables we've chosen—advertising expenditures, prices, personal disposable income, and unemployment rate—have a "statistically significant" effect on sales.

Recall that our choice of independent variables was accomplished judgmentally. The validity of the choices is now determined statistically. One of the more popular ways of doing this is the "correlation" technique, an explanation of which one can find in almost any text book on statistics. This method provides a number from -1 to $+1$ which indicates the extent of the relationship between each of the independent variables and the dependent variable— $+1$ indicates perfect, positive relationship, -1, perfect negative relationship, and 0, no relationship. A negative number means that an independent variable is inversely related to the dependent variable, meaning in this case that as the numerical value of advertising goes down, for example, sales go up (if you can imagine such a thing). A positive relationship means just the opposite: as the value of advertising goes up, sales volume rises.

Assuming that we find that there is a statistically significant relationship between each independent variable, and the dependent variable, we "estimate" the model.

Estimation means to find the value of the coefficients for each of the independent variables—each b. This is done on the basis of historical data using the regression method · Without getting too technical, this simply means that the value of each b represents a proportionate change in the value of the dependent variable. For example, if the coefficient of advertising is 2, it means that there will be a $2 increase in sales for every $1 increment in advertising expenditures, all other things remaining constant. (This raises the question of whether the relationship is linear or curvilinear, the discussion of which is beyond the scope of this article.)

The value of each X is exogenous to the system, i.e., it is a "given". The advertising budget and product price are exogenous since they are established by management, and disposable income and unemployment rate are also eXogenous, because they come from the macro model estimates provided by the forecasting service bureau (As will be seen below, the first two items can also be eNdogenous—computed internally by the model—in a simulation exercise).

Another point of possible confusion should be clarified here in relation to the values of the Xs. This has to do with the values of the historical data used in the model to compute the values of the regression coefficients: For this purpose, the value of each X is the actual historical value. The values entered into the model to *forecast next period's sales,* on the other hand, are the forecasted values from the macro model and the planned advertising expenditures and planned price.

Validation

With the model specified and estimated, and the statistical correlations established, we are ready for validation, i.e. determine whether the model is any good as a forecasting tool.

Typically, the model is tested by selecting some period in the past, and dividing it into two segments: (1) a sample period—say the first ten years of the historical period, and (2) a "hold out" period—say the next five years of the historical period. Actual data from both periods are available to the forecaster. The sample period data are used to make a prediction for the hold-out period. The predicted value of the dependent variable (sales volume in this case) is compared with the actual value of the hold-out period. If the predicted value is a good forecast of the sales volume of the hold-out period, we can say that the model is adequately specified and "estimated," and can be used to forecast the future. If not, we have to respecify and/or re-estimate the model.

What do we do, though, when we find by the validation process that the model does not predict well. We re-examine the specification, and either eliminate variables that have a low correlation, and/or add others. We might also disaggregate one or more of the variables, as for example, unemployment. Instead of using the total unemployment figure from the macro model, we might use only the unemployment data on that segment of the population representing our market segment, say married males 18-25 years of age. We must be careful, though, that we don't "overspecify," i.e., get too fine in disaggregaing the data or including too many variables.

Having computed or determined values for all of the symbols, the model produces the sales volume figure for the next period.

Faith in Forecast

The program also produces certain statistics—$\bar{R}^2$ (R-Bar Squared), Student T statistic, Durbin-Watson statistic, and standard error of regression—which serve as a guide to such things as how much of the change in the dependent variable (sales volume, in this case) is explained by each independent variable, how well the predicted values fit the actual values, and how much faith the user can place in the forecast. A detailed description of each of these statistics is beyond the scope of this article.

Let us assume that the exercise described above forecasts a sales volume of $500 million, a figure that is unacceptable to management whose goal for the period is $550 million. To achieve that goal, certain changes will have to be made in the company's plans.

Simulation is used to determine the amount by which one or more of the independent variables should be changed to achieve the desired goal. Simulation can take either one of two forms:

1. "What if?"
2. "By how much?"

Under the "what if?" procedure, the forecaster asks the model what would happen to the value of the dependent variable if the value of one or more of the independent variables were changed.

In our simple four-variable model, the forecaster has control of advertising expenditures and prices, but has no control over disposable income and unemployment. Hence, either or both of the first two variables can be changed. The model, applying the historical average relationships (coefficients) to the substituted values of the independent variables, arrives at a different sales volume figure that may or may not equal management's goal. (Note that in this context, two variables that were considered eXogenous in the earlier case—advertising and prices—because they were given by management, are treated as eNdogenous in this case, because we now assume that the forecaster has control over them.)

By How Much?

In the "by-how-much" procedure, the model is asked to compute the amount by which advertising expenditures and prices should be changed to achieve the goal. Actually, it computes the advertising expenditure and price change that, in combination, optimizes sales. This can be done only on a computer, because what is actually happening is that many combinations of expenditure and prices are being compared until the optimum combination is found. (In this case, the advertising and price variables are again eNdogenous, but for a different reason—they are computed by the model.)

Constraints

Keep in mind that we have used a simple, four-variable model, and that we have not introduced the matter of constraints into our discussion so as to keep it within manageable limits. However, in the real world there would be many more independent variables affecting sales volume and a number of management constraints, as for example, profit on sales, return on assets, unit pro-

duction costs, competitive factors, etc., all of which would set limits on the changes. Given the constraints, one may find that management's goal is unrealistic in the face of external economic forces. The answer to management's problem may lie outside the company. Perhaps the chairman should be encouraged to run for the presidency of the

U.S. Victory would give him some control over the eXogenous factors ●

Chapter 3
The Five Econometric Theories Underlying Econometric Models

A. Migliaro
Institute of Business Forecasting

A nation's economy is a system in search of stability and growth. Economists attempt to describe the system by postulating theories, or philosophies about how various groups of people and institutions behave in the face of economic stimuli.

People and institutions perform four basic economic functions: produce, buy, sell, and save (some may wish to add invest and borrow to that list; but they are part of the last three mentioned). What motivates them to perform each function, the magnitude of their performance in money terms, and the interrelationships that are created as each performer acts in his/her self interest constitute an economic system.

Government, one of the institutions involved, occupies a unique position in the economic system in that it plays two roles: it performs the four functions listed, and it also redistributes income, enabling the other groups in the economy to produce, buy, sell, and save. The magnitude of Government's performance, both as a user and distributor of income, has a profound effect on the stability and growth of a nation's economy.

Controversy

If economists succeed in correctly describing a nation's economic system, they can prescribe the role Government should play, and the magnitude of the role, so as to achieve stability and growth, i.e. prosperity for all and inflation for none. Which explains why modern political leaders search for an economic theory that will achieve that result. And, which also explains why so much controversy surrounds theories.

Economists adopt economic theories that make sense to them since hard evidence to prove one better than another is hard to come by. One cannot split an interdependent society into a test group and a control group as is possible in the hard sciences. Moreover, politicians need quick results, and they are prone to compromise which makes pure experimentation impossible.

The theory chosen by an economist as his favorite will have an effect on how he/she perceives the world and, thus, on the type of econometric model he/she will build. The five major theories underlying the models in use today, and which are shaping economic thought in Western economies are:

Keynesian
Supply Side
Monetarism
Rational Expectations
Walrasian

We present below a brief overview of the essential features of each, and outline how they might affect the models constructed under their influence. In so doing, we were impressed by the approach being taken by Nobel Laureate Lawrence R. Klein, of Wharton, and Vladimir J. Simunek, of the Kent Economic & Development Institute (KEDI); we therefore created another system which we chose to call "Totality," and which we describe briefly at the close of the article.

The reader should not expect a total exposition of each theory; volumes have been written on them. Expect only to obtain enough information to enable you, a business manager, to ask more questions when an economist comes calling to sell you his services—in other words, the basics.

Keynesian

John Maynard Keynes, a British economist, published his General Theory in 1933, at the height of the last worldwide depression. The original theory has undergone many changes at the hands of economists who adopted it—the neo-Keynesians. As originally postulated by Keynes, the theory held that a nation's economic stability and growth is dependent on demand for products and services. Changes in demand, he said, are brought about by government expenditures. Heavy government spending and lower taxes during economic downturns will spur demand, creating jobs for more people; reduced government spending and higher taxes in periods of fast economic growth will dampen inflation. The key to Keynesian economic philosophy lies in its reliance on government fiscal policy.

Interest Rate

The major change in that philosophy in recent years has been the partial acceptance by Keynesians of a modified Monetarist approach. Monetarists hold that the economy can be pointed in any desired direction by controlling the money supply (see below). Keynesians respond that money supply plays a role, but that it is not sufficient: fiscal policy is as—if not more—important. Furthermore, they say, the effect of money supply on the economy (GNP) is through interest rates, i.e. a change in the money supply affects interest rates first, and then the level of economic activity. As a result, they continue, it takes a long time for changes in the money supply to have an impact on economic activity.

The Federal Reserve Board (the Fed) can help achieve stability and growth by controlling interest rates instead of the money supply, according to the Keynesian school, because attempts to control money supply create volatility in interest rates, and contribute to uncertainty in the financial markets. Keynesians believe that the trade-off between inflation and unemployment does exist (the Phillips Curve—inflation reduces unemployment, deflation raises it).

Fiscal policy is more likely to work when the demand for money (currency and checking account balances held by people and businesses) is interest elastic (the amount held by people and businesses to meet daily transaction expenses is affected by the interest rate), and monetary policy is more effective when the demand for money is interest inelastic, Keynesians hold.

Effects on Models

Since the Keynesian theory emphasizes demand through fiscal policy, econometric forecasting models based on it are effective in describing the effects of such policies on employment, general price level, investment, and interest rates. They do not treat technology, credit markets, and interrelationships among industries, and thus, cannot adequately trace the effects on the economy of changes in technology, and of the effects of credit policies. Monetary policy changes may have some effect on them.

Keynesian-based models attempt to describe the economy in terms of macroeconomic aggregates, and thus do not adequately measure the behavior of individual markets, the microeconomic units.

Supply Side

Many people associate the Supply Side economic theory with Arthur Laffer. His "Laffer Curve" received widespread circulation in both the business and popular media when it was released in the late '70s. Actually, the theory is more than 200 years old, having first been described by Adam Smith in "Inquiry Into the Nature and Causes of the Wealth of Nations," according to John A. Tatom, writing in the May 1981 issue of The St. Louis Federal Reserve Bank monthly review.

Modern Supply Side theory uses as its point of departure the premise that aggregate demand management (Keynesian) theory produces disincentives to work, produce, save, and invest. Demand Theory, according to Supply Siders, requires that high tax rates be imposed on the more productive groups in the economy—wage and salary workers, businesses, and investors—to support Government spending, especially on transfer programs (Social Security, Aid to Dependent Children, etc.)

Since Supply Siders view reduction—if not outright elimination—of disincentives as essential to the achievement of stability and economic growth, their theory calls for a complete reversal of those monetary and fiscal policies that, they say, produce the disincentives.

Their goal can be achieved by unleashing the country's resources—capital, technology, and labor—through a program of lower *marginal* tax rates (e.g., indexing) for wage and salary workers, reduced taxes on capital, and less government regulation over businesses. In short, they call for programs that will reward the efficient use of human, financial, and technological resources.

Anyone over 50 years old will recall the phrase attributed to one of Franklin D. Roosevelt's chief advisors, Harry Hopkins: "Spend and spend. Elect and elect," he was supposed to have advised Roosevelt. Today, someone in the White House must be telling its present chief occupant: "Slash and slash. Elect and elect."

In those two phrases one can find the essence of aggregate demand management and Supply Side theory. The Supply Siders agree with Keynesians and Monetarists in defining the effects of money supply and fiscal policies on GNP. Their position,

though, is that they want them turned against expansiveness and toward fiscal restraint. They believe that standard expansionary macroeconomic policies significantly reduce the ability of the economy to produce. Both macroeconomic analysis and policy decisions of the past ignore the fact that individual choices made by economic agents (individuals and businesses) have a profound impact on the availability and efficient use of resources, they insist.

Since they have no faith in macroeconomic analysis based on macroaggregates, their approach to theorizing about how the economy operates leads them to a highly disaggregated approach to analysis and to the use of input/output analysis (see below).

Effects on Models

Supply Siders reliance on microeconomic analysis leads to the construction of large disaggregated models wherein individual market behavior is a focus of attention. Supply Side models, as described by Wharton's Klein and KEDI's Simunek, incorporate features from the Keynesian Demand Side, Leontief's input/output, and the Supply Side. A model built along strict Supply Side lines would fail in the same manner as demand models.

Monetarism

Nobel Laureate Milton Friedman, of the University of Chicago, is the leader of the Monetarists. The theory goes back to the classicists of the late 19th Century. Friedman revived it about 30 years ago when his studies led him to believe that there is a high correlation between the money supply and economic activity. A computer run using data covering an extended period of time and other studies confirmed his theory. This led to the conclusion that there was sufficient evidence to demonstrate that monetary authorities (the Fed) could achieve economic stability and growth by controlling the money supply.

Keynesians are the chief critics of the Monetarists. Although they concede a role in the economy to money supply, they do not accept the Monetarist notion that it explains everything. Basically, you can learn just about everything you need to know about Monetarism by reversing everything you know about Keynesian theory.

MS/GNP vs GNP/MS

For example, the Keynesians go right to the heart of Monetarist theory when they say that the relationship between money supply and GNP is not stable, because:

(1) The relationship between money supply (MS) and interest rates is not stable due to the instability in the demand for money—i.e. people don't always respond in the same way to the same stimulus; a rise of one point in the inter-

est rate may result in a 5% decline in the demand for money today, and a 10% decline next week or next year. That's because demand for money is influenced by more than just the supply of money—inflation, for example (Demand for money refers to currency, coin, and checking account balances held by people and businesses to meet the needs of daily transactions between pay periods and cash inflows, respectively).

(2) The relationship between GNP and interest rates is not stable either. Historically, changes in the interest rate have both spurred and dampened investment and consumption at different times, and have also remained unchanged in the face of changed interest rates.

Friedman's inference of stability, drawn from the high degree of statistical correlation between MS and GNP, would be valid, say the Keynesians, if the effect runs from MS to GNP *alone*; but it doesn't. GNP affects MS at the same time ("reverse causation effect") as MS is affecting GNP.

Money in a Jug

As for other elements of Monetarist theory, read what we've written above about other elements of Keynesin theory, take the opposite view, and you're a Monetarist. Take for example, the Keynesian view mentioned above that the effect on GNP is through interest rates, and that changes in MS affect GNP slowly. Not so, say the Monetarists: the MS/GNP link is primarily direct and fast—pumping money into an economy is like pouring it through a funnel into a jug marked GNP. The jug fills quickly.

And furthermore, argue the Monetarists, the choice between consumption and saving is not dependent on interest rates exclusively. People and businesses compare interest rates with a "rate of return" available to them from sources other than saving and participation in financial markets. Depending on the available interest rate, people may get a better rate of return in terms of convenience, satisfaction, status, etc. by buying a house, taking a vacation, or buying an automobile; and businesses may get a better rate of return from new plant and equipment. So much, say the Monetarists, for Keynesian notions about MS going through the interest rate before stimulating or dampening economic activity.

Effects on Models

Since the theory focusses on the money supply, models based on Monetarist views attempt to explain levels of output, employment, prices, and interest rates on the basis of changes in the money supply. Monetarist-based models contain fewer equations ("reduced form") than those based on other theories. In addition Monetarist equations are not structural. Their reasoning for using the reduced form in the model goes something like this: The economy is too complex for anyone to understand. The interrelationships between variables are not known with certainty; therefore, structural equations don't really measure the true structure of the relationships. Given these conditions, the best way to approach the problem is to use the reduced form equation, because it measures the impact of one variable (money supply) on another (demand) directly without any significant stopover to visit interest rate. A Monetarist model may forecast the total effect of an upturn in aggregate demand, say, four quarters after the Fed assumes an expansionary stance with regard to the money supply; the Keynesian model will predict the total effect after, say, 12 quarters, and that the rate of growth will be about one-third as large as that forecasted by Monetarists.

Macro Aggregates

Like the Keynesian model, the Monetarist model focusses on macroeconomic aggregates and, thus, fails to capture the behavior of individual markets. Incidentally, if you want to figure out who's right and who's wrong on these issues, remember that it was in 1979 that the Fed adopted a policy of contraction to combat double-digit inflation, and a policy of controlling money supply instead of interest rates. (For those who want to know more about this controversy, we recommend "Contemporary Monetary Economics, Theory and Policy," by C.L. Jain, 1981, Graceway Publishing Co., Flushing, N.Y. We are prejudiced in favor of the book, because we had a hand in writing it.)

Rational Expectations

Rational Expectations dates back to an article by J.F. Muth, that appeared in the July 1961 issue of "Econometrica." It is not a true economic theory, because its adherents have not yet succeeded in formulating a mathematical model of its effects, a deficiency being repaired by one of its adherents, Thomas J. Sargent, of the University of Minnesota. Others in the vanguard are Robert E. Lucas, of the University of Chicago, and Neil Wallace of the University of Minnesota.

Rational Expectationists (REs) focus on the behavior of people, firms, and government rather than on the economy. REs approach their subject in the Lincolnesque spirit which, as every schoolchild knows, is reflected in his remark about the ability of leaders to fool people. (You can fool all of the people some of the time; you can fool some of the people all of the time; but you can't fool all of the people all of the time.) Their theory leads them to offer some direct

and simple advice to the Fed which is, perhaps, best expressed with that quaint Southern homily: "Keep yo cotton-pickin' hands offen dat economy, Boy."

Whereas adherents of other theories advocate—indeed, insist on—government intervention to reverse a short-run aberration in the economy, REs advocate the establishment of a policy from which the Fed should not stray, no matter what. Recognition of a distinction between "policy" and "decision" is important in this scheme. A "policy" is a set of rules or guides upon which "decisions" are based. Hence, if the Fed says it will increase money supply by b when interest rates rise above X% and unemployment above Y%, and that, otherwise, money supply growth will be held at a steady rate of a% (or some such "decision rule") it has established a policy. On the other hand, when it decides to take action to increase (decrease) money supply by c, it has adopted a decision in line with the policy.

REs say that when the Fed acts to offset aberrations (stimulative decisions in periods of slow activity, and depressant decisions in periods of economic boom) its action fails, because it's based on assumptions about behavior that are deficient: in the real world, people act rationally by using all of the information they have about any systematically applied policy. They may act irrationally only if a decision by the Fed takes them by surprise.

Relative Demand

A decision to stimulate the economy by increasing the money supply usually causes inflation instead of stability and growth, REs claim. The issue revolves around "relative demand" and "aggregate demand." Assume the Fed notes a slowdown in economic activity. To offset it, it takes steps to increase money supply without making a public announcement (it may do so under the law). Orders in your sales department begin to rise (REs accept the Monetarist view that a boost in money supply has an almost immediate stimulative effect on demand). Since you don't know about the Fed's secret action, you may be led to believe that the increase in orders is due to your brilliant stroke of genius, i.e. that demand for your product is the only one that is going up relative to other products ("relative demand").

If there's an RE on your staff, he'll puncture your balloon. Demand, he tells you, is up for all products ("aggregate demand"), because the rate of growth in money supply is up. He knows, because he's been watching the numbers in the Wall Street Journal. Let's assume you dismiss your resident RE's advice, and you decide you are as brillant as you think you are: you'll do what the Fed hoped you would—increase production, hire more workers, build a new plant, buy

more equipment, even take a vacation. But suddenly you get a call from the unions— "We want more money," they say. Your purchasing department reports increases on raw materials and component parts prices. Your finance director says the bank called to ask for a higher interest rate on the loan for the new plant construction. (Investors want an "inflation premium" to protect their purchasing power.) The resident RE hides in his office: he's the only one who knows you're not brilliant, and you may chop off his head for that. What happened was that aggregate demand rose and inflation with it. The profits you expected to make vanished.

Create Shortage

Had you not been fooled by the Fed action, and realized that you were dealing with aggregate demand, you would have maintained the same production level creating a shortage in the markets for your goods. You would have thus been able to raise prices without incurring higher labor and raw materials prices and higher interest rates. That's what you'll do next time, and so will everybody else, because, as Lincoln said "you can't fool all of the people all of the time." And being a smart business manager, you'll anticipate the Fed's action the next time by keeping an eye on the economy. Given a certain situation, you'll know their secret before they do.

The Lincoln Effect

In short, you will act rationally, and so will everybody else to thwart the Fed's action. Since the Fed "can't fool all of the people all of the time" in a world populated by REs, it shouldn't try. Instead it should set a money growth rate target, let everybody in on the secret, and then step aside, and allow people and businesses to make rational decisions—or as an economist would say: the Fed should assume a "passive role in the economy."

An activist role—in which the Fed changes its decision to meet short-run goals—does not work, say the REs regardless of whether the decision is anticipated or comes as a surprise. When an expansionary decision is anticipated, they claim, it fails to stimulate investment, because business managers and investors know they are dealing with aggregate demand. And, a steady diet of surprises wears thin, since a rational person can make a good guess about the Fed's most likely response to available information.

'Rate of Return'

And furthermore, argue the REs, there's more to using money than just earning more money by saving and investing: people and businesses look for a "rate of return," and this has more than a money dimension. It is measured in such terms as convenience, satisfaction, status, which consumers get from consumer durables, vacations, college educations, and which businesses get from new plants and equipment. The result is that, depending on interest rates, people do have other alternatives on which they can earn a rate of return.

Effects on Models

Since REs are in general agreement with Monetarists in their views of the economy, they would have similar effects on models. However, their theories hold a great deal of promise for the development of more powerful models once their mathematical formulations catch up with their theories. When they do their formulations will involve non-traditional methods that will reflect supply and demand components of individual markets and/or monetary and credit instruments.

Walrasian

The Walrasian Theory dates back to the classical period of the 19th Century. It was postulated by Léon Walras in 1874 when he published a system of equations describing general equilibrium in "Élements d'économie politique pure." The final version appeared in 1926 in "Édition définitive," the English translation of which was published in 1954.

Basically, the theory explains an economy in terms of the classical view that prices are dictated by supply and demand. There are a number of significant differences however. Whereas, for example, some theorists treat the system as a whole, and talk in terms of a "general price level." Walrasians treat each good and service (i.e. each market) separately, and thus attempt to describe the performance of the entire economy through the interrelationships between businesses on the one hand, and between businesses and consumers on the other, a phenomenon captured by Leontief's Input/Output analysis (See below). "What is relevant to the individual markets is usually important to the system as a whole," they say.

General equilibrium is achieved when quantity in supply equals quantity in demand at a market clearing price negotiated between buyer and seller. Prices in the Walrasian system, however, are stated in terms of a value of 1 applied to a base commodity ("numeraire") instead of money values, and the prices of all other commodities are stated in comparison to 1 (a system of relative values). In competitive markets (the only kind considered by Walrasians), excess demand will cause a rise in the numeraie, whereas excess supply will cause a decline.

Money is 'Neutral'

Money supply, they say, is "neutral," i.e. it has no effect on the demand for goods and services: if money supply doubles, prices double and demand remains unchanged. The original Walrasian system attempted to describe the economy without taking up the problems associated with money. When money was introduced later, it was treated only as a standard of value; its two other functions—means of exchange and store of value (wealth)—were ignored. Inclusion of money as a standard of value admits only that money exists, but fails to say anything about the demand for money or how money affects prices, supply, and demand.

'Technical Coefficients'

Another important aspect of Walrasian Theory is its focus on "technical coefficients," a focus made possible by the disaggregation of the macro economy. Leontief's Input/Output analysis, which we describe below, is an extension of this feature of Walrasian theory as is Copeland's Flow of Funds system, also described below.

Effects on Models

Models based on the Walrasian Theory alone do not exist. However, as models grow in size and in detail certain of its elements have been appearing in them. The major weakness of purely Walrasian-based models would be their inability to show the effect of monetary and fiscal policies, and to treat the economy as a combination of purely competitive, imperfectly competitive, monopsonic (buyer monopoly), and monopolistic markets. Their major strength would be their treatment of the behavior of the individual markets, i.e. micro analysis, and tracking the effects of advanced technology (See Leontief below).

Leontief
Input/Output

Input/Output analysis is a practical extension of the basic Walrasian concept of general interdependence of the various units in an economy. However, for the most part, it has been combined in practice with the Keynesian system.

Input/Output analysis was developed by Nobel Laureate Wassily Leontief in the '30s while at Harvard University following his defection from Stalin's Russia. The system was used by the U.S. Government during World War II, and has since been adopted worldwide, including Russia and other Eastern Bloc countries.

Input/Output Table

As the name implies, the system divides the economic units of production (industries) into two basic components: (1) the input side which describes the factors of production and the services used by industries and shows the transactions that take place among the industries ("interindustry transactions" of "intermediate goods and services") and (2) the output side which shows what happens to production.

An Input/Output table is made up of quadrants, three of which (Northwest, Southwest, and Northeast) contain data, and one (Southeast) is blank.

The NW (Northwest) quadrant of the table shows the value of intermediate goods and services, such as raw materials and component parts, delivered by one industry and consumed by others. Example: Assume Industry No. 1 is Steel and Industry No. 4 is Auto; the point on the table where Row 1 (Steel) meets Col. 4 (Auto) shows the value of the steel delivered and consumed by Auto, and the point at which Row 4 (Auto) meets Col. 1 (Steel) shows the value of the autos delivered to the Steel industry by the Auto industry. The diagonals (Row 1, Col. 1, for example) show the value of the product retained by an industry for its own use.

Technical Coefficients

The SW quadrant of the table shows the value of the services of factors of production that are not shown in the NW quadrant, such as labor, depreciation, interest, profits, and other income, and indirect taxes less Government subsidies.

It is in these two quadrants (NW and SW) that the "technical coefficients" play a role in determining the value of goods. Technical coefficients are based on the technique used to produce a product for delivery; Example: the production of a ton of steel requires quantities of each of a number of ingredients each of which has a value, and the use of labor, capital, etc. each with a cost. As long as the technology for producing steel remains the same, input values remain the same. Technical coeffficients are at the heart of the Walrasian Theory and Leontief's method, since they allow for changes in technology which alter methods of production and/or labor and capital requirements, thereby changing input/output values.

The third quadrant—NE—shows the final supplies as goods and services for consumption, investment, and exports, for each industry. Total inputs of intermediate goods and services, and services of factors for each industry are footed in the last row, while total outputs of intermediate and final goods and services for each industry are shown in the last column. The sum of inputs along the last row equal the sum of outputs in the last column. This sum represents the magnitude of the economy. The SE quadrant is blank. (Note: A Keynesian would refer to the NE quadrant as "final demands.")

What is unique about Leontief's method is that, like the Walrasian system upon which it is based, it measures the inputs from the supply side in detail. Other methods and theories attempt to measure these elements from the demand side alone. Many economists see Leontief's method as being complementary to Keynes' demand-side orientation, while as many of them see them as competing systems.

Flow of Funds

A Flow of Funds statement shows the uses and sources of funds in each sector of the economy and in the economy as a whole. The Federal Reserve Board (FRB) publishes such a statement monthly. The development work on this system is credited to Morris A. Copeland who was at the National Bureau of Economic Research when he introduced it in 1952. He showed both the amounts and directions of the flows.

The purpose of the Flow of Funds statement is to show financial transactions between the sectors in the economy (households, businesses, governments and financial institutions). The FRB summary identifies all basic transaction categories in saving, investment, money and credit. They include such items as gross saving made up of capital consumption and net saving; gross investment made up of private capital investment (further broken down into such things as consumer durables, residential construction, plant and equipment), and net financial investment; monetary and credit market instruments such as demand deposits and currency, time deposits, U.S. Treasury securities, consumer and trade

credit, bank loans, commercial and residential mortgages and others.

Borrowing

Some sectors show a deficit which is covered by borrowing from other sectors that are in a surplus position. Because of this (plus money creation by commercial banks and the Federal Government) the totals of financial and saving-investment transactions in the economy are always in balance, i.e. total investment = total saving.

Inclusion of a Flow of Funds division, showing each of the transactions, is believed by a number of economists to enhance model performance.

Totality

In listing the five economic theories underlying econometric models, we created a sixth—"Totality"—and credited its development to Nobel Laureate Lawrence R. Klein of the University of Pennsylvania Wharton School, who developed the original Wharton model, and who has had a strong influence over subsequent changes in that and other models, and Vladimir J. Simunek, developer of the Kent Model.

Working independently, Klein starting from Keynes and Simunek from Walras, they came to the same conclusion: to combine the disaggregated Keynesian macroeconomic demand model with the Walrasian microeconomic supply and demand approach using Leontief's Input/Output model and Copeland's Flow of Funds matrix as measuring tools to develop a comprehensive explanation of the economy. Because of his Middle European background, where Walrasian theory received greater exposure

than in the U.S., Dr. Simunek used it as his point of departure. He began to incorporate the various theories with microeconomic analysis into his model at Kent in the '70s. At around the same time, Dr. Klein, starting from Keynes, was persuing the same objectives at Wharton.

Effects on Models

A model based on "Totality" is the most representative of the total economic system it seeks to describe. Such models are large, containing thousands of equations, and forecast hundreds of variables. When they incorporate findings from other social sciences, as Klein and Simunek foresee, they may even produce more accurate forecasts.

Although our information is not complete, it is unlikely that any of the commercially available forecasts are produced by models based exclusively on any one of the economic theories summarized in this article. The evidence, based on our conversations with a number of forecasters, indicates that most models are based on a mixture of non-conflicting parts of more than one theory; they are approaching "Totality."

Perhaps the best answer to the debate over theories (and one that also explains "Totality") is this statement appearing in a brochure describing System Dynamics ·

"Debates (over national economic policy) focus on competing theories of inflation or economic stagnation with little recognition that opposing theories often simply emphasize different parts of the economic system " ●

Chapter 5
ABC of Econometric Forecasting

Thomas P. Chen
St. John's University

Rodger C. Carlson
Morehead State University

A n econometric model of forecasting is based on the cause and effect relationship. It assumes that everything depends on something else. Here forecaster first identifies the factors that influence the forecasting variable, quantifies their relationships, and then uses the relationships to make a forecast.

The econometric models were initially developed to forecast the state of the economy, i.e., to forecast variables such as GNP, disposable income and business investment expenditures. All the forecasting bureaus including DRI, Chase Econometrics and Wharton Econometric Associates make extensive use of such models in preparing their forecasts. In recent years such models have found their way in company level forecasting. The objective of this paper is to explain how this type of model is used in a business environment.

Econometric Modeling

There are five steps in preparing a forecast with an econometric model which are:
1. Specification
2. Estimation
3. Evaluation
4. Validation
5. Forecast

Specification

As explained earlier the econometric model is based on the cause and effect relationship. Suppose we want to forecast the number of commuter rides in a metropolitan city. Then the number of commuter rides is the effect. Next step is to determine the factors which affect them. There are two ways of accomplishing it: One is to survey the transit authority's executives and/or industry specialists. The other is that forecaster himself, based on his judgment and experience, determines the most important factors which influence the rides. Let's say that forecaster comes up with following factors—price, population, parking rate, income and time. Then the model becomes:

$$Y = f(X1, X2, X3, X4, X5)$$

Where:

Y = Number of average weekly commuter rides, measured in thousands
X1 = Price of ride, measured in cents
X2 = Population of the area, measured in thousands of persons
X3 = Parking rate, measured in cents
X4 = Per capita income of people living in that area, measured in dollars
X5 = Time, measured in years

The above model states that Y (number of average commuter rides) is a function of X1 (price of a ride), X2 (population of the area), X3 (parking rate), X4 (per capita income of people living in that area and X5 (time). Here Y is a dependent variable and all other variables are independent variables because Y depends upon these variables. The data for the time variable is plugged as 1, 2, 3, and so on. If the data start with 1962, then 1 will be for 1962, and 2, for 1963, 3, for 1964, and so on.

Next step is to determine statistically how important these factors are. One way to do this is to compute coefficient of correlations, i.e., the coefficient of correlation between the dependent variable and each independent variable. The coefficient of correlation shows the degree of association that exists between the indpendent variable and the dependent variable. The coefficient of correlation varies between zero and one. The value of zero implies that there is no relationship between them. The value of one implies that the relationship between them is perfect. The coefficient of correlation can be positive or negative. The positive coefficient of correlation means that both the variables are positively related. When one increases the other also increases. The negative coefficient of correlation, on the other hand, implies that they are negatively related. When one goes up the other goes down.

One can establish his own criterion for accepting or rejecting a variable. Suppose a forecaster establishes a criterion of .6, then he will eliminate a variable which has a coefficient of correlation of less than .6. Let's say that the forecaster, after studying the coefficient of correlations, decides to eliminate two independent variables—per capita income and time. Then the model becomes:

$$Y = f(X1, X2, X3)$$

Estimation

Next step is to estimate the model equation. one way of doing is by the least square regression. Since we have chosen only three independent variables, the regression model becomes:

$$Y = a + b1X1 + b2X2 + b3X3$$

Where:

Y = Number of weekly commuter rides

a=Constant
X1=Price per ride
X2=Population
X3=Parking rate
b1=Regression coefficient of X1 (price per ride)
b2=Regression coefficient of X2 (population)
b3=Regression coefficient of X3 (parking rate)

Regression coefficients explain the average relation that exists between the independent and dependent variables which we will explain after we quantify them.

Using the historical data on the variables mentioned above and software package on regression, one can estimate the regression equation. Let's assume the estimated equation is as follows:

$$Y = -1477.71 - 1.76\,X1 + 1.45\,X2 + 1.46\,X3$$

The constant is the value of a dependent variable when all independent variables are assumed to be zero. The regression coefficient of X1 (price per ride) is −1.76. This means that, on the average, if the price per ride decreases by one unit the weekly rides will increase by 1.76 units. (Here price per ride is expressed in cents and weekly rides in thousands.) The regression coefficient of X2 (population) is 1.45. This implies if population increases by one unit weekly rides will increase by 1.45 units. Similarly, the regression coefficient of X3 (parking rate) shows if the parking rate increases by one unit the weekly rides will increase by 1.46 units.

Evaluation

The software package gives a number of other statistics along with constant and regression coefficients (see Table 1). Now we will explain what these statistics are and how to use them to evaluate an equation.

Standard Error of Regression Coefficient: It tells us how good a regression coefficient is. Better the regression coefficient is, better would be the forecasts. The smaller the standard error of regression coefficient is, the better. As a rule of thumb, standard error of regression coefficient should be less than half of the size of corresponding regression coefficient. In the above model, all the three coefficients are good. In each case, standard error of regression coefficient is less than the half of its regression coefficient (see Table 1).

t Statistics (t value): It is used to determine whether an independent variable has a significant effect on the dependent variable. If not, the variable may be removed from consideration. As a rule of thumb, the variable has a significant effect if its t value (with signs ignored) is greater than 2. The degree of freedom is equal to number of observations minus number of variables. In the above examples, we have 24 observations and 4 variables (including dependent variable). Therefore, the degree of freedom comes to 20 (24 − 4). All the three independent variables, used in the above example, have a significant effect on the dependent variable. In each case, their "t" value is greater than 2 (see Table 1).

R Squared (R^2): The R squared measures the goodness of fit of a regression equation, implying how good a regression equation is. Its value varies between 0 and 1—the worst, when it is close to 0 and the best, when it is close to 1. In the above example, R squared comes to .9320 (Table 1). It means that 93.20% of the variation in the dependent variable can be explained by the independent variables used in the equation. Since it is close to 1, it means that the equation is good. It would give good forecasts.

Adjusted R Squared: It is used to compare equations with the same dependent variable but different independent variables and/or different number of independent variables. One equation may have one set of independent variables and the other, another set of variables. By comparing the values of adjusted R squared one can determine which equation is the best for forecasting purposes. Similarly, one can compare equations with two different number of independent variables. One may have three independent variables while the other, four. Like R squared, its value varies between 0 and 1. The equation with a value closer to one is the best. But, unlike R squared, its value can be negative which implies that the equation (model) is no good. Forecaster has to go back to Step 1 to re-specify the model.

Validation

Next, prepare expost forecasts (forecasts for which actuals are known) for all the periods under study with the model selected above. If we have data of 1962-85, we forecast values of all these years and then compare their actuals with the forecasts. If the average error of these years is acceptable, the model is validated. Otherwise, the forecaster has to go back to Step 1, and start all over again.

Forecast

Once the model is validated, it is the time to prepare forecasts. Let's assume that the model described above is validated. We want to make a forecast of 1986. The model is:

$$Y = -1447.71 - 1.76X1 + 1.45X2 + 1.46\,X3$$

To make a forecast of 1986, we need values of X1 (price per ride), X2 (population) and X3 (parking rate) for 1986. The

Table 1			
Results of Regression Model			
(Prepared by Least Square Method)			
Dependent Variable	=		Y
Mean of Dependent Variable	=		1036.04
R-Squared	=		.932039
Adjusted R-Squared	=		.921845
Number of Observations	=		24
Right-Hand Variables	Regression Coefficient	Standard Error of Regression Coefficient	t Statistics
a	− 1477.7100	491.278000	−3.00790
X1	− 1.76454	.664982	−2.65351
X2	1.45311	.267423	5.43375
X3	1.46132	.583130	−2.50599

price per ride is pretty much an internal matter. The forecaster can get it from the executive involved. However, the values of population and parking rate have to be forecasted or obtained from other sources. The forecaster can forecast population and parking rate for 1986 by using any model including econometric. He can also obtain these numbers from forecasting bureaus such as Chase Econometrics or from published sources. There are many forecasts which are put out by the federal government. Many trade associations publish forecasts on variables of their interest. Let's assume that these values for 1986 are as follows:

$X1 = 110$ (in cents)
$X2 = 1596$ (in thousands)
$X3 = 200$ (in cents)

By plugging these values in the above equation, we get:

$$Y(1986) = -1477.71 - (1.76) \times (110) + (1.45) \times (1596) + (1.46) \times$$

$$(200)$$

$$= 934.89$$

Since Y is expressed in thousands, the forecast of average weekly rides for 1986 would be 934, 890.

Turning points are most difficult to predict. A turning point refers to a point where there is an abrupt change in the data pattern. Sales revenue sharply increased because of opening of a number of new stores, introduction of new products or changes in the line of merchandise. Or, sales revenue sharply declined for one reason or the other. Econometric models do a better job in predicting turning points than any other model of forecasting. However, they are costly as they require more time, data, and computing power. ●

PART II

Structural Changes

Chapter 6
Structural Change—An Overview

Kevin Beebe
United Telecommunications, Inc.

Jack Malehorn
United Telephone System—Eastern Group

Model development is confronted by the ubiquitous presence of structural instability. Economic/business relationships, social, demographic, and political factors comprise a complex and dynamic environment undergoing change. Consequently, the causal relationships expressed mathematically by the estimated model parameters are inherently unstable which may lead to a misrepresentation of the subject matter being investigated and ultimately unreliable forecasts.

Recognition and understanding of the problem of structural instability involves both the technician and manager. While statistically a complex issue, it can be dealt with through an intuitive and pragmatic approach.

Econometric models are used to specify behavioral relationships, an integral component of a forecast process. However, forecast models built on the premise of capturing causal associations are often unreliable due to the presence of structural instability, i.e., an unanticipated change in data patterns. Structural instability occurs when the causal relationships being modeled change either permanently or temporarily. As a result, the efficacy of a forecast model is seriously impacted due to the underlying structural shift in the data reducing the model's usefulness in forecasting. While econometric models encompass a richness of theoretical reasoning displayed through the mathematical representation of the intuitive relationships which em-body the subject matter, the problem of structural instability needs to be recognized and addressed.

The problem of structural instability is prevalent throughout many practical business applications including: sales forecasts estimates of labor force requirements, and projected budget outlays, to name just a few. Thereby, an awareness of a changing environment in model building is essential. This paper focuses on the importance of recognizing the problem of structural instability by examining the roots of the problem and subsequent tests to determine whether the problem exists. Finally, the authors offer suggestions to effectively deal with the problem of structural instability. An underlying theme throughout the discussion is the condition that both the technician and manager work together to minimize the impact of structural shift on forecast accuracy.

The Problem

Many forecast models are based on an economic system which defies clear and concise characterization. Unlike experiments in the physical sciences where laboratory conditions guarantee a controlled environment, economics is a social science dependent on the vicissitudes of human behavior. The economy is inextricably tied to the real world, a complex and dynamic system impacted by economic, social, demographic and political event(s), not easily recognizable and not divisible phenomena. This trait is best described by Albert Sommers in *The Economy Demystified:* "The mixed economy is not a beautiful structure; it defies and irritates theoretical purists of all persuasions. Complex, changing, nontheoretical, it is the real world in which we live, the world reflected in diverse and often conflicting numbers that describes the upcoming future...making good judgments about the future will continue to require not just numerical evidence but also broad appraisal of the society of which the economy is a part."

As a result, the modeler cannot depend solely upon a string of numbers—data—as evidence of a system's activities without regard to the underlying intricacies involving the individuals and institutions which comprise the system. Additionally, when an attempt is made to incorporate the dynamics of an economic system, the modeler faces several and often conflicting aggregate measures, such as Gross National Product which can misrepresent the true level of economic activity. Furthermore, the modeler faces several diversified schools of thought, such as Keynesian—demand oriented, Monetarists—an emphasis on monetary flows, and Supply-Side—incentive based analysis. All encompass strong support from a theoretical basis, but in practice each one of these schools of thought have failed to consistently capture macroeconomic behavior. Consequently, many model builders have set out in an attempt to capture and utilize the most potent aspects of macroeconomic behavior borrowed from each discipline combined in an eclectic balance. While such a model building procedure is intuitively plausible, it lacks strong theoretical support, thereby exposing the analyst to the undue risk of structural shift.

On a more detailed basis, e.g. microeconomic relationships, many analysts rely principally on linear regression to mathematically portray the subject matter being investigated. Linear regression models are popular for their ease of use and interpretation. Still, linearity assumes an underlying constancy in the relationships being modeled. For example, if a model estimates, from historical data, a relationship of eight to one between sales and advertisement expenditures, the linearity assumption implies that such a relationship will continue to hold in the future. To elaborate in detail: Take for example, a simple linear model: $Y = a + bX$— where Y and X are the dependent and independent variables respectively, whereas a and b are the estimated coefficients of the model, i.e. a and b describe the mathematical relationship between the dependent and independent variables determined from the historical data. The estimated coefficients are average values fixed over time which in essence assume a permanency in the posited relationships and in a relative sense minimize the model's current sensitivity, thus highlighting the potential problem of forecast error due to structural instability.

Causes

In general, the causes of structural instability are numerous, encompassing unprecedented changes, exogenous events, i.e, events outside the control of the decision making unit, and seemingly conflicting shifts in the theoretical underpinnings of the subject matter under investigation. Some of the causes of structural instability include:

(1) *Functional Change:* Markets and players evolve as information is gathered and incorporated into decision making processes. This phenomenon manifests itself through the market forces of supply and demand. In reality, market relationships seldom follow a hypothesized pattern for an extended period of time. Thus, a linear model may often cause unreasonable forecast errors due to its structural composition. Examples of quasi-linear projections gone astray are numerous. Some better known examples from the 1970's include forecasts for spiraling oil prices beyond 1980, and the continuation of double-digit inflation within the U.S. economy into the foreseeable future. Both forecasts, while

mathematically/statistically sound, did not include the "non-linear" impact of social, political and economic changes—structural components—within the system.

(2) *Timing:* Another cause of structural instability occurs when the inherent time framework which embodies a relationship measured by the forecast model changes, for example from a lagged relationship to a contemporaneous one. Advancements in communications and transfer of information via data processing systems have radically changed the inherent timing of events. For example, transactions in the U.S. bond and equity markets now operate within a twenty-four hour perspective, due to the magnitude and extent of foreign financial investment spanning the globe coupled with the universal ability to communicate pertinent market information and place orders.

(3) *Regulatory Change:* Regulatory change as evidenced in the banking, trucking, airline, and telecommunication industries are viable candidates for causing changes in the structural composition of markets. Changes within the banking industry with respect to the legality of operations, e.g. expansion beyond state boundaries, types of services offered, and new financial instruments, have caused significant changes in monetary and financial relationships. In recent years, some banks have assumed the position of a brokerage house. Also, banks have enhanced their financial sophistication with instruments such as SuperNOW accounts and techniques such as interest rate swaps.

The impact of such a change has had far reaching consequences. On an aggregate level, the deeply ingrained historical relationship between money and the economy has been distorted. For approximately thirty years prior to deregulation, the growth rate of nominal GNP exceeded the growth rate of M1 (the most liquid form of money) by three percentage points. However, since the fourth quarter of 1981, M1 growth has exceeded GNP growth by roughly three percentage points.

(4) *The Internationalization of Markets:* Over time, the evolutionary nature of the U.S. economy toward a universal marketplace has impacted various aspects of economic activity. During the current business cycle, the foreign sector has emerged as a predominent force in the U.S. markets and subsequently the state of

the economy. The direction and extent of foreign trade is strongly influenced by the value of the dollar. Relying on the Federal Reserve Board's Trade Weighted Index, the value of the dollar has fallen roughly 35 percent since its peak established in February of 1985 without any concurrent strengthening in the imbalance of the U.S. foreign trade deficit. However, the Federal Reserve Board's index is based on historical trade flows which do not account for the relative increase in the flow of goods and services from newly emerging trading partners, such as Canada, Mexico, South Korea, Hong Kong, Singapore and Taiwan, against which the dollar has not declined appreciatively. Due to the underlying change in the composition of foreign trade, the value of the dollar as measured by the old index is unable to explain the continuing flow of imports into this country as well as the weak flow of exports.

(5) *Market Sophistication:* The changing sophistication of the consumer and investor in the world marketplace impacts well tested relationships. For example, historically reasonable debtload of borrowers depended on such factors as interest rates, the overall economy and product demand. Today, debtload is, in many situations, primarily a function of cash flow or the ability to repay on a timely basis as opposed to palatable levles of debt, based on the collateral values of assets. As a result, the flow of agricultural debt and the debtload of some third world countries have been significantly altered.

Tests

As evidenced in the previous section, the causes of structural instability are many and varied. Nevertheless, how does one know whether a problem of structural instability exists? The following is a list of techniques to test for the presence of structural instability.

(1) *Plotting:* In many instances, a simple plot of the dependent variable— the subject matter under investigation—will illustrate a significant shift in the underlying data pattern. A sudden unexplained shift may signal a tempory or permanent problem of structural instability which must be addressed.

(2) *A time variable:* The addition of a time variable is often used to proxy the

changing nature of the system being modeled. A time variable is especially useful when intuitively a problem of structural instability has been identified, however, factors causing the problem are either elusive or quantiatively difficult to assess.

(3) *Dummy variables:* The problem of structural instability was characterized as being either permanent or transitory. Both problems can be dealt with by the use of a dummy variable. A dummy or binary variable of "0" or "1" status is used to reflect the presence of structural shift. A "0" is used when a status quo situation is anticipated, whereas the use of a value of "1" would reflect a period of change. Dummy variables are commonly used to test for seasonality, a common example being an increase in jewelry sales during the fourth quarter of the year. The significance of a dummy variable suggests the likelihood of a structural shift taking place.

(4) *Chow's F Test:* A commonly used statistical test for the presence of shifts in data is Chow's F Test. The sample period is divided into sections to test the hyposthesis that the estimated coefficients are equal across the separate time periods. An F test is used to statistically verify whether the null hypothesis of no structural shift between time periods can be accepted or rejected. If the difference between the estimated coefficients of the time periods is significant, the null hypothesis is rejected, implying there is structural instability in the data. The major weakness of Chow's F Test is the obvious requirement of a large number of observations to allow for the separation of time periods while maintaining the statistical richness of the data.

(5) *Specification/Estimation Shifts:* An underlying structural shift may be reflected during the model estimation and reestimation process by the presence of changing signs on the estimated coefficients, as well as shifts between significance and insignificance. In addition, a sensitivity test of the explanatory variables to account for past forecast error may signal a more complex or dynamic relationship than originally hypothesized.

Recommended Corrections

Recognizing the existence of structural

instability in model development involves both the technician and the manager. Once a problem is detected, steps must be taken to deal with it in order to satisfy the ultimate objective of forecast accuracy. In this area, the manager needs to understand (at least intuitively if not mathematically) the correction procedures used by the staff analyst. A basic understanding is imperative when explaining the forecast changes to other managers as a means of ensuring credibility. A condensed explanation of several procedures to deal with a problem of structural instability follows.

Judgmental

If data and/or software limitations do not warrant the use of formal statistical procedures, both manager and technician should make judgmental decisions about the impact structural change has had on forecast accuracy. For example, experiences similar in scope to the current problem can be employed to adjust the forecast. The manager and technician might also analyze other industries where changes have occurred and use their changes as a proxy for adjusting in-house projections.

It is important to note that judgment in these situations should be viewed as a temporary solution. Both manager and technician need to commit to developing more formal procedures to measure the impact, especially if the change is permanent.

Qualitative Variables

A more formal way of dealing with structural instability, when using regression techniques in model development, is to use qualitative variables in the model. (This is also a way to test for instability as mentioned previously.) This is often used when a one time shift in structure occurs, as well as when there is a recurring change such as seasonal difference. It involves adding another variable(s) to the model that equals one when the shift occurs and equals zero when it does not. Essentially, because these variables have positive numbers only when a shift in the data occurs, the resulting coefficient is a measure of the impact the structural change has on the objective function. For example, the impact of one time fluctuations due to policy changes may be accounted for in

this manner. Suppose a forecast model was built for a certain type of heavy machinery and there is concern that the Tax-Reform legislation may influence demand. A dummy variable of "0" could be used for the time period before Tax-Reform legislation and a value of "1" for the time period following, as a means to test for the effect of lost investment tax credits and shortening of depreciation schedules on market demand.

One caveat to the use of qualitative variables is that the modeler assumes the impact will be constant throughout the forecast period. In other words, seasonal impacts might very well change over time, whereas this procedure assumes they remain constant, thereby inadvertently complicating the problem of structural instability.

(The above mentioned procedures are fairly simple and inexpensive to employ. The following procedures are more elaborate and costly in computer time and interpretation. A detailed explanation of these methods is beyond the scope of this article, however, references are cited for additional reading.)

Advanced Statistical Procedures

Assuming the data collected are "rich" enough (in terms of number of observations and validity), models can be developed using advanced statistical procedures to account for structural instability. If the modeler is working with cross-sectional data, i.e., collected at one point in time for a number of specific entities (e.g., 1985 data on industry earnings for all firms in a specific industry would be one variable in a cross-sectional database), there exist some random coefficient methods that can be used (See Judge Chapter 9).

Forecasting normally involves the use of "time series" data, i.e., data collected on one specific unit over a period of time (e.g., information on one firm's earnings for the period 1970-1986 constitutes time series data). Time varying parameter models constitute techniques used to deal with structural instability associated with time series data. These methods estimate the model under the assumption that coefficients vary over specific time subsets. One procedure (discussed in Judge Chapter 10) is the Cooley-Prescott Time-

28

Varying Parameters Method (TVPM). This method estimates model coefficients by accounting for two types of structural change: a permanent change in market structure, and a temporary change (or one time blip) in structural relationships. The coincident existence of both types of change is more the rule than the exception. For example, a government policy change in the financial sector will certainly cause permanent market reaction, but initially may cause a quick-solution type reaction until the change is fully understood. (An Although the TVPM is complicated mathematically, there are PC-based and mainframe software packages designed to handle this type of problem. One of the PC-based packages is Forecast Master, Scientific Systems, Inc. This package is menu-driven and has a varying parameter regression option ●

References

Cox, Michael. "A New Alternative Trade-Weighted Dollar Exchange Rate Index." **Economic Review. Federal Reserve Bank of Dallas,** September 1986, pp. 20-28.

Judge, George R. etal. **The Theory and Practice of Econometrics.** New York: John Wiley & Sons, Inc., 1980.

Maddala, G.S. **Econometrics.** New York McGraw-Hill, 1977, pp. 194-201.

Monetary Trends: Federal Reserve Bank of St. Louis, September 1986.

Newbold, Paul and Bos, Theodore. **Stochastic Parameter Regression Models.** Sage Publications, 1985.

Rosensweig, Jeffrey A. "A New Dollar Index: Capturing a More Global Perspective." **Economic Review: Federal Reserve Bank of Atlanta,** June/July 1986.

Forecast Master (Software). Boston, MA: Scientific System.

Triantis, John. "A Way To Help You Keep Up With A Shifting Marketplace." **Journal of Business Forecasting.** Winter 1984-1985, pp. 13-16.

Chapter 7
Ways to Detect and Correct Structural Changes

Charles C. Holt
University of Texas at Austin

Jerome A. Olsen
University of Texas at Austin

All forecasting depends on estimating relationships from the past and projecting them into the future. Examples of such forecast relationships are those that exist between company sales and, industry sales; regional population and per-capita income. Typically the numbers (weights or parameters) contained in such relations are *assumed* in statistical analysis to be constant, even though business managers recognize that the relations in fact are undergoing continual change, i.e., they undergo "structural drift." To cope with these changes judgmental adjustments often are made.

However, a test is available to detect the presence of the problem and to correct it by using a statistical method: "exponentially weighted least squares (ELS) regressions." It offers a simple and economical, though approximate, way of coping with the problem. In at least one operational application (presented in detail in the Appendix) ELS provided a significant improvement in forecast performance. (The results are summarized at the end of the Appendix.)

Where business firms often must forecast the sales of hundreds or even thousands of products, the use of an adaptive forecasting method such as ELS may be attractive, even when specific evidence of structural drift is absent. There is some peace of mind in knowing that if parameter changes were to occur, ELS estimates would automatically track them. Low computing costs and data requirements may make this method practicable even where there is a large number of products to forecast. Also, the greater flexibility of regression analysis in reflecting causal structure, may offer advantages over simple extrapolation formulas which are often used for sales forecasting.

Structure Not Constant

Many business managers are aware of the forecasting problems created by changes in their business environments: good forecast relationships that have worked well in the past become obsolete, causing increasingly serious forecast errors to occur. Managers may not have recognized that the statistical methods which had long been taken for granted *implicitly* assumed that structure was *constant*—but it was not.

Although seldom stressed, the theoretical specification of the variables, functional forms and lags constitute the starting point of the estimation process that is *intended* to yield forecast relations with parameters whose values are constant. For example, a linear approximation to a nonlinear function will tend to be unstable, and hence should be avoided, if possible, by specifying a suitable nonlinear function whose parameters will be more stable. Where the slope coefficient for one variable is unstable, because it varies with a second variable, the model ideally should introduce the second variable *explicitly* so that the new parameters will be stable.

However, in spite of all efforts to achieve constancy of parameters, forecast relations for businesses, industries, and state and national economies are continually changing.

Imperfect Understanding

In contrast forecast methods usually implicitly assume *no change* in relationships. The issue is not that there is a logical contradiction. Clearly there is. The critical issue is how *much* the forecast performance of relationships and models is reduced by parameter changes. The longer the forecast horizon is, the greater the time available for important structural change to occur. Also, when the pressures which drive structural change are high, as was the case as the result of the large increase in energy prices, availability, etc., explicit consideration of structural drift is of greater importance.

The theory of marketing and economics usually supplies only imperfect understanding of the static equilibrium relations between variables. They say little about dynamics and even less about how those relationships change. Hence, any practical statistical method for measuring structural change must have minimal requirements for information about parameter-change processes.

Most statistical estimation techniques in current use simply *assume* that the theoretical specifications of relationships between variables incorporate quantitative parameters whose values remain *constant*. The estimators then use all of the available data to obtain the best constant estimates of those parameters. However, in our complex changing world, models seldom, if ever, achieve constancy of parameters. Instead, for many reasons that often cannot be identified or measured, their values drift continually. This has important implications for forecasting for how we should deal with estimation methods, parameter estimates, and data.

Data Relevance

Drifting parameters will have different values at different times and hence estimates of their values are equally dated. Since the business world maintains a set of parameter values for only a limited time, there is a corresponding limitation on the amount of data that will be relevant for estimating those parameter values. Parameter drift *inherently* reduces data sample sizes with corresponding increases in sampling variability, and raises the issue of data relevance. Both depend on the speed of structural change relative to random residuals. These conclusions are reflected in the wide recognition that forecasts from econometric models and forecasting relations often require judgmental adjustments.

The last decade has seen basic research on testing for the existence of structural change, and on continually revising statistical estimates in order to take account of that change. However, the adoption of new statistical methods that take account of random parameter variation has been very limited compared to ordinary least squares regressions, probably because the new methods are more complex, are costly in computing time, and increase the number of

29

parameters to be estimated—sometimes excessively.

We now consider a simple test for structural change and an economical, but approximate approach to adaptive estimates of drifting parameters.

Testing for Structural Change

The essence of Ashley's test[1] is to estimate the forecast relation which is being studied using the initial assumption that all parameters are constant. Then a second estimate is made using the same data, but allowing either the "constant" term or a critical impact parameter to be free to take different values during different intervals of time. Then the residual errors from the two estimates are compared. The second fit will always be better, because the larger number of parameters will make it possible to fit some of the random variation of the residuals. The likely improvement can be easily estimated from the probability theory incorporated in the F-distribution table. An improvement beyond the expected amount is an indication that the tested parameter probably had different values during the different intervals of time. This evidence of structural change calls for modifying the model, if the source of the parameter change can be identified and explained. Then the new model would have constant parameters. Otherwise, the parameter changes must be attributed to unidentified random impacts, and a statistical method used that incorporates this additional source of random variation.

ELS Estimation

A theoretical derivation by the authors, Holt and Olson[2], shows that accumulated random impacts on parameters have the effect of making older data reflect the current values of the parameters less and less accurately. To compensate for this, less weight is put on older data. The exponential decline of these weights going backwards in time is shown to give a reasonably accurate approximation to the theoretically correct weights.

Many business managers have long used and are well aware of the computational economy that derives from exponential weighting. This advantage carries over to the greater generality and power of regressions in the exponentially weighted regression method of estimation, ELS. Every time period, the new data is combined with the old, and new estimates are made of the parameters. Except for the non-critical choice of the exponential coefficient for weighting, the computation is only slightly greater than making ordinary least squares regression estimates each period. Indeed an OLS computer program may be used with minor modifications.

Not only is ELS responsive to the important conceptual issue of drifting parameters, but, as is shown in the appendix, out-of-sample forecasting was significantly improved in a practical forecasting application.

Applications

In order to make the implications of the foregoing issues more concrete, let's briefly consider how they occur in two applications, one hypothetical and the other operational.

Consider a hypothetical national company that specializes in the installation of wall-to-wall carpeting in new homes. Data have become available on new residental building permits that seem largely to "explain" and predict the fluctuations in sales of carpet installations five months later. The company could estimate the regression coefficient that related carpets and permits in the past, and then use that relation to forecast carpet installations in the future.

Now the question arises as to whether that regression parameter is constant or subject to *structural drift* as tastes change and construction times vary. By applying Ashley's test for structural change to the historical data, a conclusion can be drawn about whether there is evidence of structural drift. If there isn't, an OLS regression can be used with confidence and reestimated infrequently. If there is, and if there were no ready explanation for the cause of the structural drift, the manager may conclude that using a regression estimator which assumes structural drift, such as ELS, may be preferable to one which assumes constant structure.

Overly Erratic

In that case, some experimentation would be needed on past data to determine what value for the exponential weighting coefficient yields the best forecasts. If data is limited, a value can be guessed for the coefficient without undue risk. The trade-off is between parameter estimates that are too slow to respond, and those that are too fast to respond, and hence, overly erratic.

In using the ELS forecasts, the parameter relating carpeting and permits is reestimated *every* time period, so if that parameter changes, the estimates *automatically* track those changes rather than letting the parameter estimates become outdated and inaccurate.

This example could be readily generalized so that several variables are used in the forecast relation. In such more complicated cases, parameter changes are likely to occur in complex patterns that are not well understood. An automatic adaptive method of estimation such as ELS has much to recommend it, therefore.

Case in Point

The Legislative Budget Board in Texas, because of a constitutional requirement which limits state expenditures, needed forecasts over a three-year horizon of the growth in Texas personal income. One method which was used for making these forecasts employed a Box-Jenkins relation to link forecasts of Texas to forecasts of national income growth, obtained from a large macro model. The application to this practical problem of the test and regression methods which we have considered is presented fully in the appendix where significant improvement in forecast performance was obtained by taking structural drift into account. Strong evidence of structural drift in parameters was found, and ELS outperformed OLS even when both methods were used to revise estimates every quarter.

Technical Appendix

Mathematical relationships between measured variables contain parameters whose numerical values are estimated from historical data. Structural change is indicated when estimated parameters have significantly different values at different points of time rather than maintaining constant values. There can be as many different kinds of structural change as there are parameters and time periods, so the concept is inherently complex. However, since most statistical techniques assume no structural change, a rather general test is needed to distinguish between "change" and "no change."

Ashley[1] presents a simple new test in which the sample of observations are partioned into a number of roughly equal time intervals; dummy variables are defined for each. He then makes regression estimates under the assumption that the parameters are constant, and alternatively makes estimates using the dummies under the assumption that the constant or critical slope parameters take different values in each time interval. The residual errors under these assumptions are then compared for significant differences using an F test. Ashley shows with a Monte Carlo simulation that this simple test is powerful compared with the more complex specialized tests, and it also can be applied to testing for discrete parameter jumps.

Clearly if all of the regression parameters are undergoing random walk variations, the mean of the process will tend to be different in the different time segments. Hence, testing whether the constant term is fixed or variable offers a reasonable catch-all test for drifting structure. Alternatively, if there is reason to expect the regression coefficient for a particular explanatory variable is drifting, then the dummy variables can be used to estimate different values for different time intervals.

We apply these tests to a Texas forecasting relation next. The background of this problem is discussed above in the non-technical section.

Structural Change

In order to appraise the relevance of the statistical methods for detecting and dealing with structural change to the specific problem of forecasting Texas personal income, the Ashley test for structural change described above was applied to a Box-Jenkins time series model that had already been estimated. The model is Equation (1) in Figure 1.

In order to perform the Ashley test, we divide the sample period into six equal subsample intervals of twelve quarters each.

This partitioning of the sample gives a good compromise between maintaining a large number of observations in each subsample so that the estimated subsample parameters have some precision, and having a large enough number of subsamples so that structural drift can be detected. Two tests for structural drift were performed. The first is a test of the invariance of the *constant term* over the sample period. This test can be loosely interpreted as a test of the overall stability of the structure of the regression, since a regression relation can usually be made to track fairly accurately for short periods of time simply by making additive adjustments to the constant term, even when the coefficients are inaccurate. This test is performed by deleting the constant term in equation (1), and replacing it by a set of six dummy variables, one for each of the subsample periods. If there were no structural change, the estimated coefficients of the six dummy variables are all estimates of the same true constant term, and we would expect the estimates to cluster around that single value, differing from it only by random sampling errors. The result of executing the modified regression for testing the constant term is: Equation (2), Figure 1.

The test statistic for structural change based on the two estimates shown in Figure 1 is:

$$F_{(5, 62)} = \frac{\frac{.0040896 - .0029559}{5}}{\frac{.0029559}{62}} = 4.76$$

The critical value for this test at the 95% confidence level is $F_{(5, 62, .05)} = 2.37$. Since the test statistic is greater than the critical value, we reject the null hypothesis of an invariant constant term at the 95% confidence level. Thus we conclude that the difference between the single estimate for the constant term in regression equation (1) and the six subsample estimates of the same term in equation (2) is *not* due to sampling error, but is instead a significant difference attributable to structural drift.

The second test performed to detect structural change addressed the null hypothesis of invariance of the coefficient of gnp_t in equation (1). We are particularly interested in testing this coefficient because it represents a measure of the strength of the linkage between the Texas economy and the U.S. economy. The test was performed by deleting gnp_t from equation (1) and substituting six interaction terms, which are the products of multiplying gnp_t by the dummy variables described for equation (2). The estimated coefficients of the interaction terms are interpreted as individual estimates of the gnp_t coefficient during the corresponding time periods. The result of estimating this model is Equation (3), Figure 1.

The F test gives a value of 4.76, and the null hypothesis is again rejected. Having, by these two tests established the presence of parameter instability, we apply the ELS procedure to see how much it will improve our forecast.

FIGURE 1
Equation No. 1

$$tpy_t = .0652\ tpy_{t-1} + .2633\ tpy_{t-2} + .2561\ tpy_{t-3}$$
$$(.56) \qquad\quad (2.50) \qquad\quad (2.29)$$

$$+ .4046\ gnp_t + .0023197$$
$$(3.60) \qquad\quad (.82)$$

$$R^2 = .47,\ DW = 2.00,\ SSE = 4.089 \times 10^{-3}$$

Where $tpy = \ln(TXPY_t) - \ln(TXPY_{t-1})$,

$TXPY$ = Texas personal income in millions of current dollars,

$gnp_t = \ln(GNP_t) - \ln(GNP_{t-1})$,

GNP_t = U.S. Gross National Product in billions of current dollars, seasonally adjusted,

and the numbers in parentheses are t-ratios.

Equation No. 2

$$tpy_t = -.26181\ tpy_{t-1} - .04530\ tpy_{t-2} + .06035\ tpy_{t-3}$$
$$(-2.21) \qquad\qquad (-.40) \qquad\qquad (.57)$$

$$+ .27912\ gnp_t + .008932\ D6062 + .01726\ D6365$$
$$(2.70) \qquad\quad (2.81) \qquad\qquad (4.08)$$

$$+ .02596\ D6668 + .02026\ D6971 + .03276\ D7274$$
$$(4.63) \qquad\qquad (3.96) \qquad\qquad (4.81)$$

$$+ .03193\ D7577$$
$$(4.44)$$

$$R^2 = .620,\ DW = 1.785,\ SSE = 2.9189 \times 10^{-3}$$

Where D6062 = $\begin{cases} 1 \text{ if the observation is in 1960, 1961, or 1962,} \\ 0 \text{ otherwise,} \end{cases}$

and the other dummy variables are similarly defined.

Equation No. 3

$$tpy_t = -.11965\ tpy_{t-1} + .14184\ tpy_{t-2} + .18295\ tpy_{t-3}$$
$$(-1.12) \qquad\qquad (1.45) \qquad\qquad (1.82)$$

$$- .14376\ D6062^* gnp_t + .25897\ D6365^* gnp_t$$
$$(-.88) \qquad\qquad (1.79)$$

$$+ .51862\ D6665^* gnp_t + .25178\ D6971^* gnp_t$$
$$(3.54) \qquad\qquad (1.63)$$

$$+ .65359\ D7274^* gnp_t + .55041\ D7577^* gnp_t + .0105$$
$$(5.09) \qquad\qquad (4.74) \qquad\qquad (3.26)$$

Where: $R^2 = .616,\ DW = 1.937,\ SSE = 2.9559 \times 10^{-3}$

ELS Regressions

Brown[3] and Gilchrist[4] responded to the drifting structure problem by proposing "discounted least squares," i.e. least squares regression models in which exponential weights are applied to the observations. In the exponentially weighted regression, the observations for T periods earlier than the current one are weighted by A^t where the exponential coefficient A is less than one.**

They proposed ELS as a reasonable estimator for forecasting, but did not work backwards from that solution to determine exactly what problem they had solved. The authors, in Holt and Olson[2], have done just that and shown that ELS supplies an approximate solution to the problem of randomly varying parameters.

Since we are not likely to know much about the stochastic process that generates the structural change, a numerical search is needed to determine the value of the exponential coefficient which gives the best forecast.

Texas Personal Income

In order to compare the forecasting accuracy of the exponentially weighted least squares (ELS) procedure to that of ordinary least squares (OLS), both methods were

used to produce out-of-sample forecasts for the period 1978 through 1979, based on data from 1960 through 1977. Forecasts for multiple quarter horizons are made by repeated use of the one quarter forecast relation. The criterion for comparing forecast accuracy is the root mean squared error (RMSE) over the two years with forecast horizons running from 1 to 8 quarters. The RMSE of the forecasts tabulated in Table 1 shows forecast RMSE for eight different values of the exponential coefficient (A^2). The value 1.0 corresponds to OLS, and the smaller values represent progressively faster rates of downweighting past data.

TABLE 1
RMSE OF TWO-YEAR OUT-OF-SAMPLE FORECASTS AS A FUNCTION OF THE EXPONENTIAL COEFFICIENT

Exponential Coefficient Squared	RMSE of Forecasts
1.00*	0.006907
.98	.006430
.96	.006319
.98	.006302
.92	.006324
.90	.006356
.85	.006435
.80	.006493

*Corresponds to ordinary least squares.

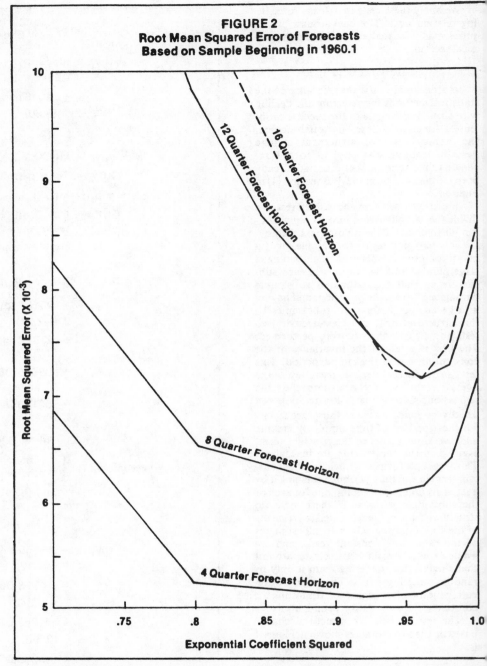

FIGURE 2
Root Mean Squared Error of Forecasts Based on Sample Beginning in 1960.1

Table 1 shows that for this model, forecasting for from one to eight quarters ahead, the optimal value of the exponential coefficient is .94.

When the RMSE errors of the forecasts for each horizon are plotted against the value of the exponential coefficient (squared) used in estimatng the forecast relations, the minimum RMSE again occurs at A 1. This indicates that the forecast errors are reduced by using ELS instead of OLS. For the 16 period forecast horizon, the reduction in RMSE at the best value of the exponential coefficient shows a 17 percent imporvement over OLS. For 12, 8, and 4 quarter ahead forecasts, the best RMSE

improvements are respectively 12, 15, and 11 percent. (See Figure 2)

To find the best value of A in your forecasting situation, you must perform a similar search over the values of A, and choose the one that gives the best result. In general a longer forecast horizon will call for a larger value of A, and the choice may be fairly critical, whereas a shorter horizon will call for a smaller value, and the choice is much less critical.

The primary implication of this work for forecasting Texas personal income is that some method of treating structural chang clearly is necessary. The more general implication of these findings is that ELS is clearl a cheap and useful tool where structural change is involved. The optimum forecast RMSE uniformly occured at $A < 1$. Whenever researchers suspect that the parameters of a forecast relation may be unstable, they should make out-of-sample forecast tests using exponentially weighted least squares with a standardized test period. ●

References

1. Ashley, R. "A Simple Test for Regression Parameter Instability with Applications to a Phillips Relation." Austin: University of Texas, July 1980.
2. Holt, Charles C. and Jerome A. Olson, "Exponentially Weighted Least Squares Regressions for Estimating Structural Drift," Bureau of Business Research BP 82-8, Xeroxed, University of Texas at Austin, 1982.
3. Brown, R.G. *Smoothing, Forecasting and Prediction*. Englewood Cliffs: Prentice-Hall, 1963.
4. Gilchrist, W.G. "Methods of Estimation Involving Discounting." *Journal of the Royal Statistical Society* 29, 1967.

Footnotes

This paper is an extension of earlier work which was supported by the Legislative Budget Board, State of Texas.

**Where $y(t-T)$ is the dependent variable and $x_i(t-T)$ ($i=1, \ldots$ I) are the explanatory variables for the period $(t-T)$ in the OLS regression, they are replaced in ELS by the weighted variables $[y(t-T)A^T]$ and $[x_i(t-T)A^T]$. Otherwise the calculations are identical.

Equivalently the cross product matrices for each period can be weighted by $(A^2)^T$ and summed. This is most easily calculated by updating the sum each period using:

$$\begin{bmatrix} \text{New Weighted Sum} \\ \text{Cross-Product Matrix} \end{bmatrix} =$$

$$\begin{bmatrix} \text{Cross-Product Matrix} \\ \text{for current period} \end{bmatrix} + A^2 \begin{bmatrix} \text{Old Weighted Sum} \\ \text{Cross-Product Matrix} \end{bmatrix}$$

Matrix inversion then yields new parameter estimates for the current period. A computer program, written in Minnesota FORTRAN, is available from the authors that preserves the cross product sum matrices and updates them each period. The program is "ELS-Regression" by Jerome A. Olson.

Chapter 8
Coping with Structural Changes— The Integrating Industry Model

Russel G. Thompson
University of Houston—University Park

In the face of policy changes, incorporating structural changes in forecasting equations improves demand forecasts of industrial electricity and natural gas. The Integrated Industry Model, as developed by the author, shows how to do it.

The primary purpose of this article is to describe how structure can be successfully incorporated in demand equations to forecast electricity and natural gas purchases by industry. Another purpose is to compare the forecasts from these equations for 1981, 1982, 1983 and 1984 with statistics observed since 1980, when the forecasts were made.

The incorporation of the structure was achieved by using the Integrated Industry Model (IIM), developed by the author. The model generates long-run price elasticities of the factor demands. The price elasticities plus the lag in adjustment from the historical data provide the forecasting equations (Composite Equations). These forecasting equations differ fundamentally from forecasting equations based soley on historical data (Historical Equations), because they also include information as to how cost-conscious adjustments would be made by managers in response to anticipated structural changes.

The industrial demand model forecasts purchases of the relevant factor in terms of its use intensity. Factor use intensity is expressed as a function of the factor price, price of factor substitutes, and lagged factor use intensity. The demand models were expressed in double-log form, as they were found to improve accuracy.

The Integrated Industry Model contained valid representation of the petroleum refining, basic organic chemicals, intermediate organic chemicals, plastics and synthetic fibers, synthetic rubber, alkalies and chlorine, and nitrogenous fertilizer industries. Linear programming procedures were used to compute solutions to the IIM and evaluate its sensitivity to a wide range of electricity and natural gas prices.

In this article, the frame of reference, as seen at the time of the study in 1980, is briefly described below. Illustrative forecasts of electricity purchases from the Composite Equation are compared with forecasts from the Historical Equation. Also, Composite Equation forecasts made in 1980 for 1981, 1982, 1983 and 1984 are compared with statistics observed since 1980 for electricity purchases in the Houston Standard Metropolitan Statistical (SMSA) and for natural gas use in the nation. (The details on the Historical and Composite Equations models can be obtained by writing to the author at Dept. of Decision and Information Sciences, Univ. of Houston, Univ. Park, 4800 Calhoun, Houston, TX 77004.)

Frame of Reference

At the time of the study, the frame of reference for developing the industrial demand models was as follows:
1. Changes in energy prices and government regulations were forcing industrial consumers to ressess their purchases of energy.
2. Industrial managers were becoming increasingly sensitive to higher energy prices and alert to overall plant economics.
3. Changes in investments in new technology were resulting in new patterns of energy purchases.
4. Both revenues and capacity expansion requirements for energy suppliers were sensitive to industrial consumer responses to prices changes.
5. Industrial growth was the driving force behind industrial energy demand.
6. Industry representatives expressed the following concerns in 1980: How will industrial demands for electricity and natural gas be affected by different prices of electricity and natural gas? How will industrial demands for electricity and natural gas be affected by national energy and clean environmental legislation?

In order to answer these questions, it was necessary to discern how industrial consumers would modify the structures of their plants in response to not only prices, but also in response to Government regulations. The economic concepts of demand provided the framework for posing the problem, and the principles of econometrics provided the framework for estimating the model.

Need for Structure

Because the policy changes were first-time experiences, the historical data available at the time of this study in 1980 did not yet fully contain industry manager's responses to these policies. In a baseball context, it would be like the Commissioner changing the makeup of the leagues and further changing how the game would be played, for example, ten players rather than nine on a team. This type of change in baseball would fundamentally affect the value of the teams and how fans would turn out to watch them play. Such a shakeup actually occurred in industry in the late 1970's with the National Energy Act and the Clean Air Act Amendments.

As a means to improvise, we came up with the idea of going back to the fundamentals of how the industries were put together from different basic technologies. Representations of these technologies allowed us to analyze how cost-conscious managers in these industries would modify their input purchases and processes used to produce a projected slate of outputs. The essence of the modifications were incorporated in price elasticities as well as in demand forecasting equations.

Basis for Generating Data

The Integrated Industry Model contained valid representations of the technologies used in the petroleum refining and large volume chemicals industries from basic petrochemicals to important end products. The representations were in the form of an operable computer code, which could be tailored to represent a production complex in a given area. That tailoring was actually done to represent the petroleum refining and petrochemicals industries in the Houston SMSA. Many cross-checks were made to ensure the accuracy of the representation at the time of the study. With that basis, variations in the prices of electricity and natural gas were systematically made; and at each step of the variations process, a new solution to the Integrated Industry Model was computed. Each solution gave the purchases of all factors, including electricity and natural gas, plus the costs of producing all end product outputs, product-by-product. All of the solutions were analyzed simultaneously to find how the purchases of electricity and natural gas would vary in response to price changes. Best fitting log-log functions were

estimated, which gave the direct price and cross-price sensitivities of these demands to price.

Composite Equations

Because industry managers, like everyone else, need time to respond to price changes, there is always a lag in the demand response to price. This lag was captured by fitting demand equations to historical data, assuming that the response lags to price would not be affected by the policy changes. The coefficient of the lagged factor demand intensity, as estimated statistically, was then used in conjunction with the estimated price elasticities from the model-generated data to develop the forecasting equations (Composite Equations).

Modeling Procedure

The Integrated Industry Model finds the feasible process options, evaluates their relative technical efficiencies, and balances the relationships between relative market prices and relative technical efficiencies. The IIM's optimal solution gives the minimum total cost of production, the marginal cost of producing each output and controlling each waste discharge (shadow prices or opportunity costs), and the economic quantity of each input used. As mentioned above, alternative solutions for different input prices give economic demand schedules for factor inputs (e.g., electricity).

Applying the above procedure gives the quantity demand of each factor by industry at different prices. Fitting regression equations to the model-generated data gives smooth long-run measures of the respective anticipated static demand function; for example, the quantity of electricity demanded as a function of the prices of electricity and natural gas. Estimates of the long-run price elasticities were the key inputs required to evaluate the demand responses to price in a period of major changes in structure.

The cost minimizing problem for the representative producer, subject to the production function, gives the representative manager's factor demand functions for the purchased inputs. Electricity and nautral gas would be two of these factor

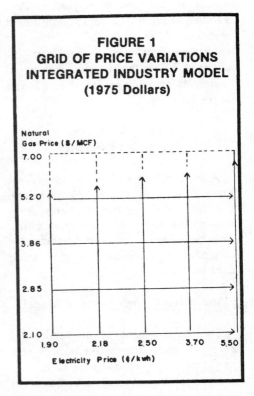

FIGURE 1
GRID OF PRICE VARIATIONS
INTEGRATED INDUSTRY MODEL
(1975 Dollars)

demand functions. Regulatory restrictions, as imposed by the National Energy and Clean Air Acts, would enter as parameters in the factor demand functions.

With the Integrated Industry Model, the production function is actually represented as linear combinations of the process vectors, which characterize the technologies. As used here, linear programming (L.P.) methods provide the mathematical means of finding the least-cost combination. Post-optimality evaluations gave step-function estimates of the purchased factor demand functions, as illustrated below.

Lag Adjustments

Another component of the forecasting basis developed for the utility studies was a meaningful measure of the lag-adjustment coefficient which reflects the frictions in adjustment to changes in the electricity and natural gas prices. A straight-forward way of getting an initial estimate of this adjustment lag is to specify a dynamic demand model to be estimated statistically from historical data. This demand equation is comparable to the static demand model to be estimated from the model-generated data except it has one more independent variable to capture the lags in adjustment responses. The estimate of the lag-adjustment coefficient is the central input needed from the historical data-based regression equation to link the short-run to the long-run.

Linking Long- and Short-Run Estimates

Assumption of a dynamic adjustment process, such as the Koyck principle, transforms the long-run price elasticities into usable short-run price elasticities. This well-known principle was actually used to develop the forecasting equation used in this study.

Industrial Energy Demand Model

The development of the industrial energy-demand forecasting model was partitioned into six separable steps:
1. Data collection for estimation of historical demand equation and service area characteristics.
2. Estimation of dynamic historical demand equation.
3. Service area tailoring of static structural industry model.
4. Use of Integrated Industry Model to generate economic process data.
5. Estimation of static demand equation from economic process data.
6. Development of Forecasting Equation by synthesis of lag structure from historical data equation and long-run elasticities from economic process data equation.

Historical Demand Data

Step 1 required collection of electricity consumption data by industrial sector of use. Annual time series data for the period 1963 through 1979 were organized in this study for the Houston SMSA. Primary focus was the large industrial customers in the 2-digit petroleum refining (SIC 29) and large volume chemicals (SIC 28) industries. With regard to electricity purchases, these data represented 98% of the total chemical industry purchases and 99% of the total petroleum refining industry purchases at the time of the study.

The annual quantity of electricity purchased and revenue paid by each customer in these two industries was developed by the Houston Lighting and Power Company (HL&P). These detailed data were aggregated by HL&P into aggregate consumption and average price data for the analysis.

The average price of natural gas for large industrial users was obtained from the Texas Railroad Commission and other public reports. This natural gas price represented the price paid by large industrial customers in the Houston SMSA.

Value-added by SIC's 28 and 29 in the Houston SMSA was the output measure used in this study. Value-added weighs the mix of products produced by each industry; and, in contrast to value of shipments, it basically removes the effects of high input prices (e.g., crude oil). Value-added equals the value of shipments (plus the change in value of inventories) less the costs of materials purchased.

Valued-added data for SIC's 28 and 29 in the Houston SMSA were obtained from the *Census of Manufacturers* and Annual Survey of Manufacturers for the years 1963 through 1977. Estimates of value-added for other years were made by regressing real value-added for the respective industries in the Houston SMSA on the index of industrial production for the nation. Regressions were separately made for SIC 28 and SIC 29. Estimates of value-added for the Houston SMSA in 1978 and 1979 were made by use of the regression equations and reported values of the national index of industrial production. Inflationary effects of changes in the price level were removed by use of appropriate deflators.

Step 2 required the estimation of Dynamic Historical Demand Equation for industrial electricity and natural gas purchases by SIC's 28 and 29 in Houston SMSA. In accordance with economic principles and the discusion above, the intensity of the industrial demand for electricity purchases (electricity purchases relative to value-added) was estimated as a function of the real price of electricity, the real price of natural gas, and the intensity of electricity demand lagged one year. A similar specifi-

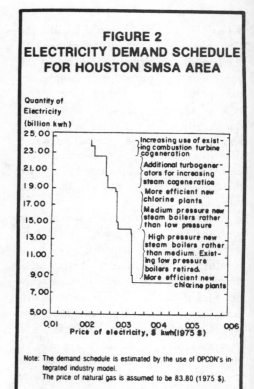

FIGURE 2
ELECTRICITY DEMAND SCHEDULE FOR HOUSTON SMSA AREA

Quantity of Electricity (billion kwh)

Increasing use of existing combustion turbine cogeneration

Additional turbogenerators for increasing steam cogeneration

More efficient new chlorine plants

Medium pressure new steam boilers rather than low pressure

High pressure new steam boilers rather than medium. Existing low pressure boilers retired.

More efficient new chlorine plants

Price of electricity, $ kwh(1975 $)

Note: The demand schedule is estimated by the use of OPCON's integrated industry model.
The price of natural gas is assumed to be 83.80 (1975 $).

cation was made to represent the modeling basis for estimation of the industrial demand for natural gas.

Regression estimates of the historical-based demand equations were made for both electricity and natural gas. The regression coefficients had expected signs and were significant at the 5% level. Over 80% of the variances in the intensity of electricity purchases and also natural gas purchases were explained by the regression equations. No significant serial correlation was present in the estimates.

Step 3 required the characterization of the Houston SMSA for economic process analysis and tailoring of structural model. Large industrial customer data represented a chronological history of electricity and natural gas purchases in the service area. This history provided a continuing pattern of these factor purchases for virtually all of the plants in SIC's 28 and 29.

Information from OPCON's data base, plus telephone queries pinpointed each plant's primary production capacities/technologies, fuel/feedstock inputs and products outputs. Investments in production capacities were estimated year-by-year from published survey reports to accurately estimate the 51 major outputs produced in the 1979 base year.

Levels of production were estimated from the 1979 capacities using national capacity and production data, as reported by the International Trade Commission. Average capacity utilization ratios were estimated from the national data for the years 1971-1979 to balance out extreme deviations for 1979. These ratios were then applied to the plant capacity data for the Houston SMSA to estimate production levels, which were not available from reported statistics. Estimates of 1979 production levels represented the initial values for projecting 1990 demand requirements in the Integrated Industry Model.

Industry projection of growth rates in demand requirements for different refined fuels and chemical products were used as one source of inputs for projecting demand requirements. Another source of information was the specifications made by Oak Ridge National Laboratories (ORNL) for an analysis of the nation's chemicals industries, which OPCON made for Oak Ridge. This analysis represented an integral part of Oak Ridge's evaluation of regulatory impacts on the chemicals industries for the U.S. Department of Energy. Because the U.S. Department of Energy was the client, Oak Ridge's specifications were generally consistent with studies by the Energy Information Administration. Still another source was OPCON's interpretation of different perspectives for the future and how the Houston SMSA will be affected by them.

Projected demand requirements for each end product and the production level for selected intermediate chemicals in the Integrated Industry Model were made for the year 1990. Cross-checks were also made to generally verify the consistency between these projections and the value-added projections for SIC's 28 and 29, which are discussed above.

The basic procedure for projecting the detailed product output requirements was as follows: First, ratios between 1979 and 1990 production rates were computed from 4-digit SIC national growth rates given by ORNL. Next, 1979 production levels were scaled upward to 1990 to give

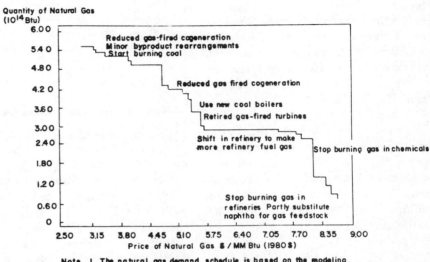

FIGURE 3
NATURAL GAS DEMAND SCHEDULE FOR PETROLEUM REFINING AND CHEMICALS

Note 1. The natural gas demand schedule is based on the modeling results for 1990, Houston Standard Metropolitan area.
2. The electricity price is assumed to be 3.25¢/kwh. (1980 $)
3. Capital cost reflects 15% rate of return on capital.

total 1990 production for each product in accordance with the growth ratio. In many cases growth ratios for certain individual products were adjusted downward if, from OPCON's experience, growth of these products was less than the group averages. For example, intermediate polymers, which are used to make synthetic fibers, would not be expected to grow as fast as similar products used to make general purpose plastics.

Input Specifications: With regard to oil liquids, heavy high-sulphur crude was assumed to be available at a world oil price of $31.30 per barrel in 1975 dollars; and high-sulfur resid was assumed to be available at a comparable Btu-equivalent price. Also, a limited quantity of light low-sulfur crude was available for use.

Availability and price of natural gas liquids were estimated from current pipeline flows into Houston. Information sources for these estimates were the National Petroleum Council and the 1979

Administrator's Annual Report (AAR) to Congress.

A relatively small quantity of natural gas was assumed to be supplied from old contracts at a very low price of $.90 per million Btu. All additional gas was supplied at the new gas price, which was a parameter in the model runs.

Regulatory Restrictions: Use of natural gas and oil products to fire boilers is not allowed in any new base load steam boiler equipment built after 1977. Such firing is allowed in new combustion turbines which have unfired waste heat boilers, in accordance with DOE rulings. It is also allowed in the hydrocarbon heaters, which are integral with many chemical processes; and it is allowed in "peaking" boilers, which are used only when the coal boilers are down for cleaning and repairs (one-sixth of the time).

Clean Air: The major air pollution emmisions modeled are sulfur oxides and particulate emissions. The effect of the

Clean Air Act Amendments of 1977 on the refining and chemicals industry is to require stricter ambient air quality standards. These standards stem primarily from the Prevention of Significant Deterioration and Nonattainment provisions of the Amendments. The sulfur dioxide standards on new industrial boilers currently remain the same as before the amendments. Primary impacts result from stricter ambient standards, which are harder to quantify because of regional and weather-related variations.

We assume a very strict particulate emission limitation on all combustion (0.3 lb. per million Btu) which translates into a requirement for fabric filters on all coal-fired equipment and electrostatic precipitators on all residual oil fired equipment. We assume that boilers must burn low-sulfur coal (1.1 lbs. SO_2 per million Btu). The limitation on SO_2 emissions from oil burning equipment is 0.5 per million Btu.

Water: We assume a level of wastewater treatment equivalent to tertiary treatment with activated carbon to remove additional traces of toxic chemicals.

Step 4 required the generation of economic process data using the Integrated Industry Model. As tailored above, solutions to the Intergrated Industry Model were computed for the following ranges of prices (1975 dollars) for natural gas and electricity: electricity (1.9¢/kwh—5.5¢/kwh) and natural gas ($2.1/Mcf—$7.0/Mcf). The endpoints of each range and three intermediate points in each range were specified to give a five-by-five grid of price variations as shown in Figure 1.

Solutions to the model were computed in the following way: (1) select an electricity price, say 1.9, and then vary the gas price over the range from 1.9 to 7; (2) select a second electricity price, say 2.18, and then vary the gas price over its range; (3) continue until all electricty price delineations are used; (4) then select a natural gas price, say 2.10, and vary the electricty price over its range; and (5) continue for remaining natural gas prices delineated.

Process economic data for marginal costs, electricity use and natural gas use are stored for each solution. These data, along with electricity and natural gas

TABLE 1
Ratio of Electricity Purchases Relative to Value Added

Year	Actual Electricity Purchases Relative to Estimated Value-Added	Forecast Electricity Purchases Relative to Estimated Valued Added	
		Hist. Equation	Comp. Equation
1980	3.959	3.957	3.959
1981	3.416	4.098	3.960
1982	3.227	4.168	3.947
1983	3.339	4.154	3.705
1984	3.235	4.069	3.511

prices, represent the starting economic process data for derivation of the process economic data equation.

However, all data from solutions with a zero consumption of new natural gas were deleted from the static demand equation estimation, in order to have all quantities well-defined mathematically. As illustrated in Figure 1, data used in the estimation result from price combinations along the solid lines in the grid, with data along the dashed lines deleted.

Step 5 required the estimation of static demand equation from economic process data. Five hundred data points generated by the Integrated Industry Model parameters are analyzed. With regard to the electricity demand, a plot of the data points for one particular gas price ($3.86/Mcf) is presented in Figure 2). With regard to the natural gas demand, another plot of data points for one particular electricity price is presented in Figure 3. Again, the results clearly follow the law of derived demand for a representative firm.

The ranges of prices chosen for the LP calculations were wide enough to induce a relatively wide range of technical adjustments in the model. The major variations occurred in the choice of whether to both generate electricity and produce high-temperature, high-quality steam (cogenerate) or not to cogenerate, and in choices of types of fuels and types of boilers (see Figures 2 and 3). Less significant variations occurred in the types of feedstocks and production processes used.

Smooth summary measures of the quantity/price points were estimated for

both the industrial electricity and natural gas demands. Very good statistical fits were found in the smoothing estimation process, for example, 88% of the variance in electricity purchases were explained.

Step 6 required the synthesis of estimates for the forecasting equation. As premised in this study, the historical data-based demand function gives a sound estimate of the lag-adjustment coefficient; and the model-generated data-based demand function gives sound estimates of the long-run price elasticities. Use of the economic principle of linkage (Koyck) gave electricity and natural gas purchases. The Composite Equations in each case were benchmarked to the latest historical data to obtain the constant terms.

Forecasts

In 1980, forecasts of electricity and natural gas prices were made for the years 1981-2000. Forecasts of industrial output levels were conditioned on forecasts of Gross National Product (GNP) and estimates of growth for SIC's 28 and 29.

With regard to electricity, forecasts of electricity purchase intensity were prepared for the period from 1981-2000 for the petroleum refining and chemicals industries in the Houston SMSA.

The graphs of ratio of demand to value-added show that the Composite Equation forecasts less growth in 1981 and 1982 than the Historical Equation (see Figure 4). Further, in the Composite

Equation, the negative electricity price effects strikingly dominate the lag-adjustment effect from 1983 through 1988; while in the Historical Equation, this price effect did not dominate the lag-adjustment effect until 1984, after which a modest domination was present. In 1988, both equations give minimum forecasts for the 20-year forecasting period; however, the minimum in electricity purchase intensity was 24 percent less for the Composite Equation than for the Historical Equation. After 1988, both equations show increasing electricity purchase intensity, with the Historical Equation giving noticeably higher values than the Composite Equation.

Using the forecast values for value-added as made in December 1980, the forecasts of electricity purchase requirements were more optimistic from the Historical Equation than from the Composite Equation (See Figure 5). The forecasts from the Composite Equation peaked in 1982; however, the forecasts from the Historical Equation did not peak until 1984. That is, on the basis of what was foreseen in December, 1980, the Composite Equation showed that the negative price effect was going to dominate the positive lag adjustment effect within two years; while the Historical Equation was showing that the positive lag adjustment effect was going to generally prevail over the negative price effect, and that any slowdown in industry's electricity purchases, because of conservation, was going to be modest indeed. However, the Composite Equation showed that the conservation effect was going to significantly decrease industry's electricity purchases starting in 1983 and continuing through 1986; further, the recovery from this recession was going to take four years to just get back to the 1982 forecast level.

In actual reality, significant conservation in electricity purchases by industry occurred shortly after the sharp increase in world oil prices in 1979/1980.

Using estimated value-added, this conservation effect is strikingly evident from the intensity of electricity purposes (see Table 1). As shown, the intensity of actual electricty purchases, relative to estimated value-added, decreased 14 percent from 1980 to 1981 and another 6%

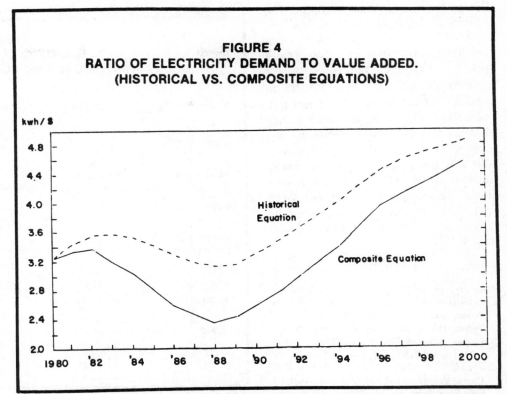

FIGURE 4
RATIO OF ELECTRICITY DEMAND TO VALUE ADDED.
(HISTORICAL VS. COMPOSITE EQUATIONS)

from 1981 to 1982. It increased toward the 1981 level in 1983 followed by a decrease toward the 1982 level in 1984. In comparison, the Composite Equation did not show an increase in the electricity purchase intensity in 1981; and further, it showed continuing decreases in these intensities from 1981 through 1984. However, the Historical Equation shows higher electricity purchase intensities in 1981, 1982, 1983 and 1984 than in 1980; and it shows an increase in the electricity purchase intensity in 1981 and another increase in 1982. Thus, to date, the Composite Equation electricity purchase intensities follow more closely the actual electricity pruchase intensities than the Historical Equation electricity purchase intensities.

With use of the Composite Equation, 981 megawatts less electricity generating capacity would be forecast for the Houston SMSA than with use of the Historical Equation. Using published estimates, construction costs would be nearly one billion dollars (in 1985 dollars) less for plans based on the Composite Equation than for plans based on the Historical Equation.

With regard to natural gas, the Composite Equation for the Houston SMSA was scaled upward to represent purchas-

ed natural gas by the petroleum refining and basic chemicals industries in the nation. This scaling assumes that the sensitivities of electricity and natural gas demand to price will be the same in the nation as it is in the Houston SMSA, which seems plausible (see Figure 6).

Several inferences can be drawn from the Composite Equation forecasts of natural gas use by the petroleum refining and basic chemicals industries. High prices of natural gas, relative to the prices of electricity, as existing in 1980 would significantly depress industry's demand for gas in the 1980's. For the 1980's, the economic growth effect was not going to be sufficient to offset the negative price effects of high energy prices.

Interestingly, the Historical Equation for industrial natural gas use in the petroleum refining and chemicals industries maintained its exponential growth pattern in the forecast period. That basis for forecasting natural gas use in these industries would have been a costly planning error for these industries in the 1981-1985 period. Actual natural gas use in the chemicals (SIC 28) and petroleum refining (SIC 29) industries decreased every year from 1980/1981 through 1984/1985, as reported by the

Energy Information Administration. The relative decreases in use for the two industries together were 8% from 1980/1981 to 1981/82, 20% from 1981/82 to 1982/83, 28% from 1982/83 to 1983/84, and 32% from 1983/84 to 1984/85. Thus, the downward trend in natural gas use by these two major industries was forecast correctly by the Composite Equation in 1980. However, this new trend would have been totally missed by the Historical Equation in 1980. Again, the data observed since 1980 lends credibility to the Composite Equation, not to the Historical Equation ●

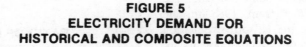
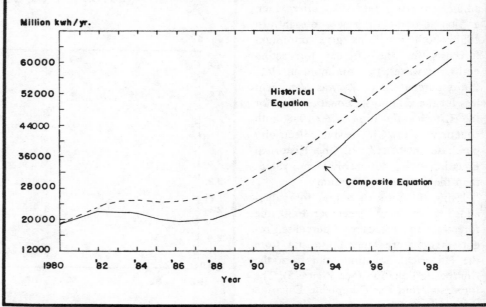

FIGURE 5
ELECTRICITY DEMAND FOR
HISTORICAL AND COMPOSITE EQUATIONS

References

Calloway, J.A. and Thompson, R.G. "An Integrated Industry Model of Petroleum Refining, Electric Power, and Chemical Industries for Costing Pollution Control and Estimating Energy Prices." **Engineering and Process Economics.** Vol. 1, 1976, pp. 199-216.

Dorfman, R., Samuelson, P.A., and Solow, R.M. **Linear Programming and Economic Analysis.** New York: McGraw-Hill, 1958.

Griffin, J.M. "Joint Production Technology: The Case of Petro-Chemicals." **Eocnometrica.** March, 1978.

Marshak, J. "Statistical Inference in Economics: An Introduction." **Statistical Inference in Dynamic Economic Models.** T.C. Koopmans (ed.) New York: John Wiley and Sons, Inc. 1953, pp. 1-52.

Marshak, J. "Economic Measurements for Policy and Prediction." **Studies in Econometric Method.** Wm. C. Hood and Tjalling C. Koopmans (eds.) New York: John Wiley and Sons, Inc. 1953, pp. 1-26.

Maddala, G.S. **Econometrics.** New York: McGraw-Hill Book Co., 1977.

Nerlove, M. **Distributed Laws and Demand Analysis.** U.S. Department of Agriculture Handbook 141, Washington, D.C., 1958.

RGT, Inc. Industrial Forecasting Model for Houston Lighting & Power Company Service Area, report to Houston Lighting & Power Company, Houston, Tx., December, 1980.

Singleton, F.D., Jr., Muthukrishan, S., Taylor, F.A., III, and Thompson, R.G. **Solid Fuels Conversion Costs for Texas-Coal and Other Industries.** University of Houston Technical Report to the Texas Energy Advisory Council, January, 1979.

Thompson, R.G., Stone, J.C., Muthukrishnan, S., and Halter, A.M. "Refinements in Energy Economic Modeling for Policy Purposes." **Computers and Operations Research.** Vol. 9, 1982, CAOR-67, pp. 1-24.

Thompson, R.G. Calloway, J.A., and Schwartz, Andrew K., Jr., "National Economic Models of Industrial Water Use and Waste Treatment." **Economic Modeling for Water Policy Evaluation.** R.M. Thrall et al. (eds.) North-Holland/TIMS Studies In the Management

Sciences, Vol. 3. Amsterdam: North-Holland Publishing Company, 1976, pp. 57-74.

Thompson, R.G. and Singleton, F.D., Jr. "Statistical Economic Aggregates for Petrochemical Industries Replicated with Linear Programming Model." **Computers and Operations Research.** Vol. 12, 1985, pp. 117-124.

Thompson, R.G. and Singleton, F.D., Jr. "Fore-casting Industrial Electricity Demand in the Face of Structural Change." Texas Public Utility Commission Files, Austin, Texas.

Thompson, R.G., Singleton, F.D., Jr., Stone, J.C. and Khosravian, K.R. "High Prices Will Dampen Industry's Demand for Gas." **Review of Regional Economics and Business.** April, 1982, pp. 9-15.

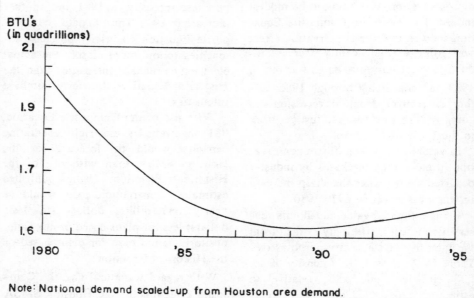

FIGURE 6
BTU's OF NATURAL GAS USED IN PETROLEUM
REFINING AND CHEMICAL INDUSTRIES U.S.
(1980-1995)

Note: National demand scaled-up from Houston area demand.

Chapter 9
When To Change a Model

George C. S. Wang
Consolidated Edison Company of New York

The 1973 oil embargo jolted the utility industry into a search for a method of forecasting short-term electricity demand which is still going on today. The most important lesson learned from this search was that industry forecasters could no longer ignore price as a significant factor affecting consumption.

In the BE (before embargo) era, preparation of a short-term forecast of electricity demand was a relatively uncomplicated procedure. A simple time series analysis in which past consumption patterns were extrapolated into the future produced accurate forecasts in the two to three year range. But the oil embargo changed all that: both utility management and regulatory authorities recognized that the sharp price increases in energy prices were having a significant impact on electricity demand.

Consider the New York City area serviced by Consolidated Edison. In 1974, real electric price in the area rose 36% primarily because of the quadrupling of oil prices in that year; in the same year, Con Edison's electric sales dropped 6%. Even by 1982, Con Edison's electric sales had still not returned to the 1973 level.

Before the oil embargo, only a handful of authorities estimated the short-term and long-term price elasticities of demand for electricity. Since the oil embargo, interested researchers [1,2] and utility fore-casters have been developing econometric models to forecast the demand for electricity. These models always include a price variable as one factor to explain sales variations.

Forecasters at Con Ed joined the trend: we developed an econometric model in which price is one of the factors used to forecast electricity demand.

Quarterly Model

The econometric model developed at Con Edison is a quarterly model using historic data from the first quarter of 1973 through the most recent quarter for which data are available. The choice of 1973 as the first year of the modeling period was based on the consideration of data consistency during the post embargo period. A different model structure is probably required for the period prior to the embargo.

An advantage of employing quarterly data is that the seasonal variations in consumption patterns and the impact of summer-winter rate differentials in the price variable can be more properly evaluated.

The model incorporates: (1) two climatic variables (cooling degree days and heating degree days) (2) the average real electric price (3) local non-manufacturing employment (4) two dummy variables, one to simulate the impacts of the 1973-74 oil embargo and the other to reflect the 1979 temperature regulations affecting commercial buildings.

The reasons for including the two climatic variables and the real electric price variable are obvious. The employment variable is included as a surrogate for the regional economy. Although the employment variable functions well in the model, the search for other economic variables for model testing and improvement is a continuing effort of the modeling staff. (The availability of regional economic data for modeling electric sales is quite limited).

Average Price

Theoretically, the marginal price rather than the average price should be used in a demand function, since the average price may be simultaneously related to quantity demand. Due to discounts based on consumption, however, the average price decreases as consumption increases.

Marginal price is also difficult to determine, because of the many consumption blocks included in the tariff schedule. It is not clear which of the block rates should be selected as the marginal rate. A recent Electric Power Institute (EPRI) publication carries two articles addressing the method of incorporating the declining rate structure into demand functions. [3]

Moreover, since the tariff structure changes over time, it is difficult to compile a consistent series of marginal prices. Recently, there has been a trend to reduce the number of blocks in the tariff. Thus, the choice between average price and marginal price is less important than it was years ago.

In the utility industry, the fuel cost for electricity generation is generally passed on to consumers in proportion to consumption. When the fuel cost component constitutes a large portion of the total bill, the simultaneity between the average price and the quantity demand diminishes. The use of average price in the forecasting model has not been found to cause any serious problems.

Forecast

A single equation is used to forecast the total sendout of electricity. The forecast is then translated into kilowatthour sales to each type of customer group on the basis of the historic sales mix. A set of pricing equations, which were separately developed, are then utilized to estimate revenues from sales to each customer group. The forecasting model is non-linear due to a restriction imposed upon the coefficients of the price variable and the oil embargo dummy. The restriction requires the model to estimate both the short-term and long-term price elasticities and the short-term and long-term impact of the oil embargo. The long-term elasticity is assumed to asymptotically approach its equilibrium over time.

(A "linear model" represents a fixed relation while a "non-linear" model describes a changing relationship between variables. This model estimates the process of the consumer's gradual adjustment of consumption of electricity in response to a price change. This gradual adjustment process will continue over time until the desired level of consumption is reached. This is a changing relationship between the electricity price and the consumption. The model is, therefore, non-linear. The gradual adjustment is termed as an "asymptotically approaching" process. The coefficient of a variable measures the degree of its impact on a forecast. A dummy variable is used to estimate the impact of the oil embargo on electricity sales. The embargo was a special event. When it occurred, it caused a drop in sales; when it was over, its impact gradually disappeared.)

For the other variables in the model, only the short-term elasticities are estimated. The model structure and the estimated coefficients are included in the technical appendix.

In forecasting, the two climatic variables are the thirty-year (1951 through 1980) average cooling and heating degree days. (The degree days can be defined as the difference between the average temperature in a given day and a reference temperature, e.g., 65°F. When the daily average is below the reference, the differ-

ence is called heating degree days; when it is above the reference, it is called cooling degree days. The reference temperature for the heating degree days may be different from that for the cooling degree days.)

Bank Economists

The employment and local CPI (Consumer Price Index) input forecasts have generally been based on local area forecasts supplied by Wharton Economic Forecasting Associates. At times, however, based on our knowledge of recent develop-

ments in the area's economy and discussions with other regional economists, particularly with those at major banks and government agencies, we have adjusted Wharton's employment and CPI forecasts.

The CPI forecast is used in the calculations of real electric price. The other component's of the electric price variable are the fuel cost for electricity generation and the base tariff rates developed by other operating departments of the company.

The accuracy of forecasting the demand for electricity depends not only on the correctness of the model specification, but also on the accu-

TABLE 1
ACTUAL VS. FORECAST
(Million kilowatthours)

Period	Actual Normalized For Weather	Forecast	Error (In Percent)
1981:			
1st quarter	8,948	8,795	1.7
2nd quarter	8,741	8,690	0.6
3rd quarter	9,982	9,760	2.2
4th quarter	8,850	8,805	0.5
Annual	36,521	36,050	1.3
1982:			
1st quarter	9,060	8,950	1.2
2nd quarter	8,789	8,760	0.3
3rd quarter	10,125	10,080	0.4
4th quarter	8,934	8,835	1.1
Annual	36,908	36,625	0.8

TABLE 2
ESTIMATED COEFFICIENTS AND t-STATISTICS

Coefficient	Estimates	t-Value
a_0	2.408	3.3
d	0.604	5.3
a_1	− 0.101	− 7.0
a_2	0.374	4.0
a_3	0.000246	14.6
a_4	0.000043	6.3
a_5	− 0.043	− 6.0
a_6	− 0.033	− 3.4

R^2 (Adjusted for degree of freedom)	=	.974
S (Standard error of regression)	=	0.011
H (Test of autocorrelation)	=	1.50
Long-term price elasticity	=	− 0.255

racy of the input forecast. The largest forecast errors are caused by weather variations, a condition that is well understood by management and the regulatory agencies.

Forecast Errors

Forecast errors resulting from errors in the other input forecasts require more in-depth investigation. Table 1 shows a comparison of actual sendouts with forecast as experienced in the past two years. The variations were largely due to unanticipated changes in the real electric price and local employment rates.

The 1981 forecast was made at the end of 1980, and the 1982 forecast, at the end of 1981.

The forecast and the sales revenue estimates derived from it are routinely furnished to the various operating departments of the Company for use in the preparation of the operating budget, cash flow analysis, fuel requirements, etc. This forecast methodology is also utilized to project the data submitted to the Public Service Commission for examination during electric rate case proceedings.

●

REFERENCES

1. Bohi, D.R., "Analyzing Demand Behavior; A Study of Energy Elasticity." The John Hopkins University Press, 1981.

2. _____(Principal Investigator), "Price Elasticity of Demand for Energy—Evaluating the Estimates." Electric Power Institute, EPRI EA-2612, Project 1220-1, September 1982.

3. Corio, M.R. (Principal Investigator) and J.S. Chipman and G.M. Duncan (Consultants), "Aggregate Residential Electricity Demand: Methods for Integrating Over Declining Block Rates." Electric Power Institute, EPRI-2767, Project 1361, December 1982.

4. Box G.E.P. and D.R. Cox, "An Analysis of Transformation." Journal of the Royal Statistical Society, Series B, 26, 1964.

TECHNICAL APPENDIX

The functional form of the forecasting model was postulated as non-linear with logarithm transformation of the sendout, real electric price, and employment data. The non-linear structure was a direct result of the model specification to estimate both the short-term and long-term price elasticities and to estimate only the short-term elasticities for the other variables in the model. The logarithm transformation was not only for the convenience of estimating elasticities, but application of the Box-Cox approach [4] to the data indicated that the logarithm transformation also improves the efficiency of the model. (The Box-Cox procedure was applied to the linear form of the model; i.e., the restriction on the coefficients of the price and oil embargo dummy variables was removed.)

The final model specification is as follows:

$$y_t = a_0 + dy_{t-4} + a_1 P_t + a_2 (E_t - dE_{t-4}) + a_3 (CCD_t - dCDD_{t-4}) + a_4 (HDD_t - dHDD_{t-4}) + a_5 D_{1t} + a_6 (D_{2t} - dD_{2t-4}).$$

Where,

y_t = logarithm of quarterly sendout of electricity,

P_t = logarithm of quarterly real electric price,

E_t = logarithm of quarterly employment,

CDD_t, HDD_t = quarterly cooling and heating degree days,

D_{1t} = oil embargo dummy
= 1 for the fourth quarter 1973 through the 3rd quarter 1974,
= 0, otherwise,

D_{2t} = Temperature Regulation Dummy
= 1 for the third quarter 1979,
= 0, otherwise,

e_t = disturbance.

The estimated coefficients, t-values and other model statistics are shown in Table 2. (The mathematical derivation of this model is available from the author.)

Chapter 10
A Way To Keep Up With A Shifting Market Place

John E. Triantis
AT&T Communications

Many forecast errors—especially large ones—can usually be traced to the failure of most techniques to recognize permanent changes in the underlying structure of the market and to account for them in the forecast. Many attempts, based both on statistical methods and judgment, have been made to overcome this weakness.

One which the author has found effective is a technique called "Varying Parameter Regression" (VPR). It is used to estimate the values of certain statistics in a forecasting model.The major difference between VPR and most other techniques is the assumption on which they are based. The VPR techinque, unlike others, entertains the notion that the underlying structure of the market may not remain stable over time; it assumes that the structure is subject to two types of changes (Note: Technical words and phrases appearing in *italics* in the text are defined in nontechnical terms in the Glossary at the end of this article. Ed.):

1. Permanent changes which are reflected by upward or downward drifts in the *parameter* values that persist over time.
2. Transitory changes which are reflected by an upward or downward blip in the *regression coefficients* caused by one-time, unusual, random events,

The author thanks John J. Cotter for his support in this project. The model used here does not in any way reflect the views, practices or policies of AT&T Communications.

such as strikes, severe weather, fire, product recall, etc.; the term "Random" is usually applied to this type of change.

Illustrations

VPR distinguishes between those types of changes, and incorporates the information into the values of the parameters to produce a more reliable forecast. VPR also:

1. Helps determine whether or not the model is properly specified (*model specification*)
2. Pinpoints the period in time when a structural change has occurred in the historical data
3. Estimates the values of the parameters *(model estimation)* one period beyond the sample (historical) period

To illustrate the difference between VPR and other techniques, we have selected as an example a *multiple regression* model. In one case, the parameters are estimated with one of the most popular techniques, *ordinary least squares* (OLS), and in another with the VPR technique.

Telephone Demand

The model constructed for this purpose assumes that the demand for telephone messages from the U.S. to another country (the *dependent variable*) depends on the values of the following *explanatory variables:* the number of messages actually demanded in the period immediately before the *current period* (denoted X_1); a price index of nominal telephone rates between the two countries during the historical period (X_2); real U.S. personal income (X_3), a general price deflator (X_4), and seasonal influences (S_1, S_2, S_3). The last mentioned are *dummy* variables.

The relationships between the explanatory variables listed above and the dependent variable are stated in the following multiple regression model:

$$Y = a + b_1X_1 + b_2X_2 + b_3X_3 + b_4X_4 + b_5S_1 + b_6S_2 + b_7S_3 + U$$

Where:
- Y = dependent variable
- a = the *constant, or intercept*
- b_1-b_7 = *regression coefficients*
- X_1-X_4 = explanatory, or independent variables.
- S_1-S_3 = seasonal variables *(dummy)*
- U = *error term*

(See Footnote below for explanation of the absence of the fourth season of the year, S_4, and how it is accounted for. Ed.)

Under these circumstances, the value of the constant is fixed as it is found by the OLS process; in reality it is an average value over the time period represented by the historical data series. The same is true of the values of the regression coefficients; they, too, remain fixed through time once their average values are computed under OLS. Only the values of the explanatory variables (Xs) change over time to represent their actual values in each of the periods in the historical data series and their forecast values in the forecast periods.

A structural change, therefore, is given short shrift by the OLS technique. Such changes will have some effect on the values of the constant and coefficients under the OLS assumption, but only to the extent that they affect the average values; their full impact at any given point in time is not reflected.

OLS statistics cannot always determine whether the model is properly specified, that is, that the explanatory variables do, in fact, properly explain the changes that occur in the dependent variable.

VPR Assumption

VPR, on the other hand, allows for the notion of changing values for each coefficient over time. Under this assumption, VPR states that the coefficients of the *present periods* are composed of a permanent component (structural change) and a transitory, or random component. The permanent part of the coefficients in the present period are expressed in terms of the coefficients of the previous period's permanent component and another *error term*.

In effect, the VPR technique computes individual values for the constant and each of the coefficients for each period in the historical record.

(VPR estimation is a complicated process. Its details, therefore, are not discussed in this article. Readers interested in learning more about it are referred to papers by Cooley, and Cooley and Prescott listed in the References. A computer program is available from Carnegie-Mellon University, Pittsburgh, PA. Consulting services are available from Evangelos O. Simos, head of International Business Resources, Inc., 24 Tennyson Ave., Dover, New Hampshire 03820.)

Figures 1a-3d

Under the VPR assumptions, we obtain the values of the parameters shown in Figures 1a through 3d. Compare those with the single parameter values found by the OLS technique shown in Table 1. Note that the parameter values found by the VPR technique change over time but that the OLS technique finds only one value for each.

The data exhibited in the charts is interpreted as follows:

1. The evolution of the constant term (Figure 1a) exhibits wide fluctuations in its pattern beginning in 1977-'78 with an increase in the average value in the period 1978-'81. This suggests that something is disturbing the market structure, a disturbance not captured by the explanatory variables chosen to ex-

plain the changes in the dependent variable. Or, as a statistician would put it, "the model is mis-specified."

2. The values of the *lagged dependent variable coefficient* (Figure 1b) exhibit a strong downward trend from 1973 to 1980 at which point they turn sharply upward. The behavior of this coefficient indicates that it adapts well to the changes in the market.

3. The plots of the price index (Figure 2a) and the consumption price deflator (Figure 2b) show that the market was quite stable during the 1971 to 1978-'79 period but appears to have experienced shocks in the 1979-81 period. On the other hand, the income

TABLE 1 OLS COEFFICIENT VALUES	
Variable	**Coefficient**
Constant Term (a)	−2.7162
Messages of Previous Period (b1)	.2949
Telephone Rates (b2)	−.1597
Real U..S personal income (b3)	1.9949
General price deflator (b4)	.9598
First quarter seasonal (S1)	−.1093
Second quarter seasonal (S2)	.1837
Third quarter seasonal (S3)	.0129

coefficient (Figure 2c) exhibits an upward trend.

The pattern exhibited by the VPR parameters suggests an evolution in telephone usage between the two countries.

4. As for the seasonal coefficients (Figures 3a through 3d), we find them to be stable until about 1974 when they begin an ascent with a strong trend until 1980 at which point they stabilize again.

The upward drift in the values of these coefficients cannot be due to seasonal changes alone; all seasonal factors cannot increase in the absence of a strong underlying cause. If these seasonal factors were, in fact, capturing the effects of seasonal influences alone, we would expect that some would increase and others decrease.

The conclusion, therefore, is that the seasonal variables are capturing the effects of some other factors (explanatory variables) that have not been included in the model. This confirms the information obtained from Figure 1a— the

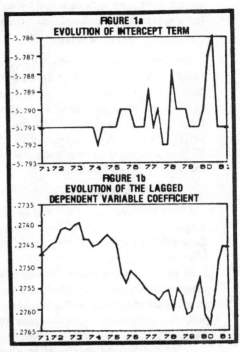

model is mis-specified.

The VPR model also measures the portion of the changes that are of a permanent nature. In this case, that portion is 40 percent, implying that the structure of the model used in this case is not adequate. It is relatively unstable and subject to outside influences originating in the U.S. and the other country. (The

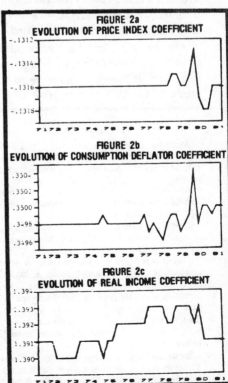

40 percent figure is determined by solving a maximum likelihood function.)

Fixed Values

Obviously, then, a forecast based on ordinary least squares with its assumption of fixed values of the parameters cannot always produce a reliable forecast. Moreover, it can lead one to believe that it does since, unlike the VPR technique, it cannot issue a warning about its own inadequacy.

Alternatives

Given that the model used in the example is mis-specified as demonstrated by the VPR technique, one can do one of three things:

1. Re-specify the model by adding or subtracting explanatory variables, and re-estimate the model by OLS, and project the dependent variable into the forecast period.

2. Re-specify the model as in alternative 1 above and re-estimate the model by VPR and project the dependent variable into the future.

3. Accept the mis-specification and the errors associated with it and project the dependent variable into the forecast period using VPR.

If the second alternative fails to provide a reasonable forecast after a number of attempts, the chances are that the model cannot be specified.

Alternatives 2 and 3 are recommended only for those occasions when one is in a hurry and does not have immediate access to the VPR technique ●

GLOSSARY

Multiple Regression Model: A model that assumes that there is a cause and effect relationship between the value of the variable for which a forecast is being prepared and two or more other variables. The major assumption of the model is that the relationships are fixed through time and will continue into the future.

Ordinary Least Squares: A statistical procedure that quantifies the past relations assumed by the regression model (see above).

Dependent Variable: The variable for which a forecast is being prepared using a statistical model. Usually denoted by the symbol Y with a subscript to denote the time period covered by the data: $t+1$, for example, denotes the period beyond the most recent period of the historical data series being used; $t-1$ denotes the period immediately before.

Explanatory (Independent) Variables: Variables that are deemed to have a significant effect on the behavior (value) of the dependent variable (see above).

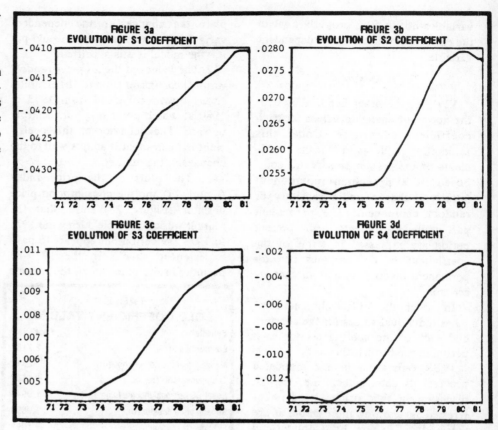

FIGURE 3a
EVOLUTION OF S1 COEFFICIENT

FIGURE 3b
EVOLUTION OF S2 COEFFICIENT

FIGURE 3c
EVOLUTION OF S3 COEFFICIENT

FIGURE 3d
EVOLUTION OF S4 COEFFICIENT

Dummy Variable(s): A substitute for an explanatory variable the actual value of which is not known but which is believed to have an effect on the dependent variable. A dummy variable is given a value of from 0 to 1, 0 when it has no effect on the dependent variable and 1 when it does. A value of 1 is assigned to the variable for those periods when it has had an effect on the dependent variable (a strike, fire, product recall, etc.) and a value of 0 when the variable has had no effect on the dependent variable.

Model Specification: Selection of the explanatory variables which are deemed to have a significant effect on the dependent variable. They are usually denoted by the symbol X with a subscript to distinguish one from another. i.e., X_1, X_2, etc.

Constant (Intercept): Roughly speaking, the value of the dependent variable without taking into account the specific effects on it of all of the explanatory variables. Example: The amount of sales a company would enjoy if it did nothing more than open its doors each morning and it was not affected by outside forces. It is usually denoted by the Greek letter alpha (α) or the letter a. It is also called the intercept because it is a point on the perpendicular axis on a graph where the "regression line" begins (See Figure 1 and "Regression Coefficient" below).

Regression Coefficient: A measure of the degree to which a given explanatory variable influences the value of the dependent variable. The value of the coefficient indicates the amount of change that occurs in the dependent variable for each unit of change in the explanatory variable to which it is applied as, for example, b_1X_1. The value of each coefficient is found by several

methods, one of which is Ordinary Least Squares (See above). Coefficients are usually denoted by the Greek letter Beta (β) or the letter b.

Error Term: The difference between the actual value of the dependent variable and its value as estimated by the model. One of its uses is to re-estimate the value of the dependent variable by incorporating it in the original model.

Parameters: A collective noun for the constant, coefficients, and other statistics associated with a regression.

Present (or Current) Period: Present period does not necessarily mean the present period in real time. It refers to the most recent period in the data series that is being used to estimate the value of the dependent variable in any period. Assume, for example, that the parameters have been estimated on the basis of 20 quarters of historical data beginning the first quarter of 1981. Using those parameters in the multiple regression model, we can estimate the value of the dependent variable for any period in time, past or future, by applying them to the actual or forecasted values of the dependent variables of the same period. Thus, if we were to estimate the value of the dependent variable in period 6 (part of the historical data), it would be the "present period.

Lagged Dependent Variable: In some situations, the value of the dependent variable in one period has an impact on its own value in the next period. The number of cars sold during the forecast period, for example, depends on car prices, personal income, interest rates, and other independent variables. And it also depends on the number of cars sold during the period prior to the forecast period. To account for this factor, the value of the dependent variable in the period prior to the forecast period is incorporated into the model as another independent variable.

Model Application: After the model is satisfactorily specified and estimated, the values of the parameters are applied to the *forecast* value of each of the explanatory variables. Hence, if one requires a forecast of the third period beyond the most recent period covered by the historical data (current period), denoted t+3, one needs a forecast of the value of each explanatory variable in that future period.

Model Estimation: The values of the parameters as computed by a statistical process.

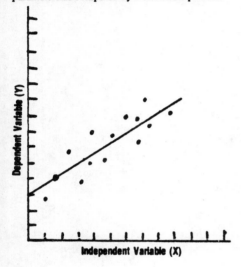

The above figure is for illustrative purposes only. It was drawn free hand without use of data. It illustrates the relationship between only one independent variable and the depedent variable. The relationships between all of the independent variables and the dependent variable would entail superimposing a number of graphs on each other resulting in a blur.

FOOTNOTE

Traditionally, seasonal *dummy variables* are introduced in a model in either one of two ways:

1. Use four seasonal dummies and eliminate the constant term from the model.
2. Use three seasonal dummies and the constant term, and allow the constant term to measure the effect of the fourth seasonal dummy.

The second approach is used in this article with a modification. The definition of the seasonal dummies under that approach is: $S_1 = (1, 0, 0, -1)$, $S_2 = (0, 1, 0, -1)$, and $S_3 = (0, 0, 1, -1)$.

The advantage of this definition is that it allows the constant term to remain in the equation and the coefficient of the fourth seasonal dummy to be estimated by making $S_4 = S_1 + S_2 + S_3$.

References

Cooley, T.F. Estimation in the Presence of Sequential Parameter Variation. Unpublished Ph.D. dissertation, University of Pennsylvania.

Cooley, T.F. and Prescott, E.C. "Systematic (Non-Random) Variation Models - Varying Parameter Regression: A Theory and Some Applications." **Annals of Economic and Social Measurement.** (214), 1973, pp. 463-473.

_____, "An Adoptive Regression Model." **International Economic Review.** (14), 1973, pp. 364-371.

_____, "Tests of an Adoptive Regression Model." **Review of Economics and Statistics.** (55), 1973, pp. 248-256.

_____, "Estimation in the presence of Stochastic Parameter Variation." **Econometrica.** (44), 1976, pp. 167-184.

Simos, E.O. "Structural Change in the Production Function: Evidence from the U.S. Private Economy, 1929-1973." **Zeitschrift fur Nationalokonomie.** (40), 1980, pp. 149-168.

Simos, E.O. and Triantis, J.E. "Human Wealth and Price Variability in the Demand for Money: U.S. Post-War Evidence." **Economic Notes.** (12), 1983, pp. 161-173.

PART III

Improving Regression Based Models

Chapter 11
Five Ways To Improve Regression Based Models

William M. Bassin
Shippenburg University

Technicians are always looking for ways and means to improve a forecast. A given forecasting model may give fairly good results. Diagnostics and search methods, discussed here, can improve the results of a regression based model further. (A regression model is based on a cause and effect relationship. The effect refers to a dependent variable, the variable that is to be forecast—sales, for example. Cause refers to independent variables—price and advertising expenditure for example—that influence the dependent variable.)

Regression diagnostics critically examine the forecast equation for weaknesses which otherwise might remain hidden. Diagnosing and correcting these weaknesses improve forecast results.

The diagnostics illustrated in this paper are:

1. The Durbin-Watson statistic
2. The turning point test
3. The time test
4. Leverages
5. A backtest

First Approximation

Before going through these tests, there needs to be a predictive equation to be tested or enhanced. The existing equation can serve as a first approximation (the one to be enhanced). If no equation exists, one can develop it based on judgement and experience and use it as a first approximation.

Suppose that a company forecasts personal consumption expenditures on radios, TVs and related appliances (RADTV). The equation is already in place. It states that RADTV depends on disposable income (INC), fixed investment in residential structures (RES), and a price deflator for RADTV (PRICE), where:

RADTV = (Dependent variable) Personal consumption expenditures on radios, TVs and related appliances, measured in billions of 1972 dollars, seasonally adjusted at an annual rate

INC = (Independent variable) Disposable income, measured in billions of 1972 dollars, seasonally adjusted at an annual rate

RES = (Independent variable) Fixed investment in residential structures, measured in billions of 1972 dollars, seasonally adjusted at an annual rate

PRICE = (Independent variable) The implicit price deflator for RADTV, deflated by the consumer price index

Quarterly data for these variables over the 1Q/73 through 4Q/83 interval were used to build a forecasting equation based on the linear regression technique. The first predictive equation is:

$$RADTV = 8.98 + .0189(INC) + .0209(RES) - .254(PRICE)$$

To forecast RADTV, simply plug anticipated values of INC, RES, and PRICE into this equation.

This first predictive equation gives fairly good results. Its major characteristics are as follows:

1. The R-squared value is .989. That is, the independent variables "explain" 98.9% of the variation in RADTV. The R-squared value can vary between zero and one. The closer the R-squared value is to one, the better is the predictive ability of the equation.

2. Each of the coefficients has the right sign. A regression coefficient is a measure of the degree to which a given explanatory (independent) variable influences the value of the dependent variable. The value of the coefficient indicates the amount of change that occurs in the dependent variable for each unit of change in the explanatory variable. Increases in INC and RES should cause the forecasted value of RADTV to rise, while increases in PRICE should have the opposite effect. The coefficients conform to these ideas.

3. Each of the coefficients is "significant." The significance of a coefficient is measured by its "t-ratio." This is the ratio of the coefficient to its standard error. (The standard error is a measure of the uncertainty attached to the value of the coefficient due to the fact that the regression is based on a sample of data.) The higher the t-ratio, the more likely that the value of the coefficient reflects a significant relationship between dependent and independent variables and not just a chance relationship caused by an unrepresentative sample. For example, the t-ratio for the INC variable is: 3.098 (.0189/.0061). This value indicates that the INC coefficient is more than three times as high as its uncertainty measure. This means that it is very likely that there is a significant relationship between INC and RADTV. The t-ratios for the RES and PRICE coefficients are 1.490 and −4.705, respectively. These ratios indicate high significance, too. Notice the signficance of the PRICE variable is negative as it should be.

4. When the equation is applied to the data for the 1Q/73 through 4Q/83 interval, the average error is only 2.54%.

However, the results of the first equation for the three quarters beyond the regression interval (1Q/84 through 3Q/84) are not as good as experienced during the 1Q/83 through 4Q/83 interval. The average percentage error rises from 2.54% to 8.62%. (See Table 1)

Table 1
Percentage Errors with the First Equation
(1Q/84 through 3Q/84)

Period	Actual RADTV	Forecast RADTV	Absolute Error	Percent Error
3Q/84	$27.8	$25.4	$2.4	8.63%
2Q/84	27.7	25.1	2.6	9.38
1Q/84	26.7	24.6	2.1	7.87
Average	$27.4	$25.0	$2.4	8.62%

The forecast errors are all positive, i.e., the actual RADTV values exceed the forecasts in all three quarters.

Durbin-Watson Statistic

The first of the diagnostic procedures is the Durbin-Watson statistic. The Durbin-Watson statistic measures the extent to which errors (actual less predicted values for each period) are correlated with each other. The ideal Durbin-Watson statistic value is 2.00, indicating no correlation among the errors, i.e., randomness. A rough lower bound, below which correlation can be considered to be serious, is 1.40. For the first forecast equation, the Durbin-Watson statistic is 0.523.

Table 2 shows absolute errors for the selected period 1Q/75-2Q/79. Notice that the errors are not random. Over the 1Q/75 through 4Q/76 interval, the errors are all positive. This means that the actual values in this interval are all higher than the predicted values. This suggests that a variable not in the regression equation is at work, boosting actual values above the predicted values. By the same token, the errors in the 1Q/77 through 2Q/79 interval are all negative, i.e., the actual values are lower than predicted. Perhaps the same

missing variable is operating in the opposite direction. In any event, the low Durbin-Watson value indicates that there are important missing variables which ought to be sought out.

Table 2
Absolute Errors With the First Equation

Period	Absolute Error
1Q/75	$0.127
2Q/75	0.141
3Q/75	0.264
4Q/75	0.499
1Q/76	0.431
2Q/76	0.304
3Q/76	0.310
4Q/76	0.086
1Q/77	−0.326
2Q/77	−0.309
3Q/77	−0.293
4Q/77	−0.037
1Q/78	−0.443
2Q/78	−0.529
3Q/78	−0.761
4Q/78	−0.337
1Q/79	−0.731
2Q/79	−0.317

Turning Point Test

Another indication of missing variables is the turning point test. The test works this way: Count the number of "turning points" among the absolute errors, i.e., the number of times in which the error is either above or below both of its neighbors. For example, 1Q/81 is a turning point because the errors for this quarter and its neighbors are as follows:

4Q/80	.040
1Q/81	.362
2Q/81	.129

The ideal number of turning points is $(2/3)(n-2)$, where n is the number of data periods. In this example, the ideal number is $(2/3)(44-2)=28$. If the actual number of turning points is close to this number, then the errors are presumed to be uncorrelated.

The actual number in our example is only 19, far too low. This also implies that the equation may be lacking in key independent variables.

The time test determines whether the coefficients of an equation vary with time. If so, the equation developed using data from the 1Q/73 through 4Q/83 interval cannot be counted on to remain stable, and the result will be poor forecasts. The test works this way:

1. Create a "time trend" variable, called TIME. In our example, TIME equals 1 in 1Q/73, equals 2 in 2Q/73, equals 3 in 3Q/73, and so on.

2. Create three other time variables: TIMEINC, TIMERES, and TIMEPRICE. These variables represent TIME multiplied by INC, TIME multiplied by RES, and TIME multiplied by PRICE, respectively.

3. Perform a linear regression over the same interval with RADTV as the dependent variable and with the following independent variables: INC, RES, PRICE, TIMEINC, TIMERES, TIMEPRICE, and TIME.

4. If the new regression has significantly less unexplained variation in RADTV (i.e., a higher R-squared value), then these new TIME variables are important. This would mean that time dependence does exist.

The results show that the addition of the time terms reduced the error from 2.54% to 1.6%. The coefficients of the first equation are therefore time dependent. This is another indication that some key independent variables are missing from the first equation.

Further evidence of missing independent variables is obtained by examining the leverage values for the first equation. The leverage value for a given period indicates the influence of that period on the values of the coefficients. The higher the leverage value, the more influential the period.

As a rule of thumb, a period has unusual influence if its leverage value exceeds 2 (m/n), where m is the number of coefficients including the intercept, and n is the number of periods in the regression interval. For the first equation, m is four and n is 44, and so the cutoff value is 2(4/44)=.182.

Other factors such as the state of the economy and changes in technology affect expenditures. Leverage values show whether these factors are accounted for in the equation. Periods in which these factors are unusually strong, such as recessions and recoveries, ought to show high leverage values. Table 3 shows the leverage values for the first equation for some periods of recession and recovery in the regression interval.

Table 3 shows that one period yields a leverage value which is significantly higher than .182, cut-off value estimated earlier. This is another evidence that the equation lacks key independent variables.

Table 3
Leverage Values for Selected Periods

Period	Leverage Value
1Q/75	.183
2Q/75	.202
2Q/80	.056
3Q/80	.049
2Q/83	101

Backtest

The Backtest simulates the use of the equation in forecasting periods at the end of the regression interval. For a Backtest of four quarters, the procedure is:

1. Re-run the regression using data only from the 1Q/73 through 4Q/82 interval, leaving the 1983 data for the simulated forecast.

2. Use the equation developed in step one to forecast the values of RADTV for the four quarters of 1983. In this way, the equation does not "benefit" from changes in the coefficients brought about by the events of 1983.

3. Compare the forecasts to the known actual values of RADTV during 1983.

The results of the Backtest are shown in Table 4. The table shows that the Backtest gives adequate warning of the ineffectiveness of the first equation. The errors are, on the average, larger than the errors in the whole of the regression interval (1Q/73 through 4Q/83). Also, the errors get larger as the quarter being forecasts become farther into the future. Both of these weaknesses imply that the equation is unreliable for forecasting. The key independent variables that the equation does not include have only a subtle effect in the historical regression interval. However, they can (and ap-

parently do) have a large impact in the period beyond the regression interval.

Enhancing the Equation

All of the diagnostic test results point to the need for enhancement of the first equation with additional explanatory variables. Without them, the equation is liable to fail.

Based on judgment and experience, the following independent variables seem to be promising additions to the ones used in the first equation:

IP367S = (Independent variable) FRB index of electronic component production, 1967 = 100, seasonally adjusted (This is a proxy for personal computer sales)

INT = (Independent variable) Interest rate on consumer loans

CIDRP = (Independent variable) Ratio of consumer installment debt to personal income

The task is to determine which combination of original and new variables yield the best predictive equation. Because of the high t-ratios of the INC and PRICE variables, it seems reasonable to keep them in the equation regardless and to try combinations of the four other variables: RES, IP367S, INT, and CIDRP.

A procedure for doing this is known as a linear search. It automatically performs regressions using equations involving INC and PRICE plus each possible combination of the above variables. It then selects the best equation using R-squared, t-ratios and the Durbin-Watson statistic as criteria. The best equation includes INC, PRICE IP367S, INT, and CIDRP. The three proposed variables have been added, but the RES variable has been dropped.

Lag Search

The equation can be enhanced further by considering the lagged values of the PRICE and INT variables. (For example, the 3Q/83 value of INT lagged two quarters is the value of INT in 1Q/83.) This is because changes in prices and interest rates make themselves felt over time A procedure for doing this is known as a lag search. It automatically performs

regressions on all equations resulting from combinations of lags (in this case, up to four) of INT and PRICE. The best equation turns out to be:

$$RADTV = 16.98 + .0229(INC)$$
$$+ .0115(IP367S)$$
$$- .218(PRICE1)$$
$$- .341(INT1)$$
$$- .749(CIDRP)$$

where PRICE1 and INT1 represent the values of PRICE and INT lagged one quarter, respectively. (See Bassin for further details about search procedures)

Table 4
Results of Backtest

Period	Actual Value	Simulated Forecast	Absolute Error	Percent Error
4Q/83	$25.4	$23.4	$2.0	7.87%
3Q/83	24.1	22.9	1.2	4.98
2Q/83	23.5	22.4	1.1	4.68
1Q/83	22.3	22.0	0.3	1.34
Average	$23.8	$22.7	$1.1	4.72%

Table 5
Comparative Results
First vs. Enhanced Equation

Period	Actual RADTV	Forecast	% Error	Forecast	%Error
3Q/84	$27.8	$25.4	8.63	$27.4	1.44
2Q/84	27.7	25.1	9.38	26.3	5.05
1Q/84	26.7	24.6	7.86	25.8	3.37
Average	$27.4	$25.0	8.62	$26.5	3.28

The enhanced equation yields conventional results even better than those given by the first equation.

1. The R-squared value is .996, vs. .989 for the first equation.

2. Each of the coefficients has the right sign and is highly significant, whereas the RES variable in the first equation was only mildly so.

3. When the equation is applied to the 1Q/73 through 4Q/83 data, the average absolute error is only 1.65% vs. 2.54% for the first equation.

The enhanced equation also performs better on most of the diagnostic tests. A summary follows:

1. The Durbin-Watson statistic is 1.254 for the enhanced equation. This is not a really good value, but it is a big improvement over the 0.523 value for the first equation.

2. There are 29 turning points, very nearly equal to the ideal value of 28. The first equation had only 19.

3. When time terms are added to the enhanced equation, the average percentage error declined from 1.65% to .91%.

4. The leverage values of the enhanced equation continue to be disappointing. Only one quarter has unusual influence.

5. The Backtest, however, yields an average error of only 2.78% vs. 4.72% for the first equation (See Table 4).

On the basis of the diagnostic test results, the enhanced equation shows more signs of taking account of important independent variables. It should therefore provide more accurate forecasts.

These conclusions are also supported by the performance of the enhanced equation in forecasting the first three quarters of 1984.

Table 5 shows that the enhanced equation cuts the error by well more than half ●

The software package which performs these diagnostic tests and search routines is available from SAGE Data, Inc., 104 Carnegie Center, Princeton, NJ 08540.

References

Bassin, W. **The Guide to SAGE.** Princeton: SAGE Data, Inc. 1983

Belsley, D.A., Kuh, E., and Welsch, R.E. **Regression Diagnostics.** New York: John Wiley, 1980.

Farley, J.V., Hinich, M. and McGuire, T.W. "Some Comparisons of Tests for a Shift in the Slopes of a Multivariate Linear Time Series Model." **Journal of Econometrics.** 3, 1975, pp.297-318.

Kendall, M.G. **Time Series.** London: Griffen, 1973.

Chapter 12
Ingredients of A Good Regression Based Model

Craig W. Slinkman
University of Texas at Arlington

Michael E. Hanna
University of Texas at Arlington

A forecasting model is good if it is not only technically sound but also acceptable to management. A model is developed to be used. If management does not accept certain relations exhibited by the model or for one reason or the other feels uncomfortable with it, the model will not be used—no matter how technically sound it may be. For example, a model may show that there exists a positive relationship between price and sales of a product, meaning that when price increases sales tend to increase. Management may not accept such a relation and thus question the validity of the model. If the model is not accepted by management the forecasts prepared using the model will not be used at all or not used as effectively as they could be. This article outlines what a regression based forecasting model needs for ultimate success and suggests ways that can make regression models more acceptable to management.

The major factors which contribute to the success of a model are (1) face validity, (2) technical validity, and (3) organizational validity.

Face Validity

By face validity we mean that the model gives relations both in direction and magnitude which, on the surface, appear to be logical and acceptable. Let's say a model shows when the price of a product decreases by one dollar the sales increase by one million dollars. The negative relationship between price and sales is understandable and thus ac-

ceptable. The model has face validity if it exhibits relations that seem reasonable to management. The magnitude of the relation, i.e., the one dollar price decrease causing a one million dollar increase in sales may also strike management as a reasonable figure. Also, to meet the criterion of face validity, the model must incorporate variables that are known to be important by management.

Consider the case of a northern utility company which wished to construct a new power plant. Permission had to be received from the public utility commission before construction could begin. As part of the company's justification for the new plant, a multiple regression model was used to predict the demand for electric power in the future. Two of the predictor variables (variables that influence the variable to be forecasted) used in the regression model were GNP and number of major electrical appliances. There were other predictor variables in the model but we do not need them for this example. There are various statistical measures for determining the technical soundness of a regression model. This model passed all of these measures. The model forecasted the demand for additional generating capacity. However, the regression coefficient for the variable, number of electrical appliances, had a negative sign. This implied as the number of home appliances increased the demand for electrical power decreased. This did not make sense to the members of the public utility commission who were not familiar with the finer points of regression analysis. Also, the model did not incorporate the variable, number of

households, which the public utility commission believed was important. As a result, the public utility commission distrusted the model and its forecasts, and denied the permit for construction of the new power plant.

Technical Validity

The second factor contributing to the success of a model is its technical validity. Technical validity means different things to different people. There are several statistical procedures for assessing the soundness of a model, though one forecaster may prefer one measure or one set of measures over others. In the final analysis, however, it comes down to how well a model forecasts. The model is technically sound if it yields forecasts with a minimal amount of error. Again, there are different ways of measuring error. The one commonly used is the average percentage error. To determine the validity of a forecasting model technicians normally split the data into two groups: one period is used to derive a predictive equation and then the second group is used to see how well the predicitive equation forecasts.

Organizational Validity

Organizational validity means that the organization as a whole (particularly those who use forecasts, say, marketing and production people) actually uses a model that makes a positive economic

55

impact on the organization. That is, a model that helps to make profit. For a non-profit organization a model is organizationally valid if it further the corporation goals.

Usually for a model to be organizationally valid it should be both technically valid and possess face validity. If it is not technically sound then it could give poor forecasts leading to lost profits. If the model does not possess face validity then the users of the forecasts may not trust it even though it gives good forecasts. Among other things users trust a model or view it as valid if they understand the basic ideas of the model and know its track record. Users normally don't have an advanced degree in statistics. Therefore, they are not interested in knowing the fine details of a model. In the case of a regression model, what they probably need to know is how, in general terms, a regression model functions, which variables were included in the model and why, etc. The more the users understand about the model the better.

Remedial Measures

Many times, in a regression based model, the presence of multicollinearity in the data weakens the face validity or the techncial validity or both. By multicollinearity we mean that two or more of the predictor variables used in the model are highly related to each other. In the above example, let's say, the predictor variables, GNP and number of electric appliances, are highly related to one another and the relationship is positive. This means that when the economy is in an upswing number of electrical appliances also rises. This is a multicollinear relationship between GNP and number of electrical appliances. Multicollinearity can cause an incorrect sign in the regression model when both variables are included. The incorrect sign of the number of electrical appliances may be due to the multicollinearity. Suppose the sign of number of electrical appliances is negative. This implies that all things being equal, an increase in electrical appliances will lead to a decreased demand for electricity. This does not make sense to a casual observer. Thus, the model lacks face validity.

Multicollinearity can also cause technical problems with a regression model. However, these are beyond the scope of this article and are not addressed here. The interested reader is referred to Montgomery and Peck in the references for more information.

There are a number of ways to remedy the problem of multicollinearity. One way is to drop one of the predictor variables which contributes to the problem. In the above example, let's say, the technician decided to drop the variable, number of electrical appliances. This would take care of its negative sign since it would no longer be in the prediction equation. However, this is a commonly used variable in regression models for the demand of electricity. The public utility commission may now say the model is incomplete because it does not contain a variable that everybody knows is important. That is, the model still lacks face validity. The solution to multicollinearity introduced a problem of face validity.

The second way to overcome multicollinearity is to average predictor variables that are related to each other. Such a procedure may improve technical validity but not face validity. The management may not accept or understand the resulting model since it is difficult to interpret the coefficient of the averaged variable.

A third way, and probably one of the best ways, to overcome multicollinearity is to use ridge regression. Ridge regression is a modification of standard multiple regression. To understand the basics of ridge regression a knowledge of the impact of multicollinearity on regression coefficients is required. (Regression coefficient measures the relationship between predictor variable and forecasting variable. If, in the above example, regression coefficient of GNP is .04, this will mean that, on the average, one unit of increase in GNP causes an increase in the demand for electric power by .04 unit.) Multicollinearity causes the regression coefficients of standard regression to become very sensitive to small changes in the data. That is, a small change in one of the predictor variables will cause a very large change

in regression coefficients. For example, a 1% increase in the value of GNP for one year may cause the coefficient for GNP to change by 100%. This causes the average absolute value of the regression coefficients to be "too large." Ridge regression shrinks the size of the average regression coefficient towards zero, overcoming the tendency of the coefficients to vary wildly. Essentially, ridge regression requires strong evidence in the data before it will believe that a regression coefficient is not zero. One way of viewing ridge regression is that the ridge regression coefficients are a weighted average between the standard regression coefficients and zero.

Ridge regression models have the property of yielding regression coefficients that have the correct sign. The coefficients that do not have the correct sign are insignificant, i.e., they do not improve the forecasting ability of the model. There are software packages such as Shazam which can do ridge regression●

References

Alter, Steve V. **Decision Support Systems.** Reading, Massachusetts: Addison-Wesley, 1980.

Armstrong, J. Scott. **Long Range Forecasting: From Crystal Ball to Computer.** New York: John Wiley, 1978.

Belsley, D., Kuh, E., and Welsch, R.E. **Regression Diagnostics: Identifying Influential Data and Sources of Collinearity.** New York: John Wiley, 1980.

Gunst, R., and Mason, R. **Regression Analysis and Its Applications.** New York: Marcel Decker, 1980.

Herman, C. "Validation Problems in Games and Simulations." **Behavioral Science.** Vol. 12, 1967, pp. 216-230.

Huysmans, J. **The Implementation of Operations Research.** New York: Wiley-Interscience, 1970.

Montgomery, D., and Peck, E. **Introduction to Linear Regression Analysis.** New York: John Wiley, 1982.

Mosteller, F., and Tukey, J.W. **Data Analysis and Regression.** Reading, Massachusetts: Addison-Wesley, 1977.

Schultz, R.L., and Slevin, D. (Editors). **Implementing Operations Research/Management Science.** New York: American Elsevier, 1975.

Chapter 13
Some Tips For Improving A Regression Model

Marion Sobol
Southern Methodist University

With the advent of computerized statistical packages it has become relatively simple to improve the predictability of a regression-based forecasting model. Many statisticians, particularly in business and economics, fail to check whether the model which predicts well for one data set will do the same for the other. If a model is good it should do well not only on a data set on which the model is based but also on a new data set. The purpose of this article is to demonstrate how the predictability of a regression-based model can be improved.

Types of Validity

By validity we mean how well a model performs on a new data set. There are two types of validity: (1) concurrent validity and (2) predictive validity. Concurrent validity is used to determine whether or not an equation (model) developed from a given data set performs well on a hold-out data set—data set aside for testing a model. Suppose we have 14 years of data. We may use first 10 years of data to develop a model and the next four years (hold-out period) to test it. Predictive validity is determined by testing a model on an altogether new set of data—data gathered at a new time period. Validation process is an important way of improving a model and yet it is often neglected.

Criteria For Validation

A model is validated if it meets all the validating criteria. When a model is

validated it means that the model can be expected to make good forecasts when used in the future. There are a number of criteria used to validate a model. The most important among them are:

- Shrinkage in the coefficient of determination
- Ratio of regression coefficient to the standard error of regression coefficient
- Sign of regression coefficients

Shrinkage in Coefficient of Determination: The coefficient of determination is one of the measure of reliability of a regression model. It varies between zero and one. The closer the value of coefficient of determination is to one the more reliable the model, and vice versa. The value of the coefficient of determination between actual and forecasted values shrinks when the original regression equation is applied to new data points (or new time period) to make forecasts. We will call it "revised coefficient of determination." (Appendix 1 gives the formula for computing the revised coefficient of determination.) How much shrinkage in the coefficient of determination can be tolerated? Herzberg has devised a formula to calculate tolerable value of the coefficient of determination. We will call it "tolerable coefficient of determination." (See Appendix 2 for its computation) The model is good (valid) if the revised coefficient of determination (coefficient of determination computed by inserting new data points in the original regression) is more than or equal to the tolerable coefficient of determination. Otherwise, the model is invalid, and the forecaster has to go back and re-specify the model. At times, one can experience a large amount of shrinkage in the coefficient of

determination due to changes in the environment, uses of different methods of data collection, and changes in relationships that have occurred since the first sample was used. Each situation calls for a specific action. In one case, the forecaster may have to eliminate certain data. In another case, he may have to adjust certain data to make them comcertain variables have to be eliminated and/or added to the model.

Ratio of Regression Coefficient to the Standard Error of Regression Coefficient: For a model to be valid, provided the sample is relatively large, the ratio of the regression coefficient for each independent variable to its standard error of regression coefficient should be approximately equal to or greater than two. Otherwise that variable is insignificant. To improve the predictability of the equation, the forecaster should either eliminate that variable or replace it with another one. The regression coefficient measures the average relation between the independent and dependent variables. Suppose that cashflow (dependent variable) depends on the size of account receivables (independent variable). If the regression coefficient of account receivables is .1, it means that, on the average, an increase in one dollar in account receivables will lead to a ten cent increase in the cashflow. If any one or more of regression coefficients are not signficiant (i.e., their ratio is less than two), this means that they have to be eliminated and/or replaced by other variables to improve the predictability of the equation.

Sign of Regression Coefficients: When different regression equations are computed from different segments of the

57

same data to test for validity, the sign of each regression coefficient for the same variable on each equation should be the same. Also, the size of the regression coefficient in each equation should be pretty much the same. If this is not the case with one or more variables, this means that the reliability of the equation can be improved by eliminating those variables. This is normally done by dividing the data into two or more equal segments. The number of segments depends upon the size of data set. The more data we have more segments we can generate. An equation is calculated on one data segment and tested using the other segment or segments.

Improving Validity

Using one or more of these techniques, a forecaster may find that the model is not valid. What can be done to improve it? Here are some suggestions:

(1) *By adding new variables and/or deleting old ones.* One may find that the equation is improved when certain variables are taken out of the equation. At the same time, forecaster may like to try other variables to see if they, by any chance, improve the model. If new variables are added the new equation should be tested for validity.

(2) *By adjusting the data of a variable.* As will be shown in the example explained in the next section where grades are used as a dependent variable, past grades are no longer comparable to the current grades. Over the period, grades have deflated. To make the model work, grades of periods from which the equation is derived and the period to which they will be applied have to be made comparable.

(3) *By eliminating certain data.* As time goes by, a company's environment may change. The past is no longer representative of the future. The company has added a number of stores (or closed a number of stores), it has added a number of new products (or abandoned a number of old products), its promotion strategy has changed, a number of new competitors have stepped into the market, and so on. As a result, what happened long, long ago is no longer valid. To improve the validity of a model, the forecaster may have to eliminate a certain amount of data.

Examining Validity

To determine the validity of a model one has to test a model with different sets of data. There are a number of ways of doing it, the most important among them are: (1) hold-out sample, (2) splitting data randomly into two halves, and, (3) using altogether new data.

Hold-out Sample: Here the forecaster holds a part of the sample aside to determine the validity of a model and uses the rest to compute the regression model.

Splitting the Data Randomly into Two Halves: This is another way of determining the validity of a model. Here the data is split randomly in two halves. First compute the regression equation with the data of first half and test it with the other half, and then compute the equation with the data of second half and test it with the first half.

New Data Set: Here one develops a regression model with the data available at the time and then tests it with new data when it becomes available. This technique is specially good for testing an equation that will be used to predict future time periods.

An Example

In 1974-75 the author developed a scale which would rate items on a graduate student application, other than GMAT score and undergraduate grade point average (UGPA), that were throught to contribute to the success of a student in an MBA program. This scale (0-12 point) included items such as:

1. Work experience (up to 2 points)
2. Activities in undergraduate school as a member (up to 2 points) and as an elected officer (up to 2 points)
3. Recommendations (up to 3 points?
4. Career patterns and personal goals (up to 1 point)
5. Undergraduate work: mathematics, engineering, business and economics background (up to 3 points)

It was felt that many of these items would help to account for lower grade point averages (work experience, high level of campus activity). Letters of recommendation and personal goal statements might be indicators of high study motivation. Enrollment in difficult undergraduate majors such as economics, mathematics or engineering might also explain lower grade point averages. The work in these courses might lead to success in mathematically oriented graduate courses such as statistics, finance, cost accounting and economics. Enrollment in a business undergraduate major may mean that the student has had prior exposure to many of the topics covered in a graduate program.

This scale which ranged from 1-12 points was used to evaluate students of the 1976-77 MBA class. A multiple regression equation, that included six independent variables, was fitted to the data of 134 full time MBA students to predict their grade point average in graduate school. The result was a coefficient determination of .188 which was significant at the .01 level. Moreover the 12 point scale, along with undergraduate grade point average and GMAT score, turned out to be a significant predictor of their success in the graduate program.

In 1981, it was decided to retest the scale on the 1980-81 full time MBA class. The same six variables were used and a new equation was fitted. This time the coefficient of determination rose from .188 to .310. This means that the variable, SCALE, became even more important during that period.

The study used grade point average after one semester in the MBA program as a dependent variable. Six independent variables used to develop the model were.

1. Undergraduate grade point average (UGPA)
2. Graduate admission test score (GMAT)
3. Scale described above (SCALE)
4. Years since graduation (YSG)
5. Previous graduate work (GW)
6. Sex

In an effort to improve the validity of the model, we tested it with: (1) hold-out sample, (2) by splitting the sample into two equal halves, (3) and with altogether new data.

Hold-out Sample

We had a sample of 129 graduate students. A sample of 80 students was used to develop a regression equation, using 6 independent variables described earlier. The remaining sample of 49 students was used as a hold-out sample. Then we computed the coefficient of determination on the basis of the original sample (i.e. of 80 students) which came to .35. The tolerable coefficient of determination came to .23. (See Appendix 1) We also computed the revised coefficient of determination by inserting the new data points (i.e. of 49 students) in the original regression equation. (See Appendix 2) This came to .09. Since the revised coefficient of determination (.09) was less than the tolerable one (.23), the model was invalidated. This meant that the model as it stands now was not adequate. Something had to be done to improve it.

Splitting The Sample

Next we randomly split the data of 1980-81 into two halves. Then we computed regression equation for each half, using once again the same six independent variables. Revised coefficients of determination were computed by inserting data points for one group in the equation of another. Original, tolerable, and revised coefficient of determinations for each group were computed. The comparison of the tolerable and the revised coefficients of determination showed that the model was invalid. In each case, the revised coefficient of determination was less than the tolerable coefficient of determination as computed by the Herzberg formula. When the partial regression coefficients of both equations were compared, another interesting thing emerged. The partial regression coefficients of only three variables agreed in magnitude and sign. These variables were UGPA, GMAT and SCALE. The coefficients of the other three variables were not significant as the ratio of their regression coefficient to the standard error of the regression coefficients was less than two. This indicated that the equation would be improved by eliminating these three variables. When the revised three variable equation was computed, it proved to be satisfactory.

New Sample

An important consideration regarding the validity of a regression equation is whether it would predict accurately when applied to an altogether new sample. This is defined as predictive validity. Predictive validity is more difficult to demonstrate than concurrent validity. There is a possibility of a large shrinkage in the revised coefficient of determination due to changes in various factors such as changes in environment. To test this validity the data of 1980-81 were tested with the equation of 1976-77, and the data of 1976-77 were tested with the equation of 1980-81. Again original, tolerable and revised coefficients of determination were computed for both sets of equation. In each case, the model was not validated as the revised coefficient of determination was less than that of the tolerable. However, a closer examination of the data revealed why the equation predicted so poorly. In 1976-77, the average grade point average for the first semester of graduate school was 3.316. In 1980-81, the average was 3.083. There seemed to have been an effort to curb grade inflation. Using 1980 data in the 1976 equation resulted in consistent overestimation of grades. This gave an indication that the validity of the equation can be improved by adjusting grades so that grades of both periods are comparable.

From the above analysis we learned that the predictability of the regression equation could be improved if only three independent variables (UGPA, GMAT and SCALE) were used. Grades should be adjusted so that grades of each period are comparable. With these two changes, we re-computed the regression equation with the data of 1976-77 and applied to the data of 1980-81. The predictability of the equation was improved as the revised coefficient of determination, for the first time, exceeded the tolerable one ●

Appendix 1
Calculation of Revised Coefficient of Determination

This is done by plugging new data points into the original regression equation. If we have fourteen years of data, we may use the first ten years to compute the regression equation and the other four years as a hold-out period. The regression

computed from the first ten years will be the original regression equation. The revised coefficient of determination is computed by preparing forecasts by plugging the data of last four years in the original equation. The formula for computing the revised coefficient of determination is:

$$\text{Revised Coefficient of Determination} = \frac{\Sigma(Y-F)^2}{N-K} \div \frac{\Sigma(Y-\bar{Y})^2}{N-1}$$

Where:
Σ = Sumtotal
F = Forecasted value
K = Number of independent variables
N = Number of observations
Y = Actual value
$\bar{Y}$ = Average of actual values

Appendix 2
Calculation of Tolerable Coefficient of Determination

The formula for computing the tolerable coefficient of determination was devised by Herzberg. It measures the maximum shrinkage in the coefficient of determination to be allowed to validate an equation. Its formula is as follows:

$$\text{Tolerable Coefficient of Determination} = 1 - \left(\frac{N-1}{N-K-1}\right) \times \left(\frac{N+K+1}{N}\right) \times \left(1-R^2\right)$$

Where:
K = Number of independent variables
N = Number of observations
R^2 = Original coefficient of determination

As can be observed from the above formula, tolerable coefficient of determintion depends, among other things, on the size of sample and number of independent variables. The larger the number of variables the larger the expected shrinkage in the coefficient of determination.

References

Armstrong, Scott. **Long Range Forecasting.** New York: John Wiley & Sons, 1978, Chapter 13, pp. 308-332.

Churchill, G.A., Jr. **Marketing Research.** Hinsdale, Ill.: Dryden Press, pp. 246-54.

Green, P., and Tull, D. **Market Research for Marketing Decision.** Englewood, N.J.: Prentice Hall, 1978, pp. 335-36.

Herzberg, P. "The Parameters of Cross-Validation." **Psychometrika Monograph Supplement.** #16, Vol. 34, #2, Part 2, June, 1969.

Larson, S.C. "The Shrinkage of the Coefficient of Multiple Correlation." **Journal of Educational Psychology.** 1931, 22, pp. 45-55.

Lord, F.M. "Efficiency of Prediction When a Regression Equation from One Sample is Used in New Sample." **Research Bulletin.** 50-40, Princeton, NJ: Educational Testing Service, 1950.

McCarthy, P.J. "The Use of Balanced Half-Sample Replication in Cross Validation Studies." **Journal of the American Statistical Association,** 71, 1976, pp. 596-604.

Montogmery, D.C., and Peck, E.A. **Introduction**

60

to **Linear Regression Analysis.** New York: John Wiley & Sons, 1982, Chapter 10, pp. 424-446.

Snee, R.D. "Validation of Regression Models: Methods and Examples." **Technometrics.** 1977, 19, pp. 415-428.

Stevens, James P. unpublished manuscript, Teachers College, University of Cincinatti, 1981.

PART IV

The Model Builders
And
Their Models

Chapter 14
A Quick Glance at Four Econometric Models

Thomas P. Chen
St. John's University

The Econometric forecasting industry is fairly new. In about two decades its has grown from practically nothing to an industry grossing more than $100 million.

The largest econometric service bureaus—as they prefer to be called—are: Data Resources, Inc. (DRI), Chase Econometrics (CE), Wharton Econometrics (WE). Kent Economic and Development Institute (KEDI) is often included in this group because of the size of its model.

DRI is the largest with gross sales of about $60 million a year from 900 clients. The company is now owned by McGraw-Hill, Inc., publishers of Business Week and other publications.

CE ranks second with annual revenues of $30 million collected from 650 clients. It is a division of Chase Manhattan in New York.

It started to issue macro-forecasts in 1970. Dr. Lawrence Chimerine heads the company.

WE is the joint production of the Wharton School of the University of Pennsylvania and Dr. Lawrence Klein (the Nobel Laureate)—financial resources of Wharton and the skill of Dr. Klein. It ranks third in the industry with annual revenues of $10 million, generated from 400 clients. Its macro-forecasts have been commercially available since 1962.

KEDI is headed by Dr. Vladimir J. Simunek. It has been issuing macro-forecasts on a regular basis since 1974.

The purpose of all of the models is the same. Each bureau uses its model to: (1) analyze structural relationships, i.e., how different variables are related to each other, (2) make macro and micro forecasts, (3) evaluate the economic impact of a given Government policy, (4) determine the effect of different policy scenarios on macro-variables.

Econometric models alone are not adequate for making forecasts; judgment, time series, current data analysis, and interaction among forecasters also play a role in the process in roughly the following proportions: econometric models 55% to 70%; judgment, 20% to 30%; time series, 5% to 10%; and current data analysis 5% to 10% (See Table 1). Methods such as regression, economic base and input-output are lumped into the category of econometric model.

CE uses the least amount of the input-output method. Instead, it uses the economic base method. KEDI makes the least use of regression, but the most of input-output.

In terms of number of variables used, KEDI is the largest with 4 4,400 variables—approximately 40 times as large as that of DRI.

All of the models use data acquired from government sources and from surveys. Forecasts are made 2 to 30 years ahead. As for the number of macro-variables fore-

TABLE 1
FEATURES OF FOUR MODELS

		DRI Model	Chase Model	Wharton Model	Kent Model
Purpose		• Structural Analysis • Forecasting • Policy Evaluation • Simulation	• Structural Analysis • Forecasting • Policy Evaluation • Simulation	• Structural Analysis • Forecasting • Policy Evaluation • Simulation	• Structural Analysis • Forecasting • Policy Evaluation • Simulation
Forecasting Techniques Used & Approx. Weights Given To Each	• Econometric Model	55%	45%	60%	60%
	• Judgment	30%	45%	30%	30%
	• Time Series	10%	0%	—	5%
	• Current Data Analysis	5%	10%	10%	—
	• Interaction With Others	—	—	—	10%
Data Base		Govt. Sources & Survey	Govt. Sources & Survey	Govt. Sources & Survey	Govt. Sources & Survey
Number of Equations Used		450	350	669	44,400 +
Number of Macro-variables Forecasted		1250	450	1,000	1,699
Classification of Forecasts		Sectors & 2 Digit Industries	Sectors & 2 Digit Industries	Sectors & 2 Digit Industries	Sectors & 2 Digit Industries
Lead Time		2-25 Years Ahead	2-30 Years Ahead	10 Years Ahead	2½ to 20 Years Ahead
Frequency of Release Per Year		Monthly	Monthly	Monthly	Monthly

Source: 1. Stephen K. McNees. "The Recent Record of Thirteen Forecasters." *New England Economic Review*. September October 1981, pp. 5-22.
2. L. Douglas Lee. "A Comparison of Econometric Models." Joint Economic Committee, Congress of the United States, 95 Congress, 2nd Session. Washington, D.C.: U.S. Government Printing Office, p. 2.

casted, Kent is believed to be the largest model. In each case, forecasts are updated monthly.

Forecasts are affected by the underlying economic philosophy of a model. The DRI regards its philosophy as "eclectic," with more Monetarist and Supply-Side factors added to its model in recent years. Dr. Simunek (the president of KEDI) makes extensive use of Walrasian philosophy in his model. Dr. Klein, once a strong supporter of Keynesian philosophy, has moved toward Supply-Side economics and is emphasizing flow of funds. This change in his philosophy is probably reflected in the Wharton model. Dr. Richard Young of CK claims that the Chase model has element of both Keynesian and Moentaris philosophies●

Chapter 15
The Chase Model

Interview with
Richard M. Young
Chase Econometric, Inc.

Q. *How many components of economic activity do you forecast on the macro level?*

A. We forecast a reasonably exhaustive set of final demand variables: consumption, fixed business investment, residential investment, inventory investment, and so on; a great deal of detail on the income side: wages, profits interest payments, and so on; a variety of measures of industry outputs; a wide variety of prices, interest rates, financial magnitudes, including loans, money supply, time and demand deposits, and so on; and unemployment and labor force. We forecast virtually every major economic variable for major industrialized countries and what runs into thousands of sub-variables.

Q. *How would you characterize the Chase Model—Monetarist or Keynesian?*

A. I don't think it is possible to characterize any of the major econometric models that are currently used for servicing the private sector—Chase, DRI or Wharton—in that simplistic manner. In many ways macroeconomic modeling has gone beyond macroeconomic theory in identifying the causal flows and relationship among different economic variables. I know that I will upset some of my theoretically oriented friends by saying that a theoretical model quite often has to be kept too simple to have any relevance to reality. We lean heavily on theoretical structures as far as they carry us, but we have discovered that at some point we have to go beyond theory. Almost all of these models have elements of both Monetarist and Keynesian theory. Remember we are a decision support service. It is not important which theory we use. What is important is that our data set come closer to the markets our clients are involved in, both in terms of products they are selling and things they are buying.

Q. *In what way or ways does the Chase Model differ from other models that are available to business?*

A. The major difference has to do with the causal structure of models and the relationships in terms of how fully various sectors are integrated. It is my impression that, in general, the Wharton Model is the most fully integrated in that the causal flows are highly elaborated. The DRI model is the least integrated and many of the flows are basically recursive in nature rather than simultaneous. There is also a distinction in terms of what sectors of the model are most elaborated; and what sectors of the economy are investigated in most detail. The Chase service tends to have a much more elaborate industry detail in terms of looking at industrial production. The Wharton Model, in the past, had more demographic and labor market detail than the other. I don't think that users interested in a decision support service are terribly concerned about the internal structure, e.g., which sectors are elaborated and which ones are not. They are really interested in whether or not we can supply them with a set of projections for variables which are important to their decisions; how good these projections are on average; whether they can relate our projections to the general environment they are operating in; whether we can give them reasons why a given forecast looks as it does; and whether they can assimilate our forecasts into their decision processes.

Q. *Do you first forecast state or regional activity and then aggregate the data to arrive at the national forecast or do you prepare the national forecast on the basis of the national accounts and allocate aggregates to each region and to each industry?*

A. We work on the basis of a large model of the U.S. economy which we disaggregate down to the regional level. The output is also disaggregated on an industry basis. But when we go to a global context, we do just the opposite: We first make a forecast for each country and aggregate them.

Q. *Are components of the model forecast by regession or by any other technique*

such as time series and input output analysis?

A. One has to distinguish between the method of building a model and the method of generating a forecast. In model building, it's not unusual at all to use input/output or time series to establish such things as lag structures. The actual forecast within a macro model, which incorporates information from other investigative techniques, generally uses a combination of methods such as input/output, time series and regression analysis.

Q. *Could you outline the procedures followed in producing the forecast, including such things as frequency of publication, updating, etc., and the form in which these forecasts are delivered to the client?*

A. Let's start backward: How does the client receive the forecast? The client receives the forecast in two parts: One is a book which contains both the forecasting data that we have generated and an analysis of that data, including where the economy appears to be at the moment and why we think that our forecast makes sense. Almost all of our clients take delivery in that form. A very large subset of our clients also has direct access to our data base. They dial up on a computer terminal to get a readout of a forecast as it currently stands. At that point, they have not only our most recent forecast and all of the analysis we have done, they also have the ability to use this information to develop their own forecast. For example, we may have assumed that Mr. Paul Volcker (Chairman, Federal Reserve System) is going to be very obdurate about monetary policy, and U.S. interest rates will remain high. On that basis, the forecast will take one form. A user may feel that the Chase analysis is valid. But he may also like to see the effect on the variables he's interested in if Mr. Volcker caves in to political pressure and allows money supply to grow more quickly.

Q. *What do you do if your model is producing a large error?*

A. A certain amount of error is always expected. We try to be accurate on average rather than on every single point. The first thing we do is to determine the size of the error the model most recently made and why it made it. The second step is to determine whether the error is an average error or large error. The third step is to see whether the error is due to noise in the system or to some phenomenon that is outside of the model's ability to track. Some years ago, I was in a situation where the inventory investment equation was making very large errors—errors I had not seen before. I felt that there must be some explanation beyond what I could capture with the model structure. Well, it turned out that there had been an enormous surge in inventories at one of the larger manufacturers of aircraft. A Middle Eastern country with which it had a contract refused to accept delivery of a large number of airplanes that were sitting on an airstrip someplace in the U.S., and were included in the inventory. After some consultation with people in the industry and others, we discovered that it was a temporary phenomenon. We could expect those airplanes to disappear shortly from the inventory and to appear in exports. So in understanding why the error was made, we gained a great deal of knowledge about what we had to do to the model to track that phenomenon.

Q. *From the story about the airplanes, I assume you frequently talk to industry people?*

A. Oh, yes. A tremendous amount of judgment is involved in producing an econometric forecast. Much of it has to do with what causes outside errors and interpreting those errors. We spend a great deal of time talking to industry people who seem to us to be knowledgeable about why traditional relationships might not be holding at a particular point in time. When there has been a strike in the automobile industry or elsewhere, we spend a great deal of time talking to people about what inventory behavior is likely to be, both in the presence of an anticipated strike and following the strike; we spend a great deal of time talking to people in government about policy actions and their consequences.

Q. *Would this include political decisions which are made outside of the economic realities such as the current (May 1982) uncertainty surrounding the Federal Budget for the next fiscal year?*

A. Yes. Perhaps the major problem confronting someone who wants to project the U.S. economy in 1983 at the moment is what monetary and fiscal policy will look like in that year. Will the third year of the tax cut go through; if it goes through, what will monetary policy be;

and if it doesn't go through, what will monetary policy be?

Q. *What other procedures do you follow in developing forecasts?*

A. Having made the initial set of judgments in terms of how we should manipulate the relationships, we then solve the model. At that point we begin to look at monitoring devices; there are certain key magnitudes in any model or in any economy that you tend to look at. One example would be to look at the share of wages in national income: the wage share is expected to have a certain behavior over the business cycle. We determine whether the current model solution gives a wage behavior that is consistent with historical experience.

Quite often there is an alternative specification of the same model. As long as the two sets of models produce roughly the same results, we don't worry too much about it. If an alternative structure that we cannot reject, as is often true in economics, produces a dramatically different result, then we begin to be concerned about the validity of the current projection.

Q. *When your monitoring devices give a signal different from that of your original model, do you query industry sources?*

A. We have in-house experts in a number of areas, such as energy, agriculture, autos, and metals. We first consult these people. They are in direct contact with industry people. Having looked at the monitoring system, one can make a variety of decisions: you might say, "Fine, this is the forecast. I'm done," You might say, "Given the way the economy is evolving, I will have to change my judgments about what economic policy is going to be. If the U.S. economy, for example, went into a massive deflation, Mr. Volcker is likely to relax monetary policy much more than expected in this forecast. Therefore, I will have to go back and make some changes in my judgments about basic monetary policies." You might also change your judgments about some of the non-policy variables that have been taken as given for the forecasting exercise.

Q. *This raises the question of probabilities. There are two types of probabilities as I see it. One is the probability that something will happen, and you apply that probability to that happening; the other probability is applied to the forecast of a component or of the GNP. The concept can be reduced to a statement such as: "There is an 80% probability that the Federal Reserve Board will continue to restrict money supply growth over the next three quarters. Therefore, the chances are 7 out of 10 (70 percent probability) that unemployment will average 9.8%, peaking at 10.8% in the final*

quarter of the period." Do you present your forecasts along these lines or do you assume the occurrence of one most likely scenario and base your forecast of each component on its occurrence without any reference to probabilities?

A. Well, I think that the essential point to be made here is that we are talking about conditional forecasting. The forecasts we make are conditional on the variables—external variables as well as domestic policy variables—that we have chosen.

Q. *You do not follow the Bayesian approach—that these are the different scenarios, and these are the probabilities of different scenarios. You use them to come up with a forecast of, say, the rate of increase in money supply.*

A. Any forecast scenario is a conditional forecast. The errors can be caused by a variety of things: One is that we were careless; two is that the conditioning agents that we chose did not occur the way we expected; and three is that statistical methods have some range of error built into them. Why the error occurred is not known; all we know is that an error occurred, and that historically errors tended to fall within plus or minus some percent of the actual value, on average. We can identify an error band, but it has no known and well defined probability distribution associated with it.

Q. *Assuming that everything in the scenario happened as you said it would.*

A. Let's assume that we are looking at scenario-based forecasts. But alternative scenarios could also occur. Money supply could grow faster or slower. Tax cuts happen or don't happen. An infinite number of things could occur and you could generate an infinite number of forecast scenarios based on variations. One of the enormous, if not the largest, single advantage of econometric models is that it's relatively easy to look at what difference it makes if the scenario changes. The question of establishing probabilities of one scenario versus another has to be purely subjective. With one scenario I establish a 60% probability that the outcome will lie within the normal error bands of standard forecast. With another scenario I might have 20% probability that the outcome will lie within the normal error bands of its standard forecast. These statements are very ambiguous. It seems to me that they are my probabilities and they might not be valid for someone else in his decision problem.

Q. *So, the client gets a single-figure forecast, but not in probabilistic terms.*

A. Not in probabilistic terms. What we do is present a standard forecast. We also present a set of alternatives which examine what we feel to be the major possibili-

67

ties for forecast risk. For example, we are making a forecast of the U.S. economy that assumes a certain pattern of the future world oil prices. But there is a large amount of uncertainty attached to the future pattern of oil prices. At the moment we feel that we are being relatively conservative, but world oil prices may turn out to be lower than we currently anticipate. So we will also determine what would happen to the U.S. economy if oil prices were even lower.

Q. *I am a businessman. You have presented me with your forecast along with what you called the forecast risk. I am in the housing industry. How do I use this risk factor, how would you help me make a decision about whether or not I should start a development next week or next year that I will be selling a year down the road? How do I measure my risk?*

A. There are a variety of services and information that we will bring to you: one is simply an acknowledgment that the risk exists. This is our best forecast as to what is going to happen to housing starts, say, in California over the next year. However, we feel that there is a substantial risk that something will happen that will alter the outlook. One of the risks might be with respect to monetary policy—it might be more restrictive, and we might expect housing starts to follow an alternative path that might be less rosy. At this point there is a variety of ways that a decision problem could go: one is you could say, "Well, I strongly believe that either the standard forecast or the alternative forecast is a true picture of what monetary policy is going to look like, and I am going to base my decision on that." If the risk is substantial, you might delay a decision, acquire additional information to refine the decision, develop a forecast of your own based upon the scenario of your own choice, or get out of the housing industry altogether. But the essence is the sensitivity of your decisions to standard and alternative forecasts and the risk attached to them.

Q. *That's a pretty rational approach.*

A. That's right. We have clients who make forecasts on their own, using our macro data and their own scenario. One morning he may say, "Ah, yes, it looks as though the budget compromise is going to go through, and there will be no third-year tax cut. Let us look at what the implication of that is for our projection as to what our costs and revenues will look like."

Q. *How do you specify the risk?*

A. At this point we produce a standard forecast and alternates. Then the discussion centers on the circumstances under which we feel that the alternate will be the more valid forecast than our stan-

dard, and whether we think these things have a high or low probability. There is no attempt to say that this one has 60% chance of occurring. What we are trying to do is give the user information on which he can base his own judgment.

Q. *As you know, we at The Journal have received a number of inquiries for some kind of help in evaluating the services provided by the econometric service bureaus. From our conversations with them, we get the impression that they do not have the kind of internal expertise that you say they need to deal with your forecasts. What can they do to improve the value of your services to them?*

A. What has happened in response to this need over the last decade is that the econometric forecasting services have evolved into a decision support service in which the forecasting activity is still a key element. In addition to that we are providing a wide variety of services that essentially brings the expertise to the company and allows them to purchase it from us rather than hiring it internally. It tends to be a lot cheaper to hire or buy it from us. What we offer is a set of services that will allow banks to do a complete asset/liability management analysis on the basis of our outlook for interest rates and any other alternatives assessing the risk of any portfolio position they may take. We do modeling work that allows individual firms to project revenue and sales much along the lines that I have just discussed. One of the advantages of a forecasting service like ours is simply that we spread the cost of producing that service over a wide number of firms down to the industry level, including when you get to the firm where things get very specific and you have to deal with the firm characteristics that differ throughout the industry. But to the extent that we have to build a model of the U.S. economy and a model of the industry, we've done that. Anyone that buys that service from us shares the expenses in supporting that activity.

Q. *But the final decision—which alternative or which scenario to use—is a management decision?*

A. It's management's decision. All we can do is make recommendations; unless they hire us to run their company. The reason that we exist is because we live in an age of information. There is too much information for a manager to assimilate. We look at thousands and thousands of pieces of data when we put together a forecast. For any manager to assimilate that information and have at his command a structure producing results that he can use to make decisions is clearly an absurd idea.

Q. *You're not giving any guarantees.*

A. We do not give any guarantees. It is a

world that is characterized by statistics and probability. What we hope to do is to come to management and identify where the probability mass lies. We think that the world will be in the vicinity of this environment and, in that environment, we expect this to happen to your industry, and if you do X, Y and Z this would happen to your firm.

Q. *Would you say that the services of an econometric service bureau require a great deal of sophistication on the part of the user?*

A. I don't think so. What it requires is that the user understand his problem and his need to make decisions. The problem that has to be worked out between an econometric service bureau (or consulting group or decision support group) and a client is what information structure is available to support his decision and what is the way he needs to have it presented so that it is usable by him. This is something that we work out between ourselves and our clients.

Q. *Do you have a price list for clients, that is, the standard forecast costs "X" dollars, data access service costs "Y" dollars, and the consulting service costs "Z" dollars?*

A. The services consist of data bases, software for processing those data bases, time sharing on the computer for processing analyses of the data that include both what is currently happening and forecasting, and support in assimilating that data. It takes a wide variety of forms. You can buy those in various packages. It would be beyond me to list all the possible combinations and ramifications.

Q. *Are your clients typically large corporations—The Fortune 500?*

A. The vast majority is at this point.

Q. *Is any attempt being made by the services to broaden the market to attract smaller companies?*

A. There are a wide variety of developments that I think are moving in that direction. One is that we have gone from strictly national to regional forecasting—more suitable for small firms that have a geographically defined market. It is much more important for a small firm to know what is happening say, in Idaho if that is their market, than in the U.S. economy. Secondly, we are doing much more industry detail work—again suitable for small and medium-size firms in a well defined industry. Thirdly, the real prices of these services are steadily declining for a variety of reasons. Competition in our industry is growing. Data processing has become cheaper over the past twenty years because of the technological breakthroughs in the computer industry. Moreover, as we spread a large amount of overhead over a greater number of people, our services will become cheaper. To attract small firms, we have also started providing specific services that a customer needs rather than the whole package. If you want simply an analysis of the consumer sector, you can buy that. If you want a detailed analysis of wholesale price, you can buy that.

Q. *In your judgment, what should a prospective client look for in selecting a bureau?*

A. If I were a client I would be interested in a basket of things. One is the accuracy record of variables in which I am interested. Of course the problem is that there is not a single unambiguous way of measuring accuracy. What is the appropriate measure of accuracy—is it mean square error? Theil statistic? or something else? Furthermore, even if you satisfy yourself that we have been accurate in the past, there is no guarantee that we will be accurate in the future. The other consideration in selecting a bureau should be whether or not it provides a wide array of decision support services. Essentially the questions are: "Am I going to this bureau for forecasting and to another for processing? Am I going to have three computer systems in house or am I going to do with one? Am I going to have the appropriate personnel support? Am I able to reach people who can give me the information I need when I need it?"

Q. *Is there much difference among the various service bureaus insofar as forecast accuracy is concerned?*

A. There does not appear to be a great deal of difference among the major econometric forecasters in accuracy when forecasting major macro-economic variables. The thing I would argue is that an econometric forecast will, on average, be more accurate than any other forecast.

Q. *Professor Victor Zarnowitz, at the University of Chicago, has been quoted as saying: "I have never been able to discover any real difference between econometric and judgmental forecasts." How would you respond to that?*

A. I am not quite sure what body of work Victor was looking at when he made that assertion. Over the last ten years there have been a variety of studies comparing econometric forecasts with other forecasts. The most comprehensive work on forecast accuracy has been done by Steve McNees, not only in terms of his own work, but also in surveying the other studies that have been done. It is clear that the longer the time horizon and wider the array of information that you are interested in, the greater is the advantage of econometric forecasting. It is difficult to believe that anyone who has studied the subject carefully would conclude that there is no difference. The problem in many respects is in distinguishing between econometric forecasting and other kinds of forecasting, because judgment enters all of them. Judgmental forecasts are based in part upon the information that has been garnered from econometric forecasts.

Q. *Does the decision support service vary significantly from one econometric service to another?*

A. I think so. I think that what you will find is that the accuracy question—at least in terms of five or six major aggregates that are closely monitored—tends to be not very great. One of us might systematically do better than the other on one variable. But there is a great deal of difference in terms of support services.

Q. *Is this on the basis of quality or quantity? Let's take quantity, because quality is rather difficult to define. Who has more people out there available to the decision maker?*

A. I don't know the exact numbers. If you take Chase Econometrics (CE) and Interactive Data Systems (IDC) as one entity—both are owned by Chase Manhattan Bank of New York—we are roughly twice the size of DRI. (CE is essentially the analytical group and IDC is the computer time sharing vendor. Ed) I'm sure CE/IDC deploys a greater number of support people than DRI.

Q. *Do you go into cash management for an individual firm?*

A. Chase/IDC does. We do asset/liability management for financial institutions, cash management for manufacturing groups in a wide variety of industries. One of the reasons why I concentrate on the decision support services is that it is the perception of the type of institution we are becoming. The econometric services are a part of the generalized decision support service.

Q. *Do you issue quarterly reports to your clients?*

A. Yes, we do. On the U.S. macro variables we issue a monthly updated report.

Q. *How about sector forecasts?*

A. They vary across services: in the international services we also issue a forecast each month, but the regular energy report is quarterly for example. In addition we give our clients a quick update on the implications of unexpected events—a sudden increase in oil prices, for example—even on these services for which we publish quarterly forecasts. This kind of update is issued when unexpected events occur that seem to us to be important in terms of uncertainty or that alter the outlook. These are special reports that tend to be less detailed than our typical quarterly reports or our regular analysis but are designed to give the clients a quick look at major developments in the outlook.

Q. *Do your clients subscribe to more than one econometric service?*

A. Yes; though there are clients who use just one service, many of our industrial clients use two services. The large companies use two services to get a second opinion. Many companies use different services for different things: there are clients who will use the U.S. macro services from us, the energy analysis from another, and so on. Quite often the choice depends on the compatibility of viewpoints. A corporate economist may buy information on the energy sector from a given service bureau, because the people who do the analysis have a viewpoint of the world that coincides with his. Personal relationships are also very important in this business. You might hear someone say, "I like the people who are doing the agricultural analysis over here. I feel comfortable with what they are saying. But guys in the same shop who do work on the U.S. macro variables are out in left field. I don't want to have anything to do with them. So I'll buy macro services somewhere else." It is an important part of what we are doing: we are not just selling numbers.

Q. *You are selling people?*

A. We are selling people, we are selling advice, and we are selling support in making decisions. The most important thing is that you trust the people from whom you buy advice.

Q. *How much historical data does a firm require to optimize its utility of an econometric forecast?*

A. There are techniques available for parsimonious use of data, that is, getting by with very few observations. Two things that are relevant here are: (1) As the number of observations become fewer, techniques tend to become more expensive and results become less reliable. (2) In general, the more data you have, the more reliable will be your results.

Q. *A large number of observations implies a lengthy period of time during which the pattern of the data may change. How does the model cope with such changes?*

A. What we are talking about here is a statistical relationship of greater or lesser complexity. We estimate demand relationships in which we leave out demographics that we know are very important, for example. Demographics don't change much over time. If you have a sample period that covers five years, leaving them out is not going to be very important. However, if the sample period covers forty years—a period during which the demographic characteristics of the market place have changed greatly—the estimates that you get, and the forecast that you make will be affected if demographics are left out. ●

Chapter 16
The DRI Model

Interview with
Christopher N. Caton and Christopher J. Probyn
Data Resources, Inc.

Q. *How does DRI forecast?*

A. Like all econometric forecasting services, DRI develops its forecasts by means of computer simulation of a macroeconomic model. Our model is based on observable relationships which are predicted by economic theory—a structural approach. After observing the behavior of a multitude of time series (historical data), DRI economists quantified these relationships using a variety of statistical techniques and combined them as simultaneous interacting equations into a model. DRI's macroeconomic model of the U.S. economy contains about 1000 equations. Solutions of the model may be used not only to produce forecasts but also to examine the effect of a variety of different economic policies on any of the quantified variables in an internally consistent way.

All econometric models—Wharton, Chase, DRI—are *conceptually* the same and have a common theoretical underpinning. They differ in terms of equation choice for the major variables, the number and quality of the professional staff who validate and maintain them, and also in terms of their ease of use by clients. While DRI's explicit goal has been to create user-friendly models which could be solved by clients, we also provide extensive client support through our regional consulting offices and our Lexington-based economic forecasting professionals.

Q. *What part does judgment play in preparing a forecast?*

A. DRI economists produce a forecast solution of the macroeconomic model once a month. The process requires about 4 days and relies equally on the model solutions and on the judgment of the Forecasting and Modeling Council, a group of about 25 DRI economists and industry experts. Simply stated, there are five steps in the process:

1. Major agencies of the U.S. government release current data at the national level. These data include such variables as gross national product, consumer spending on motor vehicles, corporate profits, production prices, interest rates, and financial flows.

2. DRI puts these new data into the model. The model is then solved using the new data.

3. The solutions are discussed at meetings of the Forecasting and Modeling Council. Specialists in various sectors (for example, steel, autos, retail sales, inflation) modify the solutions to reflect information they have (for example, union negotiations for wage contracts) which is not incorporated in the model solution.

4. The modified inputs (or forecasts) are then used to solve the model a second time.

5. The process iterates until, in the judgment of DRI's economists, the forecasts are as good as we know how to make them.

As this process makes clear, model solutions and expert judgments work together to produce the forecast. The model obviously contains nothing that was not put into it by DRI economists in the first place. It imposes an internal consistency and provides a disciplined framework for considering the complex issues which surround a forecast. The experience and up-to-date knowledge of the experts ensure that recent changes not captured by the structural equations are included in the forecast solutions.

Q. *Why does DRI forecast from "top to bottom?"*

A. In forecasting the U.S. economy, we use national data to generate national forecasts and then disaggregate the forecasts for state and industry activity. There are four good reasons for this.

First, the national economy really is a unit, a dynamic system governed by national policies, and heavily determining the fate of individual industries.

Second, there are better data available at the national level than at the state or industry level. National governments rely on the data collected by various agencies for decision making and ensure that the data are collected systematically and periodically.

Third, structural relationships are more robust at the macroeconomic—as opposed to the microeconomic or sector—level. That is, the top-to-bottom approach better incorporates the unity of the economy. For example, forecast variables such as national motor vehicle sales can be directly related to changes in consumer income, credit availability, etc. In contrast, a bottom-to-top approach which derives national forecasts adding up detailed forecasts from data at the state and industry level would not be based on a uniform set of national assumptions, nor assure consistency among sectors. A forecast of motor vehicle sales at the state level might be more affected by an idiosyncrasy—such as a shipping delay to Hawaii—then by underlying structural relationships. The fourth reason for the top-to-bottom approach is a practical one: even if it were possible to collect sufficient data at the state and industry level, the model would be difficult to solve and operate because of the number of equations required and the degree of simultaneity involved.

While macroeconomic model relies on this top-to-bottom approach, many of DRI's microeconomic models incorporate a bottom-to-top approach. For example, the energy model uses inputs from the macroeconomic model but also relies on detailed data, such as OPEC price changes for different grades of petroleum, to forecast oil production.

Q. *Why doesn't DRI do global forecasts?*

A. DRI does not forecast global variables, although all of our macroeconomic models are linked. Our approach is more strategic—to focus on the countries of real economic importance to the industrial world—the major countries of Asia, Europe, North America, and South America.

The forecasts of these countries are

closely linked. Also, the data for numerous minor countries are weak and much delayed, slowing down the timeliness of the analysis. For example, the Canadian model is driven by 40 components of the U.S. model, and the U.S. model requires inputs from the Canadian, Japanese, and European models.

Q. *What forecasting techniques does DRI use?*

A. A variety of techniques, including regression, input-output, and time-series analysis can be used to create forecasts. Structural econometric models rely primarily on regression analysis and secondarily on input-output analysis. Statisticians, on the other hand, often use time-series analysis. A brief definition of each term will indicate the reasons for these preferences and the appropriateness for different activities.

• Time-series analysis relies on purely statistical association even if no logic can be found to support it. That is, if two variables—for example profits and investment expenditures—have always moved together, it is assumed that they will continue to move together, even though changes in each may have different causes. For example, profits depend critically on the relationship between wages and prices, and on gains in productivity; consumption depends on household incomes, prices, psychology, and interest rates. Empirical research by economists suggests little to no causal relationship between the two, particularly in the short run, yet a multi-variate time-series analysis will forecast the two variables from each other. Univariate (single variable) time-series analysis is even more ingenious: a series is entirely forecast from its own history.

• Unlike time-series analysis, regression analysis, when used properly, takes into account the underlying causes for relationships. This mathematical technique is the basis of the structural approach inherent in econometric modeling. For example, accepted economic theory postulates a close relationship underlying consumer spending. Furthermore, it even predicts the way in which the relationship varies with different consumption categories. This theory is the starting point of the estimation process, which quantifies the understood relationships.

• Input-output analysis is based on government data collected at a highly detailed level for all inputs (raw materials, labor, energy) and outputs (finished products) that make up GNP. The method has less statistical foundation and is essentially based on one (admittedly enormous) data point in time. But it offers greater structural detail than the other methods. For example, input-output analysis explains how much of a particular industry's costs are energy-related. Thus, likely changes in industry costs can be predicted from changes in energy prices. DRI typically makes use of input-output analysis combining it more strictly with econometric modeling.

Q. *What criteria should be used for evaluating forecasts?*

A. Accuracy is usually thought of as the major criterion for evaluating forecasts. Steve McNees of the Boston Federal Reserve has made it a point to track the comparative accuracy across all firms. DRI generally fares well in these comparisons.

At DRI, we evaluate our forecast accuracy on a quarterly basis by publishing a track record comparing the forecasts generated for a specific period—say fourth quarter 1982 (December)—over the preceding two years. The table below (Exhibit 1) is excerpted from our client publication, *The Data Resources Review of the U.S. Economy,* and illustrates the changes which have been made to the forecast over time. We calculate some statistical measures of the error rate. Each variable has its own "acceptable" error rate. We are probably more concerned than our clients about not exceeding that rate. It is our professional score card.

On the subject of accuracy, we should point out that concepts that can be forecast with complete accuracy are usually less relevant to decision makers than are the variables affected by large unexpected events, such as political disruptions. Forecasting is not a crystal ball, nor is it a "pure science." Rather it combines a rigorous, disciplined examination of structural relationships in the economy with the informed judgments of specialists who stay in touch with actual business and political developments and talk with one another.

There are two other criteria of equal importance to users of forecasts. These are timeliness and clarity. Obviously, if you wait long enough for a forecast, it will become extremely accurate. If you, as a DRI client, must place a major purchase order by the end of the week, you may need a forecast of next quarter's demand for your product today. The forecast that will be available two weeks from now may be more accurate but it will be less valuable. Recognizing this, DRI generates frequent forecasts that are immediately available on-line to our clients.

The clarity of the forecast is also important. DRI does not just provide numbers; we comment on them. We publish—in hard copy and on-line—monthly interpretations of the as-

EXHIBIT 1
DRI FORECASTING RECORD FOR FIRST QUARTER 1982

	Actual BEA Prelim Estim.	1982 3/22	1/25	10/27	1981 7/26	4/26	1/27	10/23	1980 7/24	4/22	Average Absolute Percent Error
				Billions of 1972 Dollars — SAAR							
GNP	1,483.6	1,481.5	1,488.0	1,499.0	1,532.1	1,555.9	1,512.2	1,529.6	1,520.0	1,532.6	2.3
Consumption	966.8	962.8	962.7	970.5	980.9	985.3	967.3	964.5	949.4	960.9	0.8
Nonresidential Investment	162.4	156.7	159.9	160.1	164.0	167.4	160.0	157.3	154.4	160.2	2.4
Residential Investment	38.3	38.9	38.6	41.9	48.3	50.4	52.5	55.8	59.5	56.5	28.3
Inventory Investment*	-17.5	-7.6	-0.6	-4.0	6.2	7.6	3.0	5.5	8.5	6.1	115.7
Exports	153.7	154.8	155.3	158.6	156.6	162.2	163.0	165.9	168.7	172.3	5.4
Imports	115.8	118.8	116.5	118.8	117.0	116.4	114.8	111.6	115.8	116.4	1.4
Federal Spending	118.3	117.1	114.8	108.6	110.5	113.3	105.8	110.7	115.9	110.3	5.4
State and Local Spending	177.5	177.7	178.2	177.5	181.4	181.8	182.3	179.7	180.3	183.4	1.6

* These items are not restated for data revision, either because there is little or no revision, or because the restatement method cannot be applied.

sumptions and of the logic that underlie the forecast. Those independent judgments of DRI's professional staff that went into the model are explained to our clients. We are also available by telephone and in person. In fact, economists at DRI probably spend 15% of their time answering individual questions about what went "into" the forecast.

Q. *Does DRI create alternative scenarios? and, if so, do you assign probabilities to each?*

A. The answer is yes to both parts of the question. DRI's forecasts start with the most likely. This forecast—we call it "CONTROL"—always has, in our judgment, at least a 50% chance of occurring. Once we have created this forecast, we ask the question "where are we most likely to be wrong?" The answers to this question produce a variety of scenarios. A probability is assigned to each scenario, and a forecast is prepared for each scenario.

This chart (See Exhibit 2) illustrates this point. In a recent month, we developed four forecasts of GNP growth. The CONTROL scenario, with a 50% probability, was our "best guess" as to how the economy would unfold over the next 3 years. Another scenario, with a 20% probability, assumed continued stagflation for the next 3 years. A depression scenario, with a 2% probability, assumed a sharply depressed economy, with the unemployment rate exceeding 12%. The optimistic scenario, with a 13% probability, assumed growth according to the Administration's plans and low inflation. A further scenario, with a 15% probability, assumed a deeper recession and a sharper bounce back.

In addition to these judgments about probability, we use a statistical technique known as stochastic simulation to generate ranges for forecast variables. This technique uses the error terms of the equations to run one hundred simulations to trace out the probability distribution of outcomes, and shows them for the two dozen most important variables.

Our clients often use our forecasts as the basis for decisions. The probability rates are our way of telling them what we think is the likelihood of any given scenario. We often help our clients play "what if" games with the forecast. By posing these questions, the client can see the impact of changes in the forecasts on variables important to his business. We do not tell any company what its future will be like. We do work with clients to develop customized models which forecast variables of interest to them, for example, sales of individual product lines.

Q. *How can clients maximize their use of forecasting services?*

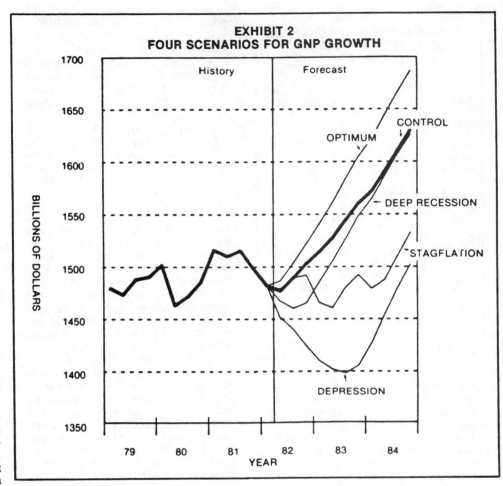

A. We can best answer that question by quoting from a speech given to the Joint Meeting of the New York City Chapter of The Institute of Management Sciences and The North American Society for Corporate Planning, Inc., on January 22, 1981, by Dr. Otto Eckstein, DRI's president. He said "The use of quantitative analysis to improve corporate planning in an increasingly complex environment is mushrooming. According to a recent survey,[1] 61% of all corporate planning groups use the services of Data Resources, Inc., and our competitors provide service to additional units. Econometric models play a central role in this work, but unlike earlier product-line forecasting applications, the models today are part of an elaborate system of data bases, analytical software capable of producing planning analyses, and consulting support.

"As I observe these planning activities, it is evident that the typical planning process of our users does not yet analyze the external environment efficiently, and that quantitative analysis must still be fully integrated into the work of business planning; the goal of such quantitative systems is, after all, to help produce the best possible business decisions for large organizations in a changing and unstable economic environment."

Q. *What specific areas of business planning did Dr. Eckstein have in mind?*

A. He identified seven:
- Monitoring the environment
- Identifying growth markets
- Analyzing costs and productivity
- Setting growth and financial targets
- Analyzing a corporation's portfolio of businesses
- Evaluating international strategy
- Strategic financial planning

Q. *Could we choose one of those areas as an example, and demonstrate how, using one or more of DRI services, a client might maximize the value of the service? Would business portfolio analysis be a good example?*

A. Yes. The repositioning of a company through acquisition and divestiture is, perhaps, the dominant theme of strategic planning. A good portfolio of businesses diversifies against such risks as the business cycle, credit crunches, oil crises, changes in international costs and exchange rates, and shifts of technology. A

EXHIBIT 3
SET OF FIRMS SELECTED FROM COMPUSTAT® BASED UPON FINANCIAL CRITERIA

Ticker	Firm Name
RUSS	Russell Stover Candies, Inc.
DOC	Dr. Pepper Co.
CRC	Crompton Co., Inc.
GFD	Guilford Mills, Inc.
RML	Russell Corp.
TCX	Ti-Caro, Inc.
MEG.A	Media General - CL A
FRK	Florida Rock Inds.
VAC.A	Vermont American - CL A
FLS	Florida Steel Corp.
PRE	Premier Industrial Corp.
MYG	Maytag Co.
OVT	Overnite Transportation
SBP	Standard Brands Paint Co.
MLW	Miller-Wohl Co.
PST	Petrie Stores Corp.
CHU	Church's Fried Chicken, Inc.

Criteria for selection:
• Sales between $100 and $500 million
• Profits in excess of 5%
• Low sensitivity to financial conditions

good business portfolio also has the proper balance between mature, cash-producing units and high-growth potential cash-absorbing units. Finally, the portfolio must have an overall level of risk which is consistent with the financial community's expectations of earnings stability and with management's staying power to survive through surprisingly tough times. If there is a substantive business synergism, such as the application of a new technology to old businesses, shared marketing organizations or production facilities, or the achievement of economies of vertical or horizontal integration, so much the better, but that is not usually the focus of the strategic planning portfolio optimizing work.

The decision support systems for business portfolio analysis have consisted mainly of the ability to do elaborate financial modeling, to condense large amounts of information in intricate graphics displays, and to access lots of data and scenarios to test out the portfolios created by the strategy. One example of such graphics is displayed in this chart (Exhibit 3), the typical "bubble" chart. It is produced by the DRI EPS Graphics Package, using models and databanks for sales and return on net assets to provide the information inputs.

Once the basic strategy is developed, the enterprise turns to acquisition analysis. The Compustat® (or Value Line) data, searched by a program such as DRI's DRISCAN, can identify companies that have the desired requisites. In the

example chosen (Exhibit 4), the criteria selected for the search were a company with sales in the $100-500 million range, a profit margin in excess of 5%, and an exceptionally low sensitivity to financial conditions. The latter criterion was expressed by requiring a strong balance sheet, defined as debt less than 30% of sales, with short-term debt less than 10% of sales. Criteria can of course be more complicated. The particular search that was run turned up a number of very conservative and closely-help companies that might prove difficult or costly to acquire.

Divestiture has usually not received comparable quantitative attention. Because of the desire to grow, companies have a lot more enthusiasm for acquisitions than for selling operating units. Sales usually occur under distress conditions, with the modest volume of business sales in ordinary times reflecting a company's failure to make a success of a particular unit or to integrate that unit successfully into the company's business structure. Nonetheless, it must be recognized that the analysis of potential sales is as challenging a task as the analysis of potential acquisitions, and that the tools are similar. Of course the data are internal, and it is elaborate financial modeling and projections of sales, costs, capital charges, and NOI which are the ingredients of the quantitative support system for the sales decision. Econometric projections of markets, costs, and in-

terest rates are inputs to that work.

Q. *What criteria should be used in evaluating a forecasting service firm?*

A. A forecasting service should be evaluated on the basis of its ability to provide assistance in the seven planning areas mentioned earlier, in addition to the more standard economic forecasting activities. The expertise of the client consultants is critical to this support as the expertise of economists is critical to the forecasting activity. Prospective clients of any forecasting service should investigate the capabilities of the firm with regard to both planning support and economic forecasting strength.

Q. *Is DRI doing anything to broaden its market beyond the Fortune 500?*

A. Advances in computer technology are opening up new markets of users who can access DRI's data, forecasts, and planning applications via personal computers and microcomputers. We have committed significant resources to developing applications for these new users—some of whom are in smaller companies than we have heretofore served. Some of these new users will be similar to our current clients in their desire to conduct their own analysis; others will require more assistance. All will benefit from the ability to conduct sophisticated analysis—drawing on DRI's analytic software, forecasts, and data—in a local microcomputer environment. ●

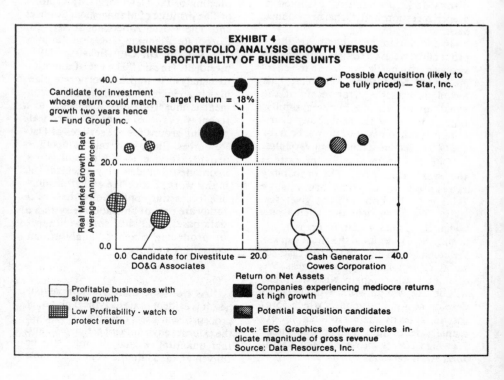

EXHIBIT 4
BUSINESS PORTFOLIO ANALYSIS GROWTH VERSUS PROFITABILITY OF BUSINESS UNITS

Note: EPS Graphics software circles indicate magnitude of gross revenue
Source: Data Resources, Inc.

Chapter 17
The Wharton Model

Interview with
Howard J. Howe and Gene D. Guill
Wharton Econometric Associates, Inc.

Q. *Generally speaking, what services does Wharton Econometrics provide?*

Guill: Each of Wharton's services provides extensive databanks recording historical data for the relevant sector or aspect of economic activity. We provide professional consulting in all areas to help people understand what is happening in the economy and why it's happening in a particular way. In addition, of course, we provide regular forecasts of economic activity and supplement those with analysis that explains our forecasts, that is, why we believe the future is going to develop in the way we foresee it.

Howe: Forecasts are provided in hard copy, written form. They are also provided on the computer, through timesharing. We provide them on tape for certain clients who want to bring the information onto their own systems to use either large-scale computers within their own company—or increasingly, mini-computers and micro-computers are in use—to do certain manipulations with the data. It may not be full-fledged model simulations and forecasting, but it is often such things as report-writing, table-making, graphics, or other applications of historical or forecast information that are useful in solving business problems on a day-to-day, week-to-week, month-to-month basis.

Q. *What role does an econometric forecasting service play in the decision-making of business people? Why do clients buy your services?*

G: All business plans are based on forecasts, whether they are explicitly or implicitly recognized. What we attempt to do is develop standard tools, scientific tools, to be used in producing these forecasts. We use the tools ourselves, combining them with information obtained through personal experience and other sources,

to produce forecasts that we consider to be the most likely path for the economy in the quarters or years ahead.

Our forecasts are presented to clients at regular meetings, where they have an opportunity to evaluate them. Client participation is a key element in our forecasting process; this is, by the way, something that distinguishes us from our competition. The clients find this useful in helping them shape their ideas about the future business and economic environment, what the pulse of the business cycle will be, the particular timing of swings in the business cycle, timing of interest rate peaks and troughs . . . all of this can be quite important in determining the timing of business decisions.

For example, housing starts and construction activity may well depend upon demographic variables in the long-run sense. But in the short run, they are strongly impacted by interest rates, that is, by financial conditions. If clients have a clear picture as to what interest rates may be in the months ahead, it would surely affect their decisions for certain types of investments or projects related to conditions in the housing and construction industries.

Q. *How do Wharton Econometrics' models and services differ from the other major econometric forecasting firms?*

H: One principal way in which Wharton differs is that we use different models for different purposes; you might say "the right model for the right purpose." For example, the Wharton Quarterly Model, a short-term cyclical model, is used to arrive at quarterly cyclical movements of the U.S. economy—for capturing the timing and strengths of those upturns or downturns in the very short run.

Yet, for our long-term U.S. forecast, rather than extrapolate and run out the Quarterly Model to 40 or 80 periods in order to forecast over a 10 or 20-year horizon, we go to an entirely different model. We use the Wharton Long Term Model, which is based on annualized

rather than quarterly data and provides much richer detail on the industrial sectors of the economy. It also gives a heavier emphasis to demographics and much stronger role for long-term responses rather than short-term cyclical responses.

Second, while we and other forecasting firms turn out numbers that extend 12 quarters, 10 years, or 20 years into the future, the quality of the models behind those numbers is quite different. This is another principal way in which we differ from our competitors. We do a lot more research. While all firms do some amount of this work, Wharton has traditionally done much more of it. We think this shows up on the bottom line. Our philosophy of spending a higher proportion of our time on research, along with our use of specialized models for specialized purposes, results in a superior forecast record. This record is borne out in the McNees Reports, both the one done three years ago and the one done last fall, which show Wharton as being the "best" forecaster.

Q. *What kind of research does Wharton Econometrics do?*

H: Reestimating equations, reformulation of parts of a model, checking to see that equations that behaved well over an earlier historical period continue to behave well. We examine any equations that are beginning to break down as shifts occur in the economy.

If I may, I'd like to add one more way in which we differ from other forecasting firms, something Gene just briefly mentioned already. One aspect of our services, really unique to Wharton, is the way we meet with our clients on a regular basis. The short-term service (Wharton Quarterly Model), for example, meets four times yearly with its clients. The Long Term Forecasting Service meets twice a year with clients. The World Economic Service has two meetings a year with its subscribers.

Those meetings attract anywhere from 50 to 150 attendees, depending on the size of the client base, the meeting location . . . and often, attendance depends on what state the economy is in. What sets these meetings apart from other kinds of presentations is that they are bona-fide, working, forecasting meetings with the clients. They are a day and a half to two days in duration, at which the Wharton people present the forecast. It's gone over in detail and then it's taken apart by the clients with comments from their particular industry or business point of view. Clients are asked to present their views in cases where they might know more than Wharton does.

For example, in a Long-term Forecast Service meeting, when General Motors wants to talk about automobiles, we sit down and take notes! The same thing is true in the aircraft industry, and the same in steel. We sit and take notes in all these cases. When it comes to putting all of this together into the overall economic picture, we see things that clients may not. So, these working meetings give us the best blend of detailed, business information and the overall consistent view that one gains from the model. We return from our meetings, rework the forecast, and distribute an updated forecast after the meeting.

This interaction among the Wharton economists and forecasters and our clients—business people, chief economists, strategic planners—give us, we feel, the best combination of modeling and practical information.

Q. *You mentioned the McNees Report. It has elicited the reaction from many business people that even the best of forecasts is wrong all the time, meaning that even the best estimate of the future is not the future by a long shot. How do you respond to that?*

H: We are not fortune tellers. Econometric forecasting is an art, a developmental science. As a user of a forecasting service, I would rather be closer to the outcome than farther away. With all due consideration to the facts and figures as we know them now, our forecast number is still not going to turn out to be *the* number. But I would still rather have *a* forecast, conditional though it may be.

These forecasts are based on as much model integrity as possible, as much outside information as possible, as much studied judgment as possible, and on a highly qualified staff with a great deal of depth. Given all of this, then if a policy assumption proves to be wrong, if a given equation goes off track, then the forecast is going to be wrong; we just cannot foretell the future exactly. But I would still rather be closer than farther away from the outcome in a forecast or a strategic plan.

G: I think, too, that forecasting has to be seen as a continuous process, a continuous exercise. Having a model and going through the exercise of forecasting has great benefit in that it forces you to formalize procedures and be explicit in making assumptions, and in evaluating how those assumptions are actually going to impact on the economy or one's business.

Try to stop time and say, "I'm going to evaluate this forecast to see how realistic it turned out to be three years into the future," is the only one way of evaluating a forecast. While it is the most common way, there is also a great benefit to clients in the fact that the forecasts *do* change. Events change on a day-to-day basis and we change our forecasts on a month-to-month basis to incorporate recent change. An evolution of a forecast happens over time. For example, we might have made a forecast for a recession in 1980, three years in advance, and then we might need to change the timing of that recession in our forecast from the first quarter to the third, depending on what more recent factors have affected that outlook.

H: What Gene says in terms of this ongoing process and the continuity that grows out of it is very important to us in terms of the delivery of economic forecasting services to our clients. It's the ongoing consulting, working relationships as much as any single number that counts.

Q. *In your forecasting process, how do you cope with political decisions, made by politicians, not for economic reasons although they may be dressed up that way, but for what are really political reasons?*

H: You couldn't have asked that question at a better time. Over the past two years, we've seen enormous changes in U.S. economic policy. It has had, and still has the potential for, strong effects on the U.S. economy. As those political decisions have unfolded day to day, week to week, month to month, we've had to find a way to give our best guess of outcomes in terms of fiscal policy.

For example, let's take the Reagan fiscal policy package and see how we attempted to cope with it over the horizon of our Long-term U.S. Forecast. After November 5, 1980, after the presidential election, we had to re-do a forecast. We had not based our forecast at that time on the assumption that Ronald Reagan would be elected or that his Reagonomics program would be fully adopted. We didn't think that his program would be adopted, at least not in its entirety. We didn't believe that the 5-10-10 personal tax cut would be adopted. Well . . . we had to learn fast in that case because as the next several months unfolded, we saw that the President did

get his program through Congress far more intact than we, as economists and forecasters, had believed he would . . . and more intact than a lot of the business and financial press were anticipating.

Q. *Was this because Wharton economists were, perhaps, not politically attuned to what was happening?*

H: No, I think not. We are quite well attuned to politics and especially economic policy matters. We have a strong Washington office. The people there are part of our Economic Policy Analysis Group. They are our government-watchers, and they are people with experience in government and on Captitol Hill. They are very good at monitoring what develops on the Hill.

If you had to pick a reason why we didn't guess that the Reagan policy would be adopted almost in its entirety, I think it was because we foresaw some of the disruptive effects of that type of policy. We thought it was really strong medicine for any economy, even one as robust as the U.S. economy. It was very difficult, with the odds that existed at the time on passage of the total Reaganomics package, to say, "We will assume that these rather drastic, radical policies will be put into place and then see what effects they will have."

This is not to say, however, that as political probabilities changed that we didn't adapt rather quickly, working new policy assumptions into our forecasts. Today, we have gotten to the point where we must consider the 1983 budget. Here's a case where being reasonably politically attuned, based on our eyes and ears in Washington, we bet that a major part, but not all, of the President's budget would be adopted by Congress. The recent budget passed by the House and Senate (June 1982) is very close to what we expected. While we are probably going to miss on some details, our best guesses on the overall budget have proved to be correct.

Q. *Do you assign probabilities to your forecasts?*

H: Yes, but no. We don't assign numbers. We know that not all of these policies are certain to go through. One certainly has to investigate the alternatives. What if there is a budget cut? What if there is some monetary relaxation? What if we do rescind the last tax cut? What if we do have earlier natural gas price decontrol or a windfall profits tax to help the budget? We evaluate all those alternatives. But to hand the client a set of alternatives and say "pick your own" places too great a burden on the client. We do know that the probabilities of certain alternatives are higher than others. We pick a policy outcome as our best guess, and say: "This is our best estimate of what the outcome is going to be." And then we present the other alternatives to back our best guess. We don't go on to say that one alternative has a 65 percent probability and that alternatives A, B, and C have 10, 15, and 10 percent probabilities.

Other forecasting firms make a valiant attempt at giving the right numerical value, but assigning a number to any alternative suggests a quantitative value that is not justified. In any event, we don't know how to put a probability number on a political decision. That's why we don't do it. However, we do indicate in the commentary accompanying the forecast the areas where we believe there is more certainty and where there is less certainty.

Q. *How does a business manager cope with that risk?*

G: Let me say first that our clients do not use our forecasts as a substitute for thinking or a substitute for analysis: it is a tool of analysis. If I, as a client of a forecasting service, were faced with the problem of developing generating capacity to meet electricity demand 10 years into the future, for example, the first thing I would want to know about the forecast I received is how Wharton derived it; what their primary assumptions were concerning those factors that determine demand for electricity. I would analyze that and come up with my own informed opinion and compare it to the Wharton forecast. I would then talk to the Wharton people to exchange viewpoints. At this point, we would help a client to incorporate some idea of the risk on the up-side and the down-side concerning this forecast.

Proper use of a forecast involves a thorough study of the major factors determining and underlying the forecast, and how they affect my particular problem in my particular industry. We do some kinds of analysis to help clients evaluate that. For example, there are major uncertainties regarding fiscal policy, monetary policy, and world economic events. Econometrics does not lend itself to determining political decisions or forecasting political decisions—that involves a very strong judgmental factor. We will perform alternative forecasts of the future in which we incorporate different assumptions regarding fiscal policy, monetary policy, the world environment, world energy supplies, etc. Clients can then see how one alternative might affect their decision for the partic-

ular problem at hand. The client can either make an independent decision or can discuss with us the likelihood we would attach to the alternative path. Although we hesitate to say that there's a ten percent probability that this pessimistic forecast is going to be the forecast for the U.S. economy, we can say that our forecast for world oil prices is such and such. We are assuming this, and it is likely that some other assumption might be just as realistic or some other outcome might occur. That kind of sensitivity analysis helps a client analyze how dependent his solution or the profitability of his action is on alternative growth paths.

H: Suppose we have, for example, a case of someone who wants to make a business investment and wants to see how vulnerable he is. We have a base case, a high growth case, a low growth case, and other more disruptive shocks like an oil price run-up in 1986 and so forth. Whether that client has a sophisticated modeling system of his own to which he applies our forecast information or whether it goes all the way down the range to some kind of qualitative back-of-the-envelope, or paper and pencil operation, or a team of industry analysts to do his company planning, he can use a broad range of alternatives as assumptions. He can evaluate his project under all these different alternatives, which we have provided from the point of view of the external environment in which he is operating. He might find out that the rate of return on the investment is relatively insensitive to a broad range of political possibilities. Or, he might learn that the thing is so sensitive that a change in fiscal policy or monetary policy, or a change in interest rates of 2 percentage points will make the difference between red and black ink on a particular project. So we don't run his business, and when it gets down to that point, it's up to him to make a business decision. We are providing him a broad range of information on the external environment to help him make that decision.

G: Another important thing is that we provide a tool to help people produce forecasts of the future, and to analyze what the future might look like under alternative assumptions. It could well be that the standard forecasts or alternatives that we have produced really do not capture what this client feels are the basic assumptions or the most likely assumptions for the next 10 years. We would then be willing to work with that client to develop a special alternative forecast, which captured and included what he feels is the most likely projection of the U.S. economy. He could take that information and perform his own analysis to

determine the profitability of this particular venture.

Q. *Many companies subscribe to more than one service. Do you think this a good idea?*

H: That depends on how one uses the information. It's a good idea if your purpose is to reduce the risks of acting on the basis of one forecast. A second or even a third forecast—especially at the macro level—gives one a full range of opinion and more confidence if these opinions are close. It's also a good idea if one finds that one bureau is better than another in some aspects—software, data base, consulting service—that are important to the client. Also, one bureau may be better than another in forecasting one set of variables while another may excel in others.

However, one may create problems by going to one service for one part of a forecast and to another for another part, because of the differences in the modeling system—you would get one view out of two modeling systems that are not consistent with each other. If a client, for example, doesn't like what one service says about interest rates but agrees with their views about the rest of the economy, he would be better off going to the service and ask to run the model incorporating his own assumptions to see how the picture unfolds. This would provide a different picture out of the same modeling system and be consistent.

Let me give you a case in point. One of our clients—a sophisticated economist who sees a lot of forecasts—said: "I don't see the U.S. economy coming into the 1990s with high inflation. There are a number of factors both with regard to government policy, and the structure of the economy itself, that are going to bring inflation down, below your baseline forecast. So, I don't like that aspect of the forecast. However, I like, respect, and need the kind of consistency that your model forces on the overall environment. So will you work with me in changing the assumptions to get us to the point of 2 or 3 percent inflation by the end of the decade? Then, I will be assured that I have my prior information built into the forecast and I will also gain the benefits of the consistency of bringing the whole system into line with the low inflation rate." He is, therefore, using a different set of assumptions to tie that back to this spectrum of risk in the forecast. He sees inflation at 6 percent by the end of the decade as being way outside of his range of assumptions. So, to reduce his risks, he wants to see what things look like under 2 or 3 percent inflation.

Q. *Does Wharton Econometrics provide industry forecasts, regional, state or*

SMSA (standard statistical metropolitan area) forecasts?

G: Wharton's Long-term Forecasting Service, which Howard represents, does produce industry forecasts, roughly at the 2-digit SIC classification level. The Long-term Model identifies 56 producing industries in the U.S. economy. When that model was developed in the early 1970s, its level of disaggregation was considered to be as extensive as possible in a state-of-the-art model. But, since then, clients have asked for more detail on industry, more disaggregated information. And it has been a challenge to econometricians to provide that type of information.

Now, we offer an Industry Planning Service, for which individual industry models have been developed for use in monitoring, analyzing, and forecasting industry performance in about 110 producing U.S. industries. It is more detailed than the Long-term Model, operating at the 3-digit SIC classification level in most cases—in some cases, at even greater detail.

In developing the Wharton Industry model, we paid particular attention to trying to identify the primary relationships which affect industrial performance. That forced us, in essence, to give a quite realistic interpretation of how each industry operates. It also caused us to build a model much larger than we originally anticipated—to include measures of inventory behavior, capacity utilization, and new and unfilled orders. I think, compared with the competition, it is a much more elaborate presentation of industrial behavior. Generally, the competition does not identify inventories by stage of fabrication or explicitly identify capacity utilization. They use "proxy" measures to capture these effects in terms of industry performance.

Q. *What specifically does the Industry Planning Service forecast?*

G: We forecast industrial output, industry prices, commodity prices, wages, inventories by stage of fabrication, new and unfilled orders for outputs of industries, as well as employment, productivity and capacity utilization.

Q. *How far in advance?*

G: We forecast on a quarterly basis, twelve quarters into the future. Then, once a year, we do a ten-year forecast.

Q. *How would an individual company use this information provided by your Industry Planning Service?*

G: One of the major applications is in development of short-term operations plans, and also in developing longer-term strategic plans. For the shorter term, it's important that companies be aware of the general economic environment in which they operate. What is going to happen

with interest rates? When will the major swing occur in economic activity? This information assists them in maintaining optimum inventory levels, in hiring, or in scheduling production processes.

Industry Planning Service clients can also use specific industry forecasts to identify supply bottlenecks. If the economy, for example, were rapidly expanding, we might experience shortages in certain markets and, as a result, industries might not be able to produce the output demanded. Therefore, industries that had a means of identifying potential shortages and bottlenecks would be induced to buy necessary input farther in advance, prior to the bottleneck occurring.

Q. *Can the Industry Service help in identifying growth markets?*

G: Yes, we identify those industries that are growing more rapidly than others; we forecast the output of 110 industries. Frequently, we work with clients in developing their own company forecasts. Then, based on a comparison of the company forecast with the total industry forecast, analysts can determine whether their market share is expected to increase or decrease over time.

Another useful comparison can be done in investigating a given industry's cost structure. Again, we prepare an analysis of the cost structure industry-wide. This might include such things as the relative importance of labor costs in overall costs, or the importance of energy cost share. A company might then take that information, compare industry-wide performance to its own, and determine whether its cost structure is likely to rise or fall relative to the industry's. From that, it could decide to change its input mix so as to achieve cost advantages for the future.

Q. *Does Wharton Econometrics have in-house expertise on various industries and sectors?*

H: Yes. Let me give you an example. Demographics is extremely important in terms of the long-term outlook for the United States. Energy is also extremely important. Wharton's experts in these two areas spend more time related to the long-term forecasts than any other area. In the short-term service, the Wharton Quarterly Model, there is a strong role for the financial side of the economy. A financial expert resides and spends more of his time on the Quarterly Model staff than any other area, but contributes his expertise throughout the firm.

G: Within the Industry Service, we specialize much further as far as industry expertise goes. We have developed specialists for labor markets, ferrous and nonferrous metals, construction materials,

chemicals, rubber and plastic, and transportation.

We also talk frequently with clients and through participation in forecast review meetings, we attempt to keep informed about specific industry developments.

Another important way in which Wharton attempts to develop its expertise is through its Contracts Research Group. Through participation in contracts research—special studies for particular industries and on particular industry issues—we develop our own human capital. This specialization is in turn contributed back to other industries and other publications.

Q. *Now let's turn to regional and state forecasting. What does Wharton Econometrics do in these areas?*

H: Wharton has a Census Region Model, which is used to provide regional capacity. The United States is divided into nine census regions and the Wharton regional model looks at each of them in terms of employment, industrial activity, price levels and market growth.

At the present time, we do not do state-by-state modeling. The one exception to that is for the State of New York, and for a selective group of clients there, the New York State Power Pool.

Q. *I assume then that you don't do Standard Statistical Metropolitan Area modeling and forecasting.*

H: Only in the case of New York City and Philadelphia. We do have models of both of those SMSAs.

Q. *Does Wharton Econometrics have a global model? Do you provide a global forecasting service?*

H: Yes, we have the Wharton World Economic Service—an outgrowth of Project LINK, founded by Professor Lawrence Klein and continuing to operate under the auspices of the University of Pennsylvania. The World Economic Service itself, however, is the premier global service in the business in terms of country coverage, in terms of consistency, in terms of how the world trade flows are linked together, and in terms of guaranteeing that the sum of World exports equals the sum of world imports.

Q. *Is the World Economic Service used primarily by those in the export market, capital markets, things of that nature?*

H: Yes, it's used by multinational corporations, large financial corporations, and increasingly, by clients in foreign countries who are interested in how their economies relate to the world economy.

Let me add something about the World Economic Service and its global nature. Under the umbrella of the World Economic Service, which covers largely the OECD (Organization for Economic Cooperation and Development) countries—basically the United States, Europe, Canada, and Australia—there are several regional services. The Centrally Planned Economies Group, which covers Eastern Europe, the Soviet Union and the People's Republic of China, is unique in the field. There is also Pacific Basin coverage, including Japan and Southeast Asia. There's the Middle East Economic Service, also unique in the field, which is based in Washington and covers seven Gulf nations.

And there is the Latin American Services Group—again, something unique. It provides the premier model of Mexico and actually has more Mexican than U.S. clients. I think that's the hallmark of a model of a foreign country; when the nationals are buying it more than the U.S. clients are, you know you have something special. The same is true, although it hasn't existed as long, of the Brazilian Forecasting Service. The younger Latin American Service is not yet as detailed as these other two, but it is comprehensive in its coverage of the major developing nations of South America.

Q. *Can I assume that you take all of these country and regional models and then aggregate them into a global forecast? As opposed to what you do in the domestic models, which is to take the national accounts, the aggregate data, and prepare your forecast for the country.*

H: That really is not the case with the U.S. macro models; the macro models are built up from very detailed information. Yes, GNP is the single most important number that comes out of the U.S. models, but that GNP figure is literally built up from detailed forecasts on 90 categories: consumption of autos, consumption of new autos, consumption of auto parts, residential investment, business fixed investment, etc.

Q. *Then you don't take industry-by-industry forecasts and then aggregate them into a U.S. forecast?*

H: In the long-term forecast, we do. What I just described is the breakdown of the 90 final demand categories, that is, how industrial output is used. But at the same time, simultaneously with what is going on in the final demand side of the model, we have an input-output model which addresses the production side. Here, outputs and prices of 56 industries are determined.

The whole system works simultaneously. We add up the production side, we add up the demand side, and guarantee that it's consistent, that it all adds up to the same number. In the same sense, the final demand prices are consistent with the industry selling prices, when one takes into account material inputs, producers' margins, prices of imports and prices of exports, to derive the prices for the final demand categories.

Q. *Does this differ from the Chase Econometrics Model?*

H: Yes, absolutely. In its entirety. What we are talking about is an integrated supply and demand system. This Wharton Long-term Model has what in the jargon is known as an "embedded input-output model," linked simultaneously with the final demand model. The final demand side is the stock in trade of most econometric forecasting. Having that linked to the production side of the economy is what's unique in Wharton's Long-term Model.

Q. *Does Wharton publish a price list for its various services? Can you give us some idea of what various services cost?*

G: We recently revised our prices, mainly in an attempt to combine some of our products into packages and offer substantial discounts for these combinations of services. It makes good sense from our point of view as well as the clients' to be able to present our products in this organized way so the client who's interested in Wharton's U.S. services can see what's available in terms of total services and then, based on that, decide what they are specifically interested in and perceive how much it will cost.

I can give you some specific prices, but keep in mind that clients do have several options. For example, one may want to purchase data via the timesharing computer system and another may not. One may want to purchase more consulting time than another.

For the U.S. macro services, the combined Wharton Quarterly Model and the Long-term Forecasting Service as a package would be in the $18,000-to-$19,000-per-year range. For the Industry Planning Service, the price is in the $15,000-to-$16,000 range.

We are in the process of unbundling some of these services so that we can be accessible to some of the companies further down the Fortune 500 list. I do think it's true that in the past these services have been most useful to the larger companies—the Fortune 500 or perhaps the Fortune 100—namely, the companies with staff economists and economics groups. Small companies' concerns are less closely related to the overall performance of the U.S. economy. They are more likely to be related to the performance of their region. In an attempt to reach that market, though, I suspect the econometric forecasting industry will be unbundling services to offer, for example, smaller packages at substantially reduced cost.

Q. *I've heard that Wharton Econometrics is becoming more aggressive in marketing its products. Just how are you accomplishing that? What markets are you trying to open?*

H: We are moving ahead aggressively in just about every market that we cover—in some, of course, faster than others. But in order to best characterize this new aggressiveness, I think you have to look back at the "old Wharton." We have always had a lot of confidence in the quality of our work, the quality and integrity of our models and forecasts—we still do. But perhaps because of our academic roots, our research antecedents, we felt that because we had a better mousetrap, the world would beat a path to our door! Now we know differently; we know that business just doesn't work that way.

All you need to do is pick up a forecast done 18 months ago and compare it with the forecasts we are producing today. While the integrity, the quality, the numbers, and so forth, are found in both examples, the readability, the usefulness, the incisiveness—just the overall utility to the client—are much greater now than before.

It's basically a question of delivery. But when you are in a service industry, an information industry, it's the delivery that matters a lot in terms of usefulness of the product to the client. Along those same lines, we have now a much larger and stronger field support group and team of marketing representatives. We are providing prospective clients with more thorough information and presentations on our products before they sign up, and we're supporting their ongoing use of our products and services better once they've become Wharton clients.

As for which markets we're pursuing, we are striking out with our upgraded products and services to get at the domestic market, to increase and open up further the market niche we already occupy. We do have a competitive advantage in that we're very strong in the international area. We are capitalizing on that. And we're opening up new areas, too, such as the Industry Planning Service, where detail and applications are important.

We feel we have the background, the techniques, the depth, and the expertise to do all of this. But it does take the right delivery to bring these advantages to the marketplace.

G: If you look back over the history of the company, you see that most of the people that came to work here in the early and mid '70s came to do research, to work with Professor Lawrence Klein in model development. At that time, the industry itself was very young and demands were primarily for economic forecasts only. Today we see an industry that has changed significantly. It is looking for much more than just a forecast. It's looking for the analysis behind it, access to analytical tools, informed opinions, decision support systems—that is, all manner of tools and information to aid in the business decision-making process.

These tools include analytical software, forecasts, extensive databanks, and personal consulting time. Wharton is moving ahead to address these needs—we're moving ahead as rapidly as possible, put-

ting resources into bringing our products to the marketplace through a much stronger and more professional marketing strategy than ever before ●

Chapter 18
The Kent Model

Vladimir Simunek
St. John's University

The Kent model is a large economic forecasting system of the the U.S. economy. It performs forecasts and simulations of 43,935 variables. The model was built by the author. It is currently managed by the Kent Economic and Development Institute, Inc.

The model forecasts 42,236 variables of interindustry division, 1,184 of aggregate division, and 515 of financial division. Forecasts data are presented in quarterly values. Forecast horizon is usually two years which can be extended up to ten years.

It is a comprehensive model of major flows of commodities, services of factors of production, income and financial instruments in the economy. Figure 1 gives a condensed version of the model. Variables and equations are grouped into three divisions: (1) interindustry division, (2) aggregate division and (3) financial division.

Interindustry Division

The interindustry division is categorized into three sections: (i) services of factors of production (labor, depreciation, etc.), (ii) intermediate commodities (production and consumption of intermediate commodities), and (iii) final commodities (production of final goods and services).

Sections (ii) and (iii) of the interindustry division are subdivided into 85 industries and 85 groups of commodities. Classification of industries and commodities corresponds to the classification of the U.S. Department of Commerce used in its input-output tables. Compared to the data of the Department of Commerce, the Kent model data are more detailed at the 85 by 85 levels: the model's data are presented in quarterly values both in constant and current dollars for production and consumption of intermediate commodities and for production of final commodities. The outputs of data are arranged in traditional formats of input-output tables.

Aggregate Division

This division covers areas of the U.S. economy that appear in current macroeconomic Keynesian-type models. The division is subdivided into four sections: (iv) primary income covering components such as compensation of employees, profits, depreciation charges, and other types of income; (v) income distribution including receipts and expenditures of households, government and the rest of the world; (vi) final spending of income on personal consumption, government consumption, investment, and net exports; and (vii) the saving and investment account (see sections iv-vii, Figure 1). Thus, the data in the aggregate division represent the flow of income in the economy, originating as primary income in section (iv), distributed in sections (v), and (vii), and spent in section (vi). Output data of the aggregate division are formatted in tables that correspond to the income and product data tables of the U.S. Department of Commerce.

Financial Division

The format of the financial division corresponds to the format of the U.S. flow-of-funds tables of the Board of Governors of the Federal Reserve System. This division contains variables and equations of 42 markets for financial instruments and 22 financial sectors that participate in these markets. Financial sectors are households, business, Federal government, state and local governments, rest of the world, Federal Reserve Banks, and commercial banks including 15 other financial intermediaries. Classification of financial sectors and financial markets of the Kent model corresponds to the classification used in the Federal Reserve's flow-of-funds tables. Sections (viii) and (ix) in Figure 1 represent financial division and are formatted to contain equal numbers of rows and columns—one row for one financial market and one column for one financial sector in each section. Section (viii) contains variables of financial sectors' demand for financial instruments, and section (ix) variables of financial sectors' supply of financial instruments. Thus values of variables in section (viii) are summed up by rows representing aggregate demand for financial instruments, and values in section (ix) are summed up by rows representing the aggregate supply of financial instruments. In equilibrium, total demand equals total supply in each of 42 financial markets in the model.

Interrrelationships

As can be seen in Figure 1, variables of the interindustry and the aggregate divisions are interrelated by two market simulation systems. The market simulation system links section (iii)—production of final commodities—with section (vi)—consumption of final commodities. The variables of interindustry division enter as supply (sales) and of aggregate division as demand (purchases). In the market simulation process, values of demand and supply are adjusted to obtain forecast data of expected equilibrium prices and quantities for each macroeconomic market. The market simulation system generates forecast values of purchases and sales and of prices (price deflators) resulting from the interaction of demand and supply in the markets. Section (i)—services of factors—of the interindustry division is linked with section (iv)—primary income—of the aggregate division by the market simulation mechanism of demand and supply of services of factors of production. In Figure 1, markets for final commodities as well as for services of factors are indicated by traditional demand-supply diagrams.

The basic linkage of aggregate and financial divisions is provided by the saving-investment relationships of sectors in the aggregate division and the net saving and net financial investment relationships of financial sectors in the financial division. In equilibrium, total of net changes in financial assets of financial sectors equals total of net changes in their financial liabilities, thereby implying the equality of aggregate saving and aggregate investment in the aggregate division.

Types of Equations

A large portion of the Kent model's equations are the accountancy or identity equations. They express the equilibria of demand and supply in markets; sources and uses of commodities and financial instruments; totals of assets, net worth and liabilities of financial sectors; and equilibria of receipts, expenditures and surpluses/

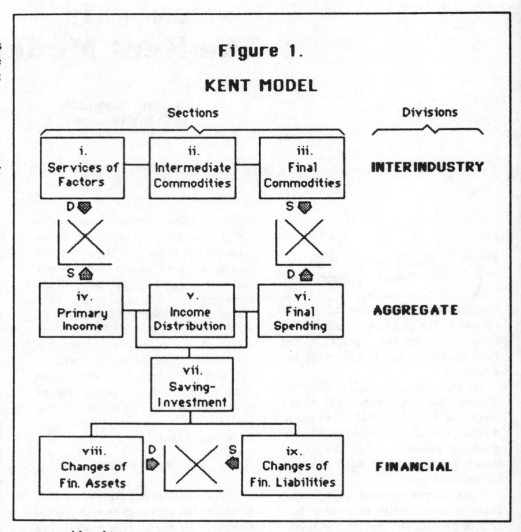

Figure 1.

KENT MODEL

Notes: 1. ╳ represents market. 2. "D" stands for demand and "S" for supply.

deficits of sectors. These equations contribute to the accuracy of the model's forecasts; they guarantee the consistency of forecast outcomes by balancing values of the model's thousands of variables. Another type of equations used in the model is technical equations. They are in the interindustry division and relate values of consumption and production by technology relationships. In the Kent model, coefficients of technical relationships are derived from constant values rather than from values in current dollars. This feature in the model adds to accuracy of predictions because it eliminates the impact of price changes. Coefficients of technical

relationships are also calculated in current values comparable to those appearing in the Department of Commerce input-output tables. The model's institutional equations are mostly in the aggregate and financial divisions. They pertain to tax rates, social security rates, and reserve requirements of the Federal Reserve System. The Kent model's behavioral equations are futuristic in nature. To avoid risks and vagaries of mechanical projections of the past into the future, estimates based on methods of futuristic assessments are used. For example, the model's market simulation equations are based on buyers' and sellers' expectations of quantities and prices (buying and selling intentions) as determinants of their behavior in markets.

References

Ruggles, R. and Ruggles, N. D. "Integrated Economic Accounts for the United States, 1947-80." **Survey of Current Business,** Washington, D.C., Vol. 62, No. 5, May 1982, pp. 1-55.

Simunek, Vladimir, J. **Kent Model of the U.S. Economy.** K.E.A., Inc., Kent, Ohio, 1974.

Simunek, Vladimir, J. "Simultaneous Price and Quantity Adjustments in a Commodity Market." Faculty working paper No. 1. **Business Research Institute.** St. John's University, New York, N.Y., 1986.

Young, A.H. and Rice, H.S. "An Introduction to National Economic Accounting. **Survey of Current Business.** Vol. 62, No. 4, April 1985, pp. 59-76.

Flow of Funds Accounts, Z. 1. Board of Governors of the Federal Reserve System. Washington, D.C. Monthly publication.

U.S. Department of Commerce, Bureau of Economic Analysis. **The Detailed Input-Output Structure of the U.S. Economy.** Vol. i and ii, 1979.

"The Input-Output Structure of the U.S. Economy, 1977." **Survey of Current Business.** Vol. 64, No. 5, May 1984, pp. 42-84.

Chapter 19
A Nobel Laureate Looks To The Future of Econometric Models

The use of econometric forecasting by both public and private organizations will continue to grow as costs decline, computing power increases, forecast accuracy improves, and as more prospective users recognize that the track record of the forecasters "is not as bad as the occasional horror story...would suggest." Those are the views of Nobel Laureate Lawrence R. Klein, Benjamin Franklin Professor of Economcs at the University of Pennsylvania and Chairman of Wharton Econometric Associates, Inc.

Dr. Klein, who was awarded the Nobel Prize in Economics in 1980 for his pioneering work in econometrics, identifies a number of significant, structural changes in world and domestic economies that are influencing model builders. Among these, he says, is a recognition of the fact that the "principal shocks to the world economy have largely been supply-side shocks—crop failures in the early '70s, and two huge oil price increases in 1974 and 1979."

"Econometric model builders," he continues, "have begun to respond to this change in the environment, and are constructing models that are considerably more oriented to supply-side influences . . . models of a decade hence will incorporate more supply influences in their analytical descriptions of modern economies."

Dr. Klein sees a switch to the Monetarist viewpoint regarding the influence of financial transactions on the economy. On this point he says:

"Financial influences have not always been given an adequate role in the simplified description of Neo-Keynesian models. This is one of the salutary lessons from the Monetarist critique. With a flow-of-funds accounting of financial transactions, including the determination of associated interest rates, we could continue to model price (interest rate) and quantity (liquidity) effects on the real economy. Already, financial variables play a larger role in the current versions (of models) . . . than they did a decade ago. These trends will continue."

The third issue raised by the Nobel laureate concerns the role of other social sciences in economic forecasting: ". . . the next generation of macro-econometric models," he says, "will have a great deal of multi-disciplinary content."

Pointing out that a macroeconomic forecasting system is set in a social and cultural context, and that it attempts to describe human behavior, Dr. Klein concludes that models "should bear a proper relationship to demography, psychometrics, criminology, quantitative political science, cliometrics, and other social disciplines."

"For the most part," Dr. Klein continues, "econometric modelling has taken the results from other disciplines as given, but a certain amount of work on the frontier has gone on in an effort to build more general social systems in which mutual feedback relationships exist between the pure economic variables and the variables generated mainly by other disciplines."

Accuracy is a sensitive point to econometricians, as it is with Dr. Klein, the world's leading authority in the field. He, however, is less defensive than most in discussing the subject.

"It must be admitted," he says, "that Robert J. Gordon and Edmond Malinvaud stress the limitations of econometric models as suggested by the experience of the 1970s. Gordon speaks of 'the failure of forecasting' during this period. Malinvaud places the emphasis on the inability of econometric models to suggest policies to take the Western economies out of the morass of stagflation, particularly in the medium term." (Both men published their views in 1980. Ed.)

It soon becomes evident, however, that Dr. Klein doesn't have a high regard for these views, for he continues:

"However, it should also be pointed out that the views of two other observers . . .

(Stephen McNees of the Federal Reserve Bank of Boston, and Victor Zarnowitz, of the University of Chicago) are somewhat *more qualified* (emphasis added, Ed.) and definitely less pessimistic." (It is not exactly clear whether Dr. Klein means that the "two other observers" are professionally "more qualified" than Gordon and Malinvaud, or whether the criticism of the "two other observers" is "more qualified." Ed.)

Dr. Klein says that McNees, writing in 1979, "concludes that the (econometric) forecasts were relatively 'good' during this decade—aside from a mediocre spell in the middle of the decade—although there is always room for improvement . . . Zarnowitz (writing in 1978) stresses an improvement over time in the forecasts of annual percentage change in nominal GNP, although he also points out that there has been a pervasive negative correlation between errors in forecasting real growth and those in predictions of inflation."

In response to criticisms about accuracy, Dr. Klein says "the track record of macroeconometric modelers is not as bad as the occasional horror story of an unsuccessful forecast would suggest," adding:

"Compared to alternatives, such as naive models, time-series analyses of single series, or judgmental forecasts, the econometric models do reasonably well, particularly as the forecasting horizon lengthens."

Dr. Klein says that "the principal lesson (learned) from over a quarter of a century of forecasting with econometric models is that the combination of good judgment and a functioning model will do better usually than either by itself."

Contrary to the implications of Makridakis and Wheelwright in their book ("Forecasting Methods for Management," 3rd edition, 1980 John Wiley & Sons, N.Y.) that econometric models did a poor job of detecting turning points in the economy, Dr. Klein points to evidence of "their ability to pick out the turning points in advance . . . For example, the Wharton model picked out the recessions starting in 1969 and in 1974 well in advance, as well as identifying the lower turning points.

"Even in the most recent episodes—the recession of 1980—one can make the argument that the forecasts were more successful than is commonly believed." He cites Robert L. McLaughlin's paper in the May 1980 issue of Business Economics: "McLaughlin argues that, in general, calendar year 1979 was one of business forecasters' better performances. In particular, he points not only to the Wharton Model forecasters' very close forecast of average real GNP growth for the entire year, but also to a highly accurate prediction of the quarterly patterns of change of this important variable." (A.M.) ●

PART V

Evaluation And Use
Of
Models

Chapter 20
What Econometric Models Can and Cannot Do

C.L. Jain
St. John's University

Econometric models are a powerful forecasting tool, though not a panacea. They can do certain things and not others. Listed below is a sampling of the important "can dos" and "cannot dos."

• *Can give insights to interrelationships:* Since econometric models identify and quantify the cause-and-effect relationships between many or a few variables, they can show how variables such as advertising expenditures, product price and personal disposable income are related to sales.

• *Can allow you to change scenarios—* the "what if" game: The model will provide a different forecast when the internal and/or external environment is changed. One can determine the effects on sales, the balance sheet, or income statement with different amounts of advertising expenditure and selling price, for example. Such information helps management select an optimal strategy with respect to advertising expenditure, inventory level, product prices, manning, etc. Also, if one is uncertain about the assumptions one is using as input (e.g., whether the prime rate will stand at 15%, 14% or 13%), a range of possible outcomes can be determined by solving the model with alternative inputs. The range identifies the best/intermediate/worst case outcome.

• *Can identify turning points:* Although econometric models still leave a lot to be desired, they are better than any other method in forecasting turning points. That's because they are based on cause-and-effect relationships and not on rolling forward past numbers.

• *Can help you react quickly to changing environment:* An econometric forecast can be revised quickly to reflect changes in the external or internal environment. An unexpected increase in raw materials prices can be plugged into the model to determine effects on the balance sheet, for example.

• *Cannot produce error-free forecasts:* Like any other method of forecasting, econometric models cannot provide perfect forecasts. In some cases they may improve the forecast, in others, they may not. Error arises because:

1. The predictive equation is not correctly specified. The variables which are believed to be the causal elements may not be, despite good statistical relationships. High statistical correlation (one of the indicators of cause-and-effect relation) can be deceiving.

2. *Multicollinearity* (effect running not only from the independent to the dependent variable, but also the other way around) exists in the data. Multicollinearity weakens predictability.

3. The relationships between the dependent variable and the independent variables, as indicated by the coefficents of the predictive equation, have changed.

4. A great deal of judgment goes into the computation of econometric forecasts. One expert claims that econometric models require 20% to 50% judgment.

5. Many micro-econometric models incorporate forecasts of macro-variables (e.g., unemployment rate and inflation), which may not be accurate.

• *Cannot be used mechanically:* Econometric models cannot be used mechanically and indefinitely in the same form. Since each forecast is based upon certain assumptions about exogenous variables, the forecast changes as the assumptions change. Econometric models cannot be used in the same form indefinitely, because the historical relations reflected in the coefficients change over time.

• *Cannot be easily developed:* The development of an econometric model is an extremely challenging and expensive undertaking. The forecaster has to resolve immense theoretical and statistical problems before he develops one. Once the model is completed, a considerable amount of resources have to be devoted to maintaining and updating the data, acquiring macro-forecasts, and restructuring and re-estimating behavioral equations.

• *Cannot detect promptly changes in historical relationships:* Regression analysis, on which most models rely to measure the coefficients, assumes that future behavior will be like past behavior. When economic agents (consumers, investors, etc.) behave differently than in the past in response to some stimuli, regression fails to capture the changed behavior promptly.

Here are some of the key elements to remember in preparing and using econometric forecasts:

• Don't ignore a forecast just because its predictions fail to come close to the actuals. Many times even bad forecasts provide a better strategy in an uncertain environment. Moreover, error in a forecast is not only a source of annoyance, but also a source of information. Some times error provides the first clue to an emerging new development or technology.

• If resources permit, develop two sets of forecasts by two different methods, and reconcile them. Such an approach provides a check on the accuracy of each method.

• It is not a simple task to judge the forecasting accuracy of a method. One way is to look at results in terms of average error, probability of an especially large error, and ability to predict turning points.

• The model is as good as its underlying theory of how the firm operates. If the basic theory underlying the model is invalid, the model cannot be expected to yield good results.

• Make sure the model does not confuse cause and effect. For example, if GNP is closely related to the sales of a medium-sized company, GNP is the cause and the company's sales are the effect, and not the other way around.

• There is no guarantee that a large model will give better results than a small one. Most of the models currently used in business are small models.

• Don't accept model output at face value. Think about it critically and/or test it. ●

Chapter 21
Six Questions to Ask Forecasters And How To Use Answers

Stephen K. McNees
The Federal Reserve Bank of Boston

The one thing we know about the future is that it will turn out different from anyone's forecast. No one can prophesy the future with perfect accuracy. The temptation is nearly irresistible, therefore, to ignore professional prognosticators. The only thing worse than a bad forecast, however, is no forecast. The decision to "let things ride" amounts to an implicit forecast that doing anything will make things turn out worse. They payoff from econometric decisions hinges critically on what happens in the future. Intelligent actions should be based on an "informed" hunch of what the future will bring. Even though your ultimate decisions cannot be delegated to some soothsayer, before you make up your mind, be sure you have milked all the information you can from the modern-day econometric prophets. Here are six questions you can ask and some hints on how to use the answers:

What Is The Forecast?

Try to pin the forecaster down to specific *quantitative* estimates. *Qualitative* forecasts—"things are going to be bad"—make easy listening, but their implications for current action are seldom clear. Qualitative statements often have different meanings to the forecaster and the forecast user. A "weak" recovery can mean anything from no further declines to 7.2 percent economic growth, the postwar average for the first year of recovery. Different users often interpret the same qualitative statement in vastly different ways. "Disinflation" has been used to cover anything from 9 to 0 percent price increases. Quantitative forecasts, even though they turn out wrong, are necessary to be sure everyone understands just what the forecaster's view of the future is.

Why Is That The Forecast?

Tables of forecasted figures down to the third decimal point may not be of much use in economic decisions. To use these projections it is usually important to understand *why* the future will look that way. To be of much use, a forecast must be accompanied by a *story* that ties the pieces together in a coherent whole and explains, in words, why that particular forecast may come about. No matter how the forecast was derived—no matter how many equations, theories, or statistical and mathematical techniques underlie the final set of numbers—there should always be an intelligible common sense story that motivates a forecast.

A necessary ingredient in any convincing forecast story is some connection with *historical precedents*. Parallels with past experience are the most powerful way to try to predict and understand the future. The forecaster should be able to point to analogous episodes when things happened roughly similarly. The future will never be an exact copy of the past, but whenever a forecast anticipates a drastic departure from all previous experience a detailed description of the precise reasoning underlying the departure must be supplied.

What Could Go Wrong?

Probably more important than the forecaster's best guess of what will happen is some feel for the probable *risks* in the forecast. What things may well come out worse than expected and what things may well turn out better? Similarly, in what areas, if any, is the forecast relatively insensitive or robust to future surprises of all kinds? When all the experts are saying about the same thing—in a minute I get to when they disagree violently—I get a little nervous. That suggests to me that no one has had a convincing, original idea for a long time about what tomorrow's big issue or the next major change of opinion will be.

The most common way of illustrating risks in the best-guess forecast is to develop a few alternative forecasts. These alternative scenarios could be based either on alternative assumptions—what if a war breaks out?, what if the oil glut dries up?, what if there is a crop failure?, what if there is a tax increase?, what if wage and price controls are imposed?—or on different views of how the economy works—what would a monetarist, a supply-sider, a Keynesian, or a "rational expectationist" expect? The key factor here is to present only the more likely contingencies. We all know almost anything is conceivable in the social sciences. To be useful, the alternative(s) must be confined to the more probable scenarios.

What Do Others Think?

Another way to pinpoint the risks in a forecast is to ask a forecaster to compare his views with those of others. The official Administration forecast issued by the President's Council of Economic Advisors is often the most natural point of comparison. Ask your forecaster to describe and explain any major differences between his outlook and the Administration's. Other times, you may also want to contrast a forecast with those of other prominent forecasters. I have published quantitative measures of the accuracy of the prominent economic forecasting organizations over the past decade.[1] This track record of previous performance provides a quantitative estimate of *the degree of accuracy one can reasonably expect* in current forecasts. This historical track record of forecasting performance always raises the question "Whose forecast is best?"

Who Is The Best Forecaster?

Several broad conclusions emerge from the track record: No one forecaster has been best for all variables. The best forecaster depends on which variable(s) you care most about. To make things more complex, even for a single variable, a forecaster's ranking often depends on the *horizon* of the forecast. The best (worst) near-term forecast can easily go along with the worst (best) long-term forecast. Thus, a major difficulty in saying which forecaster is best (or worst) is that different forecast users have different needs. Traders in financial markets care most about very short forecast horizons—months, weeks, days, hours, or even a few minutes. Capital spending decisions, on the other hand, require forecasts several years into the future. Because the rankings of the different forecasters vary with both the economic variable and the forecast horizon, it is impossible to construct an overall ranking of the forecasters that will be accurate for all forecast users.

If a forecast user has specific, numerical weights reflecting the importance he attaches to each variable and forecast horizon, he could use the published track record to construct an index ranking the forecasters from best to worst. But, before you burn out the battery on your calculator, bear in mind several limitations a ranking index will have:

(1) The *differences* in the performance of different forecasts has *typically* been fairly *small*—too small, in many cases, to attach a great amount of significance.

(2) There is no guarantee that future performances will exactly mirror past performances. Sometimes there may be reasons to expect an individual forecaster's relative performance will improve or deteriorate in the future. At the same time, there is no clearly superior alternative guide to the future than the record of the past.

(3) Forecasters often offer much more than specific, numerical forecasts—data bases, industry reports, policy analyses, and software packages. In addition, as was stressed above, the coherence and logic with which a forecast and its risks are explained can be more important to a forecast user than the exact accuracy of the numerical forecast.

What's The Bottom Line?

Let me close by offering two final pieces of advice about how to use macroeconomic forecasts as an input. First, remember *all* useful *forecasts are conditional or contingent*. They all depend on certain assumptions, economic and noneconomic. A forecaster should identify the most important assumptions and explain why he made them. But his assumptions are only assumptions. Your own assumptions, especially the noneconomic or political-economic ones, may be more realistic. A forecaster should be able to explain how his forecast would be changed under *your* most likely assumptions.

Secondly, the most important questions are probably those the forecast user must ask and answer for himself. What are your most urgent goals? How important are the risks? Which objectives are you willing to sacrifice if things go sour and which ones must be met at all costs? Is the forecast itself worth its costs? A thoughtful, explicit assessment of your basic aims and objectives can be more important in making the right decisions than knowledge of the future economic environment ●

[1] See, my "The Recent Record of Thirteen Forecasters," available on request from the Federal Reserve Bank of Boston.

Chapter 22
How to Evaluate Econometric Forecasts

Roy H. Webb
The Federal Reserve Bank of Richmond

When confronted with economic forecasts, potential users often react in opposite ways, either taking them too seriously or ignoring them altogether. The view taken here is that neither extreme is tenable. For while it is true that it is virtually impossible to forecast the future with complete accuracy, it is also true that even a forecaster whose record shows obvious errors may still provide projections containing usefull information. That said, however, it should be noted that the task of extracting useful information from forecasts is far from trivial. These issues are explored below.

At first glance it is easy to overvalue forecasts. Since they are normally stated as point estimates and are often advocated with a good deal of authority, a natural inclination is to treat these numbers as having the same precision as others that are often encountered. A little experience, however, demonstrates that forecasts can be very imprecise. Table I, for example, presents median forecasts and actual outcomes for representative variables from *Business Forecasts*.[2] The average magnitude of the forecast error in each case is a sizeable fraction of the variable that was forecasted.

Formidable Task

When predictions fail to approximate actual outcomes, some observers proceed to summarily reject all forecasts. As *The Wall Street Journal*[5] put it, "[W]e see no reason to defer to them [econometric models] on anything so complicated as an economy. . . . [W]e are not going to take economic predictions about the day after tomorrow as more than food for reflection." Similarly, as the chief executive of one large company said about economists' predictions,[1] "I go out of my way to ignore them."

Although the temptation to ignore forecasts may be strong, it is another matter to propose a better strategy for making decisions in an uncertain world. Individual households, firms, and government bureaus must act on the basis of their anticipations of future quantities to be exchanged and future prices for transactions in commodity, labor, and financial markets. Each individual decision-maker could, of course, form such anticipations in a haphazard, unsystematic manner. But many individuals have found that systematic study can improve the quality of forecasts. In forecasting, as in most productive activities, there are potential gains from specialization and exchange. That a $100 million forecasting industry has developed and prospered should therefore not be surprising, past errors for every individual forecaster notwithstanding.

In fact, the large number of forecasters and the quantity of data that each generates can make it difficult for potential consumers of forecasts to condense the information flow to a usable volume, and then employ that information to make better decisions. An obvious strategy is to identify a particular forecaster that has been especially accurate in the past and hope that his future results are as good. This, however, is not as easy as it sounds. On the contrary, identifying a superior forecaster is itself a formidable task.

Identifying Superior Forecaster

One difficulty is that users will seldom agree on the exact criteria for ranking forecasters. Different users, of course, require forecasts of different variables. And superiority in forecasting one variable does not necessarily carry over to other variables. Even users interested in one particular variable may find different error measures most relevant to their own needs. For example, one user might prefer a low average error, whereas another might prefer a low probability of an especially large error. Still another might prefer a low probability of "turning point" errors. (A turning point is the time at which a growing variable begins to decline or vice versa.)

Even if there were agreement on a particular error measure for a particular variable, it is not clear that current data could support a meaningful ranking. One problem is that different forecasters have excelled at different times in the past. In addition, there is little agreement on what constitutes a statistically significant difference in forecasting records (that is, what can be judged with a certain degree of confidence to be real performance differentials rather than mere chance). Stephen McNees[8,9] has studied in depth the problem of identifying superior forecasts and presents valuable data for the interested reader.

Reducing Uncertainty

Another approach is to adopt the philosophy that the primary purpose of a forecast is to reduce the user's uncertainty. This approach explicitly recognizes that not only are users never completely uninformed about past trends, but also that they can never be perfectly certain about future events. Accordingly, the first step in employing this approach is to examine a user's initial knowledge and specify his initial uncertainty. The next step is to then use available forecasts to reduce that uncertainty. Henri Theil[10] has examined both problems and presents a discussion of these issues with several specific, detailed examples.

Taking the easier problem first, a user's existing knowledge about future movements of one particular variable can be described by the best point estimate he could make together with an estimate of that forecast's precision. ("Precision" is defined as the reciprocal of the standard deviation of the *ex ante* distribution of forecast errors; thus that definition and the informal meaning coincide, in the sense that the greater the precision of a forecast, the greater the likelihood that the realization will be within a given distance of the forecast.) It may be objected that many people do not have the information to make such a forecast. However, it is not necessary to have much information in order to make judgments on rela-

TABLE I
MEDIAN FORECASTS[1]

	Real GNP (Percent Change)			Inflation Rate (GNP Deflator)			Treasury Bill Rate		
	Actual	Predicted	Error[2]	Actual	Predicted	Error[2]	Actual	Predicted	Error[2]
1971	4.7	3.8	1.0	4.7	3.6	1.1			
1972	7.0	5.6	1.4	4.3	3.2	1.1			
1973	4.3	6.0	1.7	7.0	3.3	3.7			
1974	-2.7	1.2	3.9	10.1	5.5	4.6	7.3	6.0	1.3
1975	2.2	-0.6	2.8	7.7	7.1	0.6	5.7	7.1	1.4
1976	4.4	6.0	1.6	4.7	5.4	0.7	4.7	7.1	2.4
1977	5.8	5.0	0.8	6.1	5.7	0.4	6.1	5.8	0.4
1978	5.3	4.2	1.2	8.5	5.9	2.6	8.7	6.5	2.1
1979	1.7	1.5	0.2	8.1	7.1	1.0	11.8	8.1	3.7
1980	-0.3	-0.8	0.4	9.8	8.2	1.6	13.7	8.6	5.1
1981	0.9	2.4	1.5	8.9	9.1	0.2	11.8	10.8	1.0
Average Error			1.5			1.6			2.2
Root-Mean-Square Error			1.8			2.1			2.6

[1] Predictions are from Business Forecasts, published annually by the Federal Reserve Bank of Richmond. The error is the absolute value of the difference between predicted and actual values (although calculations use several decimal places, rounded values are presented in the table). The root-mean-square error is the square root of the average squared error. Real growth and inflation are from the fourth quarter of the previous year to the fourth quarter of the stated year. The Treasury bill rate is the average value in the fourth quarter.

[2] Signs ignored.

tive likelihoods, which can be equivalent to a subjective probability distribution (see, for example, Morris DeGroot[3]). Hence it is likely that a cursory inspection of newspapers or television news would permit at least a very imprecise forecast.

Thus, when comparing forecasts, the one that could best lower uncertainty would be the one that had the highest probable precision accompanying the point estimate. Equivalently, a forecast could be presented as an interval centered on a point estimate together with a statement of the probability of the realization lying outside that interval. Presented this way, less uncertainty would be represented as a narrower predicted interval.

As an example of how uncertainty could be characterized in a particular case, suppose that before consulting a forecaster, a user's best estimate of inflation over the next four quarters would be the inflation rate experienced over the preceding four quarters for which data are available. Using the root-mean-squared (RMS) error (that is, the square root of the average squared error) from a sample of previous forecasts as an estimate of the standard deviation of the current forecast error, the precision of that method is shown in Table II. Also included is an 80% confidence interval that was estimated from the RMS error. Thus there would be an 80% likelihood that the forecasted variable would come within that interval (assuming that the RMS error and the ex ante forecast error are equal).

As Table II indicates, simple extrapolation of past inflation provided relatively

imprecise forecasts. Table II also shows that one could have done better, since the median forecast (reported in Table I) would have provided forecasts that were about 30 percent more precise. But extrapolation may not be the best technique at a user's disposal and thus may be too easy a comparison. As Robert Hetzel[6] has noted, inflation can be easily forecasted by using lagged growth of the money supply (M1). By estimating inflation over an interval as equal to money growth two years earlier, one can construct a record of simulated inflation forecasts that performed relatively well. As shown in Table II, from 1971 to 1981 the simple

TABLE II
ESTIMATED PRECISION OF SEVERAL FORECASTING METHODS

	RMS Error (In Percent)	Precision
Method of forecasting inflation		
Extrapolation of past inflation rate	2.7	0.37
Median forecast	2.1	0.47
Lagged money growth rate	1.3	0.74
Method of forecasting real GNP growth		
Always predicting trend rate (3.4%)	2.8	0.35
Median forecast	1.8	0.53

Forecasts are for percentage increases, fourth quarter to fourth quarter, 1971 to 1981.

money growth prediction would have increased forecast precision by about 50 percent relative to the median forecast.

Another Example

Consider another example in Table II. If a user's best estimate of real GNP growth had been the historical trend rate of growth, then the median forecast would have raised that user's forecast precision by about 56 percent. Also note that simple extrapolation would have outperformed the median forecast over the eight-year sample.

These examples show that receipt of a forecast can considerably lower uncertainty relative to an alternative such as extrapolation or use of the historical trend. But individuals may employ other methods that have such a degree of prospective accuracy that a typical forecast would not reduce uncertainty. Thus, the examples illustrate the importance of careful examination of existing information before attempting to determine the value of economic forecasts.

(We have viewed forecasts as unconditional statements regarding future conditions. However, some forecasts are presented as statements of the future provided that a specific condition is fulfilled. An example of such a conditional forecast would be a projected inflation rate between 5 and 7 percent if M1 grew between 3 and 5 percent. While a reliable conditional forecast could be especially useful for some decision-makers, the reliability of existing conditional forecasts has not been proven. Perhaps the most obvious use of conditional forecasts is in formulating national economic policy. It turns out, however, that such forecasts have often proved highly misleading. Robert Lucas[7] has explained why conventional methods cannot provide reliable conditional forecasts for government policymakers.)

Estimates of Forecast Precision

Although forecast precision was estimated in Table II by looking only at recent forecasts and the actual outcomes, other information could also be useful. To illustrate, note that the economic environment can change so as to alter the predictability of economic events. Forecasters of interest rates, for example, have found their task more difficult since the October 1979 change in Federal Reserve operating procedures. Thus a statement on the anticipated precision of interest rate forecasts might well give more weight to post-October 1979 data than would a mechanical calculation of RMS errors over a longer time-span. Individual forecasters, with detailed knowledge of the strengths and weaknesses of their own methods, would arguably be in the best position to make such subjectively adjusted estimates of future precision. Therefore, it is possible to imagine forecasters providing both point estimates and estimates of the precision of their forecasts.

If forecasters were to estimate both future values and their forecasts' precision, then forecasts would for the first time be verifiable. Point estimates by themselves are not verifiable since practically every forecast is wrong (that is, the realized value is not equal to the forecast value). But since an estimate of precision would also imply a confidence interval attached to a forecast, evaluating a forecaster's record would be straightforward. For example, if 50 percent of actual values fell outside a particular forecaster's published 95 percent confidence intervals over a reasonably long time, further forecasts would be highly suspect.

If estimates of precision would indeed be useful, why do not forecasters generally provide such estimates? There are at least two relevant considerations. First, while proper verification of a forecaster's product would require a reasonably long sample period, consumers might choose among forecasting services on the basis of a fairly small number of forecasts. Thus, a good forecaster could lose customers if his forecasts were off-target simply due to a run of bad luck. Secondly, it was noted above that a comparison of past forecasts with realized values is only a starting point for assessing the probable accuracy of current forecasts. A more complete method for estimating a forecast's

probable precision has been used by Ray Fair.[4] The price of additional completeness is a set of more complex procedures which, although feasible, would certainly increase the cost of providing forecasts. Consequently, reasonable estimates of the demand for routine but careful analysis of forecast precision may well indicate that introduction of such a costly and risky product is not currently justified.

Conclusion

The foregoing discussion provides an approach to using economic forecasts that evaluates a forecast by the extent to which it can reduce users' uncertainty about future economic conditions. While a thorough examination of the subject is beyond the scope of this article, an example was given that illustrates how estimates of a forecast's value will critically depend upon the knowledge held by a user prior to receipt of a forecast. In addition, the importance of a forecast's prospective precision was emphasized. Besides its value in reducing an individual forecast consumer's uncertainty, such an estimate of precision would make forecasts verifiable. Although final judgment on the value of forecasts is not attempted in this article, it is hoped that some readers will have a new perspective on evaluating forecasts for their own purposes ●

References

1. Allen, Frank, "Chief Executives Have Little Use for the Predictions of Economists." *The Wall Street Journal,* December 4, 1980.
2. Baker, Sandra D., Ed. *Business Forecasts.* Richmond: Federal Reserve Bank of Richmond, 1971-1981.
3. DeGroot, Morris. *Optimal Statistical Decisions.* New York: McGraw-Hill, 1970, ch.6.
4. Fair, Ray. "Estimating the Expected Predictive Accuracy of Econometric Models." *International Economic Review* (June 1980), pp. 355-378.
5. "Forces of Reaction." *The Wall Street Journal,* December 14, 1981.
6. Hetzel, Robert, "The Quantity Theory Tradition and the Role of Monetary Policy." *Economic Review,* Federal Reserve Bank of Richmond (May/June 1981), pp. 19-26.
7. Lucas, Robert E. "Econometric Policy Evaluation: A Critique." Karl Brunner and Allan Meltzer, eds. *The Phillips Curve and Labor Markets,* supp. to *Journal of Monetary Economics,* 1976, pp.19-46.
8. McNees, Stephen. "The Forecasting Record for the 1970's. *New England Economic Review,* Federal Reserve Bank of Boston (September/October 1979), pp. 33-53.
9. "The Recent Record of Thirteen Forecasters." *New England Economic Review,* Federal Reserve Bank of Boston (September/October 1981), pp. 5-21.
10. Thiel, Henri. *Applied Economic Forecasting.* Amsterdam: North-Holland, 1966.

This article has been excerpted from "Forecasts 1982" published in the Jan./Feb. 1982 issue of "Economic Review of the Federal Reserve Bank of Richmond."

Chapter 23
How Union Carbide Uses Macroeconomic Forecasts

James F. Smith
United Carbide Corporation

Union Carbide Corporation is among the 30 largest industrial companies in the United States, with sales in 1981 of slightly over $10 billion. Our major lines of business include commodity and specialty chemicals and plastics, industrial gases, carbon products, electronics, metal mining nd milling, and a line of consumer products.

We are a major multinational company with about one-third of our sales coming from international operations. The company employs over 100,000 people, operates about 500 plants, mines, and mills in 38 countries and has more than 150,000 shareholders.

From the foregoing brief description of our varying and widely-dispersed activities, it should be clear that we have great need for information about future economic trends both in the U.S. and in other countries. We get some of this information from our memberships in various economic services including Chase Econometrics, Inc.; Data Resources, Inc.; the Research Seminar on Quantitative Economics of the University of Michigan; and Wharton Econometric Forecasting Associates, Inc. Much other information comes from less formal sources such as attendance at economic conferences, reading journals, magazines, newsletters, newspapers, and the time-honored economist's method of talking with other forecasters and analysts in academia, business, and the government. Frequent communication with senior management, business planners, and operating executives is also an important part of the information-gathering process.

Two Types of Forecasts

Of course, all of this information is only useful if it can be incorporated into the corporate forecasting procedure, and disseminated to those responsible for developing business plans. We produce two to four quarterly, short-term U.S. economic forecasts every year and one long-term forecast. Because the procedures used are quite different for these two types of forecasts, they are discussed separately below.

It should be noted that the forecasts discussed here are pure macroeconomic forecasts, containing estimates of the future levels and rates of change of a large number of variables, all of which relate to the entire U.S. economy. No company-specific variables are produced in this forecasting process. Rather, the corporate economic forecast serves as one of many possible sources of information to those who develop financial projections, the outlook for raw materials prices, the cost of future plant and equipment expenditures or specific business plans.

To produce forecasts over a two to three year horizon for a large number of economic variables that are both internally consistent and capable of being subjected to analyses of the effects of alternative external developments, one has no viable alternative to using a reasonably large-scale econometric model.[2] We start our forecasting process with the Wharton Quarterly Model of the U.S. economy.

Wharton Feedback

We use this model primarily because it is the only forecasting service that relies heavily on feedback from its members. A large part of each quarterly meeting with the members is devoted to dialogue between members of the Wharton staff and various model users about what is happening in particular sectors of the U.S. economy, and where the model is too high, too low, or about right on the outlook for a particular sector or variable. Then, the staff returns to Philadelphia and incorporates many of these comments into the following month's forecast release. The Wharton quarterly model of the U.S. is also the only one in which it is reasonably convenient to tie in with both a long-term U.S. forecast and a consistent worldwide forecast.

All of the forecasting services use judgment to temper the results of the models. The unadorned model is responsible for 50-70 per cent of the forecast in the four model services we follow.[3]

Whenever possible we use the output from the Wharton quarterly model released just after the most recent meeting of members. At least once a year, the necessary timing does not permit this procedure, so we use a solution prepared prior to a meeting. In either case, we usually make a few adjustments in consultation with the Wharton staff to incorporate new information or differences of opinion about the values of particular exogenous variables. Since there are more than 700 variables that are exogenous, it is not hard to see where differences may arise.

Best Case/Worst Case

The quarterly model is then run, and after a final correction or two, we usually have our base solution. Then, we work with the Wharton staff to develop a "best case" and a "worst case" scenario. The purpose of this exercise is to attempt to bracket the base forecast within the range of probable error.

The Wharton World Model staff then takes this base case solution and runs it through their model to produce a simulation that shows the effects, if any, of our base solution for the U.S. on the rest of the world when compared with the Wharton base solution. This solution is then distributed to the economists in our area companies around the world. They make any changes in the outlook for the country or countries for whose economic forecasts they are responsible and return the results to Wharton. A final simulation by the Wharton staff takes these changes into account in producing our final base forecast for the U.S.

Only this base forecast is distributed to those people who use our forecast of macroeconomic variables in their own work. The alternate scenarios are reviewed with senior management in considerable detail, with special attention to the changes in exogenous factors that have the greatest impact on the outlook.

Long-term Forecast

The long-term forecast that is done once a year is a more complicated process. It is more of a collective effort, involving the work of more than 25 people. Most of these people require at least a few variables from the U.S. economic outlook before they can prepare their part of the work.

Accordingly, about three months before the publication of the report, I meet with the staff of the Wharton Long Term Model to go over the general shape of the outlook for the coming decade. They then produce a base forecast which is used by all the other people involved in our project as one of the starting points for their work. The results are also used to run a Wharton World Model long-term outlook which is used internally by the various area company economists as one of the bases for their own long-term forecasts.

Any changes from the area economists are then run back through the World Model, and if they cause significant changes in the U.S. outlook, the Long-Term Model is run once again to replicate those changes and produce the necessary industry and economic detail.

Much of the work by the people involved in our annual long-term release is related to the development of alternate scenarios. To the extent that these alternate scenarios have economic content that can be quantified, we run alternate versions of the long-term model. In a typical annual exercise, we may produce 2-5 such alternatives. These alternatives are distributed to users of the annual release along with the base solution.

The purpose of all of these forecasts is to provide business planners, marketing and operating executives, purchasing agents, and financial planners a background and a range to consider when preparing their own budgets, forecasts, and plans. It is also a process designed to save them the time and effort of developing these base forecasts and alternatives on their own.[1]

Steve McNees has summarized the need for such a process succinctly:
"All decisions—decisions to do nothing as well as those to do something—are contingent upon a prior assessment of the probable consequences of the status quo. The only thing worse than a bad forecast is no forecast."[3] ●

References

1. Corbett, John. "Econometrics: 'Often Wrong, Never in Doubt.'" *Chemical Marketing Reporter,* Part 2 of two Parts, "Chemical Business", May 31, 1982, pp. 39-46 contains a brief description of the forecasting process at several different companies.
2. Klein, Lawrence R., and Young, Richard M. *An Introduction to Econometric Forecasting and Forecasting Models.* Lexington, Mass.: D.C. Heath & Co., 1980.
3. McNees, Stephen K. "The Recent Record of Thirteen Forecasters." *New England Economic Review* (September/October, 1981): 5-21.

Chapter 24
Economic vs. Survey Forecasts

Daniel T. Walz
Trinity University

Diane B. Walz

Econometric models are better than the survey of ASA/NBER (American Statistical Association/National Bureau of Economic Research) as far as short-term forecasts are concerned. However, the quality of these forecasts deteriorates as the forecast horizon lengthens. Econometric as well as the survey forecasts are superior to the no-change naive model (the model that assumes that the next period value is the same as the current one). And their superiority also diminishes as the span of forecast increases. These are some of the findings of the study recently conducted by the authors.

Econometric forecasts are generally more costly than survey forecasts. Their additional cost may be justified if they produce better forecasts. The purpose of this paper is to see how econometric forecasts stack up against the survey ones, and how econometric and survey forecasts stack up against the no-change naive model forecasts. If no-change naive model forecasts are as good or better than the others, then forecasting will be a simple task. The value of the current period will be the forecast for the next period.

Data

The data consists of the forecasts of nominal U.S. GNP, real GNP, GNP deflator, and U.S. unemployment rate from five well known econometric models and one survey. The five econometric models are: (1) the Merrill Lynch Economics Model, (2) the Conference Board Model, (3) the Chase Econometric Model, (4) the Data Resources Model and (5) the Wharton Econometric Model. The survey data employed in this study were collected from the ASA/NBER Business Outlook Survey. The ASA/NBER forecasts are the result of questionnaires sent each quarter during the period to a regular panel of 160 economists. Generally, 60 to 80 responses were obtained. This study analyzes forecasts for each economic variable one, two, three, and four quarters into the future.

All forecasts represent the most recent estimates of each econometric model and the ASA/NBER survey as of the month before the end of the first quarter forecasted. All forecasted values (except unemployment rates) were analyzed in terms of percentage change, e.g., percentage change in nominal GNP from one period to the next. Data used were from the first quarter of 1977 through the second quarter of 1984.

Methodology

As a measure of relative forecasting efficiency, Theil's statistic was used. The precise formula used for comparing survey forecasts with those of econometric ones is given in Equation 1, Appendix 1. Here, a U^2 of one implies that the survey predictions are perfect, while the econometric ones are not. Decreasing values of U^2 indicate increasingly better forecasting ability of the econometric model(s) relative to the survey. A U^2 of zero indicates that the two sets of predictions are equally accurate. Negative values of U^2 indicate that the predictions of the econometric models are more accurate than the survey predictions.

To see how survey and econometric forecasts compare with no-change naive model forecasts, another set of U^2 statistics were computed. The formula used for such statistics is given in Equation 2, Appendix 1. The no-change naive model assumes that the next period value is the same as the current one. Here a U^2_i greater than zero implies that the survey forecasts ($i=1$) or the econometric model forecasts ($i=2$) are more accurate than the naive model forecasts. U^2_i less then zero implies that the no-change naive model produces more accurate forecasts.

Several results emerge from the values of the U^2 statistics derived from Equation 1, for the comparison of the survey forecasts of nominal GNP, real GNP, GNP deflator, and unemployment rate with those of the five econometric models. First, every econometric model (and the average of econometric models) is superior to the ASA/NBER survey in predicting nominal GNP, real GNP, and unemployment rate when the span of forecast is one quarter. For each econometric model and every variable being predicted one quarter ahead (save the GNP deflator), the U^2 statistics are negative and very different from zero. However, the superiority of the econometric models in forecasting these variables disappears as the span of the forecast increases beyond one quarter. The individual econometric models, as well as the mean econometric forecast, show no systematic superiority to the ASA/NBER survey when the economic variables are predicted two, three, or four quarters into the future. Finally, the econometric model forecasts of GNP deflator are not, by and large, better than those of the ASA/NBER survey for any

Appendix 1

Survey VS.
Econometric Forecasts

$$U^2 = 1 - [MSE_1/MSE_2] \quad \ldots\ldots(1)$$

Where:

MSE = Mean squared errors, where error is the difference between the actual and predicted values

MSE_1 = The mean squared forecast error for the ASA/NBER survey

MSE_2 = The mean squared forecast error for one of the 5 econometric models (or their average).

Survey/Econometric VS.
No-Change Naive Model Forecasts

$$U^2_i = 1 - [MSE_i/MSE_3] \quad \ldots\ldots(2)$$

Where:

MSE_i = The mean squared forecast error for the ASA/NBER survey (i =1) or an econometric model (i =2)

MSE_3 = The mean squared forecast error for a no-change naive model

time span. (The Table of U^2 Statistics Values for each model and for each quarter can be obtained by writing to Dr. Daniel T. Walz, Trinity University, 715 Stadium Drive, San Antonio, Texas 78284.)

The U^2_i statistics that compare the survey and econometric forecasts with those of the no-change naive model indicate rather clearly that both the survey and econometric forecasts are superior to the naive model in predicting one period ahead for each of the four economic variables analyzed. However, when the span of forecast is increased to 2, 3 or 4 quarters, their superiority significantly diminishes, and in a few cases completely disappears. The five econometric models and the ASA/NBER survey are much less accurate in predicting GNP deflator than other variables. For the one quarter forecast span, the U^2_i statistics for all predicted variables, with the exception of GNP deflator, are slightly higher for the econometric model forecasts than for the survey forecasts. Again, though, when the span of forecast is increased beyond one quarter, the difference disappears. This result reinforces the results reported earlier, that is, the econometric model forecasts are superior to the survey forecasts for a one quarter span of forecast. Finally, the U^2_i statistics that compared the individual econometric models to the no-change naive model in-

dicate that no single econometric mod performed noticeably better or wor than the other models ●

REFERENCES

Ahlers, A. and Lakonishok, J. "A Study Economists' Consensus Forecasts." **Management Sciences.** 29, (1983), pp. 1113-1125.

Brown, B.W. and Maital, S. "What D Economists Know? An Empirical Study of E perts' Expectations." **Econometrica.** 4 (1981), pp. 491-504.

Cargill, T. and R. Meyer. "Forecast Evaluation c Livingston Data on Inflation Rules and Infla tion Uncertainty." **Decision Sciences.** (Spring 1981), pp. 161-176.

Grether, D.M. "Bayes Rule as a Descriptiv Model: The Representativeness Heuristic. **Quarterly Journal of Economics.** 95 (1980) pp. 537-558.

Malkiel, B. and Cragg, J.L. "Expectations and the Valuation of Shares." **NBER Working Paper** No. 471 (April, 1980).

Theil, R. **Applied Economic Forecasting.** Chicago: Rand McNally & Company, 1966.

Zarnowitz, V. 'The Accuracy of Individual and Group Forecasts from Business Outlook Surveys." **Journal of Forecasting.** 3 (1984), pp. 10-27.

PART VI

Simulation

Chapter 25
How Monetary Policy Affects National and Industry Forecasts

Jerrold M. Peterson
University of Minnesota—Duluth

One of the basic sources of industry and firm forecasting errors stem from the potential errors that are introduced into industry forecasts from inaccurate national forecasts. All industry and firm forecasts explicitly or implicitly are developed from an examination of one or more national economic forecasts. Obviously, if these national forecasts are inaccurate, these errors will ripple through the firm or industrial forecasts often being compounded into a catastrophic company level forecast errors. This paper explores one simplistic approach for analyzing the implication of these national forecast errors for industrial and firm forecasts. In this paper, the implications of changes in monetary policy are analyzed for long-term interest rates, aggregate real rate of return, and the general value of business equity.

To illustrate how important this problem may be, review for a moment Chamber of Commerce Forecasts presented in their publication, *Economic Outlook* newsletter, January-February 1986 edition. WIthout reviewing the entire forecast, its problem is highlighted in a footnote of Table 1, January-February 1986. In this footnote the forecast assumptions are outlined. For example, in January-February 1986, the money supply as measured by M1 is assumed to rise by only 8.3 percent in 1986 and 6.9 percent in 1987 (on a fourth-quarter over fourth-quarter basis.) As of June 18, 1986, the Money Supply M1 was rising at an annual rate of 13.3 percent. It is dif-ficult to assess the national, industry or firm implication that this forecast error in growth rate of money supply has had for these other forecasts. It can be noted that forecast of automobile sales, for example, increased between November 1985 and January-February 1986 from an annual rate of 10.9 million units to 11.3 million units. As many economists might surmise, the more rapid-growing money supply in the first quarter of 1986 would lower actual interest rates with the ultimate impact of increase in automobile sales. Obviously this is an over-simplistic analysis with no direct evidence offered to support these conclusions.

The Model

In this paper FORESAL (IBM-PC Compatible package—distributed by J.P. Consulting, Inc., P.O. Box 3053, Duluth, MN 55803) has been used to analyze the implications of a change in the assumed monetary policy. FORESAL is a micro computer based model used to analyze the implication of policy changes on forecast of the interest rates and economic activity.

FORESAL is a quarterly model which simulates the U.S. economy using 1977-1984 data to set the initial conditions. In this model, the economy is segmented into a real sector and a financial sector. In the real sector, four major institutions are simulated: they are the household or public sector, the business sector, the government sector and the foreign sector. Each of these sectors is presumed to have certain institutional characteristics and identifiable economic goals. To achieve these goals each sector will make important economic decisions affecting their income and general economic activity. In addition to the real sector, the model also simulates a financial sector. The institutions comprising the financial sector include a banking system and a central banking system (i.e., the Federal Reserve System). These institutions interact with various institutions of the real sector through financial markets and financial instruments. The financial instruments include short-term and long-term bonds as well as demand and time deposits. These financial institutions also have an implicit set of goals and make important decisions. As might be expected, the financial decisions and markets impact on the economy and real sector institutions.

The model itself is a modified general equilibrium model which simulates the interaction between the financial and real sectors of the U.S. economy through a complex set of mathematical equations. Both monetary and fiscal policy are powerful tools which impact the national economy in different ways. Monetary policy has a greater impact on prices and indirectly on wages than fiscal policy. On the other hand, fiscal policy has a greater impact on real demand and output than does monetary policy. Each policy tool may be used separately, but as is true in the actual world, the policies should be coordinated for maximum impact. In FORESAL, both policy tools have certain unspecified lags.

This forecast simulation model is an electronic laboratory which simulates the U.S. economy through time and displays the results of those simulations on a micro computer monitor in balance sheet and income statement form. The simulation presents the income statements and balance sheets for business sector, public sector, government sector, commercial banks and the Federal Reserve System. In addition, the model also estimates a number of aggregate economic variables including GNP, the money supply, M1, interest rates, employment and real output to mention a few.

Because the model is interactive the simulation can highlight the impact of changes in one sector of the economy on another. In addition, the user can set up his forecast using one set of assumptions on his forecast and ultimately on the decisions based on this forecast.

Analysis of Changing Assumptions

In Table 1 the results of two forecast simulations are illustrated. In the first forecast, the economy is believed to be influenced by a relatively tight money policy. The Federal Reserve System initiates open market operations that ultimately results in growth of the money supply (M1) to average 5.07 percent over Qtr. 4, 1985 and Qtr. 1, 1986. The second forecast simulation is influenced by an easier monetary policy. In this simulation, the Federal Reserve System initiates open market operation that ultimately results in the growth rate of the money supply to average 6.2 percent over Qtr. 4, 1985 and Qtr. 1, 1986. The remainder of both forecast simulations remain unchanged so that the changes in the economy soley reflect the differing monetary policies.

As can be seen from Table 1, the relatively tight money policy results in fairly stable interest rates. Long-term bond rates is 11.11 percent in Qtr. 3, 1985, remains stable at 11.11 percent in Qtr. 4, 1985, and then rises to 11.31 percent in Qtr. 1, 1986. The rate of return on business equity is shown as 13.44 percent in Qtr. 3, 1985, rising to a peak in the foruth quarter of 1985 and then falling to 13.33 percent in Qtr. 1, 1986. The present value of the equity investment of the business sector is estimated in the third quarter of 1985 to be $5,175 billion. By the first quarter of 1986, the present value of the equity is estimated to have risen to $5191.3 billion.

TABLE 1
RESULTS OF SIMULATIONS

Assumption and Variables	Quarter 3 1985	Quarter 4 1985	Quarter 1 1986
Slow Money Growth (Assumption)	Money Supply Grows At An Annual Rate of 5.07%		
Long Term Bond Rate	11.11%	11.11%	11.31%
Real Rate of Return	13.44%	13.53%	13.33%
Capital Value of the Nation's			
Business Equity (in billions)	$5175	$5114.6	$5191.30
Faster Money Growth (Assumption)	Money Supply Grows At An Annual Rate of 6.20%		
Long Term Bond Rate	11.11%	11.00%	11.11%
Real Rate	13.44%	13.52%	13.28%
Capital Value of Business Equity (in billions)	$5175	$5118.34	$5210.84
Difference in Equity Value of the Nation Under the Fast Growth Scenario (in billions)			$19.54

If the Federal Reserve System initiates an easier money policy, long-term bond rate will first fall and then rise back to 11.11 percent. The real rate of interest will again rise to a peak in Qtr. 4, 1985 and then fall to 13.28 percent. The capital value of business equity increases to $5210.84 billion—evidence of such an equity increase could be a stock market rally during the first quarter of 1986.

In this model, therefore, the more rapid growth of money supply during the last quarter of 1985 and first quarter of 1986 results in relatively lower long-term bond interest rates and significantly higher equity value of stocks and business assets. The alternation of one assumption in national forecast about monetary policy would appear to have impacts on the forecast of the cost of credit and the financial wealth of the nation. If either of these two variables are important determinants of an industry product or service demand forecast, this change in the assumption of monetary growth may have significant implications for the forecast sales of that industry. Thus, a business or industry forecast ought to be revised to reflect rapidly changing monetary policy of the Federal Reserve System. These forecasts should then be re-analyzed to determine the implication of these changes in policy on business decisions ●

References

Chamber of Commerce of the United States. **Economic Outlook.** Washington: Forecast Section, U.S. Chamber of Commerce, Nov. 1985, Table 1, p. 4; and January/February 1986, Table 1, pg. 4.

J.P. Consulting, **FORESAL-An Economic Simulation of the U.S. Economy Now and in the Future.** Duluth, Mn., 1986.

Ruggles, Richard and Ruggles, Nancy D. "Integrated Economic Accounts for The United States 1947-80." **Survey of Current Business.** May 1982, Vol. 62, No. 5, pp. 1-75.

Chapter 26
Interest Rate Forecasting

Francis H. Schott
The Equitable Life Assurance Society of the U.S.

Forecasting interest rates is as treacherous as it is important. There is no financial decision without an implicit interest rate forecasting content. Even if you declared yourself an agnostic and ignored rate variability, the path of the financial consequences of that decision would in all likelihood be significantly different from zero on average over any substantial period. The pronounced and prolonged uptrends and downtrends of interest rates over the past decades have not been a random walk. Logical reasoning and analysis should have enabled you to make these variations work for you rather than against you.

Fundamentals

It is, in fact, not difficult to define the fundamentals of interest rate forecasting. The business cycle is one factor of obvious importance. Economic expansion is "credit and liquidity driven" in a modern financial economy. As the demand for funds strengthens during an expansion, upward pressure on interest rates will occur. The reverse will happen during a business slump.

Although the demand side is emphasized in this explanation of the cyclical effect on interest rates, it is possible, indeed necessary, to refer to the supply side of credit and liquidity as well. While in the initial phase of an upswing the growth of savings may be stimulated *pari passu* with income,

shortfalls relative to demand will occur as the expansion proceeds and buoyant business and consumer spending strain that supply.

This imbalance will be accentuated by monetary policy. The Federal Reserve is supposed to "lean against the wind." Thus, the Fed's net addition to liquidity (growth of the monetary aggregates) will tend to raise interest rates near cyclical peaks and diminish them at cyclical troughs.

What are the "basics" of the interest rates around which they move with the cycle? First there is the "real" rate—compensation for consumption postponed or forgone. This rate will tend to drift downward with society's increasing wealth but has to continue to be a positive figure, such as the 2½%-3% real rate the U.S. has averaged over the past century. To this must be added an inflation factor—compensation for anticipated inflation that would otherwise erode the purchasing power of principal and interest (and hence ruin the supply of savings.) Inflation compensation has been important indeed in the sharp rise of market rates of interest, with inflation itself, in the late 1970s and early 1980s.

The elements of our logical edifice are now in place. Interest rates are the dependent variable in a multiple regression equation in which the state of the business cycle, monetary policy and inflation anticipations are the right-hand explanatory variables. Immense practical difficulties stand in the way of using this simple scheme. But nothing in what follows should divert the reader from clearly fixing in mind these ex-

planatory factors and the appropriate sign of the coefficients.

Problems

Now to the difficulties. In the first place, the correct measurement of the explanatory factors is hard to find. Obviously the "business cycle" is an abstraction—perhaps more precisely a short-hand summary term for a multitude of conditions and their statistical representation—that is in search of a necessarily imperfect proxy among the available data. A similar comment applies to Federal Reserve policy, which is characterized by multiple "operational proxies" for such ultimate objectives as steady growth and full employment with price stability. Perhaps most difficult in recent years has been the quantification of inflation expectations: It is the potential future loss of purchasing power for which the current saver has to be compensated to induce continuation of the activity, not any past inflation, relevant as that may be to the formation of future expectations. Thus, the need for trial and error in finding just the right proxies arises, and a great deal of the differences between technically equally qualified forecasters working with the same data base may be traced simply to the selection of different proxies for the same variables.

A second major difficulty is that the "fundamentals" may well be in need of supplementary explanations at specific times and for specific periods. For example, the inflation factor, although always "fundamental," could be dismissed in actual measurement for

101

the decade of the 1960s. Now, in the mid-1980s, following the major swings of interest rates in the past 10 years, it may well be necessary to add a volatility measurement to interest rate forecasts. (The risk of capital loss on financial instruments is materially enhanced in a volatile interest rate environment. This extra risk raises the required yield to generate savings, all other factors equal.) In addition, the increased openness of financial markets strongly suggests that an "interest differential" factor ought to be an additional independent variable. (The higher "home" interest rates relative to those abroad, the more will be the net foreign savings that will help to alleviate upward pressures on domestic rates, and vice versa.) Again, these considerations invite extensive experimentation.

A third difficulty is that the term "interest rates" is itself a proxy for several hundred prices quoted at any one time in the financial markets. To take just one—probably the most important one—of the distinctions among interest rates, there are short rates, intermediate rates and long rates. Extensive theories of the "term structure" of rates have been developed. The bottom line, for purposes of most analysts, is that "the normal yield curve slopes upward" (interest rates usually but not always rise with the term to maturity of the fixed-yield instrument). This brings up the question whether the forecaster ought to focus on short rates, long rates, or perhaps "the shape of the yield curve" (the spread between long and short rates). There is no single answer for all the purposes to which rate forecasts are put, but any point of departure permits the eventual construction of a model of all maturities.

Example and Uses

Despite these difficulties, quantitative interest rate forecasts are regularly attempted by a great number of forecasters and frequently structured along the lines of the sample equation

TABLE 1
MODEL AND VALUES OF PARAMETERS

MODEL

20 YEAR T-BOND = C0 + C1 × LOG (UNEMPLOYMENT RATE) + C2 × % CHANGE IN M1 + C3 × % CHANGE IN CPI, ANNUALIZED + C4 × VOLATALITY

Where C0 is constant and C1, C2, C3 and C4 are regression coefficients and C3= the sum of the polynomial distributed lag coefficients L0, L1, L2 and L3.

VALUE OF PARAMETERS
(Period 1961:1-1986:2, Quarterly)

Independent Variable	Coefficient	T-Value
1) Constant	11.137 (C0)	4.36
2) Log (Unemployment Rate)	−3.297 (C1)	−3.65
3) % Change in M1	−0.026 (C2)	−2.16
4) Polynomial Distributed Lag of the % change in the CPI, annualized; lag of 4 quarters, 2nd degree polynomial, tail restriction.	Σ=0.24 (C3)	2.73
5) Volatility = 4 year moving average of the absolute value of the change in the 3 month T- Bill.	1.726 (C4)	2.05
S.E.R. = 0.4709	D.W. =1.64	R²=0.975

TABLE 2
ACTUAL VS. FORECAST
(QUARTERLY)

	1985 III	IV	1986 I	II	III	IV	1987 I	II	III
	ACTUAL				FORECAST				
20 Year T-Bond	10.74	10.22	8.92	7.7					
20 Year T-Bond (fitted)	10.95	10.55	10.06	8.68	7.49	7.18	7.04	6.91	7.02
Unemployment Rate	7.2	7.0	7.1	7.1	6.9	6.8	6.8	6.9	7.1
% Change in M1	15.3	11.1	7.9	16.6	17.0	10.0	9.0	8.0	8.0
CPI (% Change)	2.6	4.3	1.4	-1.7	2.5	3.0	3.5	4.0	4.2
Volatility	0.96	0.77	0.73	0.74	0.57	0.48	0.49	0.48	0.45

Sources: Federal Reserve, U.S. Dept of Commerce, Equitable Calculations

and forecast shown in Chart 1 and Tables 1 and 2. We are showing the 20-year U.S. Treasury bond rate as a function of the unemployment rate, the money growth rate, a weighted average of past inflation and recent past volatility. There is as yet no international rate relationship factor in our equation. All coefficients have the expected sign, are statistically significant and yield a good combined correlation with the rate in question. The equation tracks the past with a standard error of only about half a percentage point but tends to lag actual developments by about a quarter. As will be seen, on assumptions as stated for 1986 III-1987 III, the equation forecasts further modest declines of the long-term rate in question until mid-1987. The projected

turnaround at that time reflects slightly worse inflation and lower money supply growth.

No reasonable business person will act on the basis of such a quantitative appraisal alone. Differences among forecast methods and assumptions regarding the independent variables can give vastly different results from forecaster to forecaster. At Equitable, we use the method here described and compare our results with econometric model builders. Further, we use business procedures to reduce our exposure to interest rate forecasting mistakes (e.g., asset/liability maturity matching and hedging with futures). Most important, we bring experienced senior management judgment to the table in deciding on our market actions.

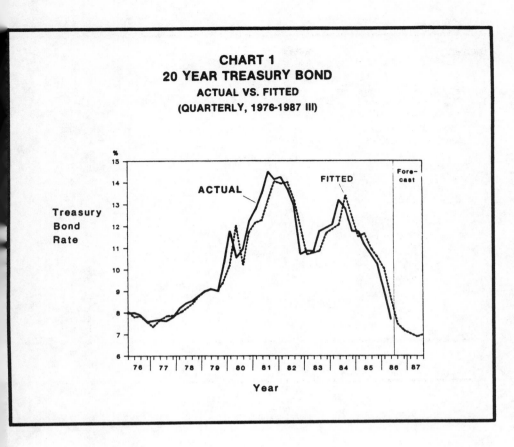

CHART 1
20 YEAR TREASURY BOND
ACTUAL VS. FITTED
(QUARTERLY, 1976-1987 III)

Nevertheless, as noted at the outset, structure of thought is of tremendous help in checking on one's judgment ●

References

Friedman, Benjamin M. and Roley, V. Vance. "Models of Long-Term Interest Rate Determination." **Journal of Portfolio Management.** Spring 1980, pp. 35-45.

Pindyck, Robert S. and Rubinfeld, Daniel L. "Econometric Models and Economic Forecasts." New York: McGraw-Hill Book Co., 1976, Chapter 10.

Schott, Francis H. "Forecasting Long-Term Interest Rates." **Business Economics.** Vol. VIII, No. 4, Sept. 1973, pp. 46-53.

_____. "Interest Rates." in **Encyclopedia of Economics.** Douglas Greenwald (ed.). New York: McGraw-Hill Book Co., 1982, pp. 538-554.

Sinai, Allen and Rathjens, Peter. "Deficits, Interest Rates and The Economy." **Data Resources U.S. Review.** June 1983, pp. 27-41.

The helpful assistance of Mary Helen McSweeney is greatly acknowledged.

104

PART VII

Econometric Service Bureaus

Chapter 27
A Guide To Selecting An Econometric Service Bureau

C.L. Jain

St. John's University

Econometric service bureaus offer three basic services—forecasts, data base access, and economic consultation. Together, the services constitute a decision support service for company management.

The forecasting service includes forecasts of macro variables (e.g., GNP, unemployment, interest rates), industry forecasts, and company forecasts. The last mentioned is typically provided on a custom basis.

Access to the data base containing historical and current data on thousands of economic activities is offered to those companies who prepare their own macro forecasts, and who need more recent data than is available in the monthly or quarterly updates. This service is also used by clients who wish to use input assumptions of their own in a simulation.

The consulting service is the keystone of the decision support service, and is purchased by companies requiring expert advice in the use of the model output, and on constructing company models. It is also used by top management as an aid to planning and development of business strategy. Depending upon the services one selects, the cost runs anywhere from $8,000 to $75,000 and more a year. Great care is required in selecting the bureau and the services appropriate to the company's requirements. Here are some tips that could be helpful to those considering the employment of a bureau:

Acquire a working knowledge of econometric modeling: Before you start looking for a service bureau, make sure that either you or someone on your staff knows how an econometric model is built and used, and what it can and cannot do. You don't have to be an expert in the area, but you should know enough to distinguish a good econometric model from a bad one. Of course, the more you know about econometric modeling, the more wisely you can choose a bureau and the more effectively use its services.

Company Needs: Determine clearly your requirements in terms of the type of service and data you need. If you need forecasts of macrovariables, determine specifically the variables you want, the kind of details you want, and the frequency with which you want them. You may find one service bureau is better in one area while another excels in another. If the budget is adequate, buy some services from each. Study each bureau's past performance on those variables that are important to your business. Remember though, that:

1. Some variables are harder to predict than others. GNP is relatively easy to predict; inventory investment and interest rates are among the most difficult variables to forecast.

2. No bureau does well in all, or even nearly all, variables; concern yourself with the variables you are interested in.

3. Timing regarding the availability of forecasts is important; a slightly greater error in forecasting may be acceptable, provided forecasts are available at the time you need them.

4. No model or bureau can forecast accurately for every period. So, evaluate accuracy on the average, and not on every single point.

5. Government data are frequently revised. In determining accuracy, make sure you compare forecasts with the latest revision. From the standpoint of a company, what is important is not the accuracy of macro-forecasts, but of its own forecasts (e.g., sales forecast) where macro-forecasts are used as input. Irrespective of the level of accuracy, macroforecasts are good as long as they produce reliable forecasts for the company.

6. Large error is not a sign of incompetence in periods when all other forecasts are even worse. Ideally, forecasting ability should be judged comparatively and not absolutely.

Free forecasts: Find out what types of macro-forecasts are available at little or no charge. Government agencies issue forecasts of a number of variables that are free of charge. Many academic institutions and private organizations make their forecasts available for a small fee. For example, periodic forecasts of food and energy prices are issued by the U.S. Departments of Agriculture and Energy, respectively. The American Statistical Association in cooperation with the National Bureau of Economic Research conducts surveys of all major macro-variables. The results (forecasts) are available at a nominal charge. Of course, one has to determine whether these forecasts are as good as the ones commercially available.

Decision support: It is important for the company to know what types of decision support is available from a bureau. Has the bureau qualified people in your business area? Can the company get help from the bureau when it's needed and where it's needed?

Underlying economic philosophy: Each model is based upon a certain economic philosophy or a combination of philosophies. The major economic philosophies are: (1) Keynesian, (2) Monetarist, (3) Rational, (4) Supply Side, and (5) Walrasian. It is difficult to say which philosophy is better. Users normally select a bureau whose models use the philosophy which is similar to their own.

Forecast form: The form in which forecasts are furnished is important. If forecasts are furnished on line, they become available instantly. If provided only in printed form, forecasts may be old by a few days, a week or more by the time they reach the user.

Details of forecasts: It is important to know whether forecasts provide just numbers or numbers with some explanation. There are some bureaus that provide alternatives to most likely forecasts. Also, study how well forecasts are disaggregated, e.g., national income into disposable income, disposable income into consumption and saving, consumption into durable and nondurable goods, and so on. Whether or not such refined details are necessary depends upon the need of the user.

A PARTIAL LISTING OF
DOMESTIC AND FOREIGN ECONOMETRIC SERVICE BUREAUS
Domestic

Company	Contact	Macro Forecasting	Data Access	Consulting	Other
1. A. Gary Shilling & Co. 111 Broadway New York, N.Y. 10006 (212) 349-6000	Dr. Glenn C. Picou	Yes	No	Yes	Industry Level Analysis
2. Center For Economic Research Chapman College Orange, CA 92666	Dr. James L. Doti	Yes	Yes	Yes	
3. Data Resources, Inc. 29 Hartwell Ave. Lexington, MA 02173 (617) 861-0165	Sandy Bragg	Yes	Yes	Yes	
4. Economic Forecasting Georgia State University Atlanta, GA 30303 (404) 658-3282	Dr. Donald Ratajczak	Yes	No	Yes	Regional Analysis
5. Indiana University Bloomington, IN 47401	Dr. Eugene A. Brady	Yes	No	Yes	
6. Kent Econ. & Dev. Inst. 1700 East Main Street Kent, Ohio 44240 (216) 673-8249	Dr. Vladimir Simunek	Yes	Yes	Yes	Special Economic Studies
7. Merrill Lynch Economics 165 Broadway New York, NY 10080 (212) 637-6211	Dr. Raymond Cosman	Yes	Yes	Yes	Special Economic Studies
8. UCLA Business Forecasting Los Angeles, CA 91436 (213) 825-1623	Dr. Larry Kimbell	Yes	Yes	Yes	
9. Wharton Econometric 3624 Science Center Philadelphia, PA 19104 (215) 667-6000	Dr. Lawrence Chimerine	Yes	Yes	Yes	
10. Williams Trend Indicators 6 Devon Dr. Orangeburg, NY 10962 (914) 359-1129	Dr. Roger Williams	Yes	No	Yes	

Foreign

Company	Contact	Macro Forecasting	Data Access	Consulting	Other
1. Informetrica Limited P.O. Box 828, Station B Ottawa, Ontario Canada KIP 5P9	Dr. Michael C. McCracken	Yes	Yes	Yes	Software Application Packages
2. Centre For Economic Forecasting London Business School Sussex Place, Regents Park London, NW1 4SA England 01-262-5050	Dr. Bill Robinson	Yes	Yes	No	On-line access to large econometric model of the UK economy
3. Henley Centre For Forecasting London, England 01-353-9961	Dr. Aleck Kellaway	Yes	Yes	Yes	Forecasting Services & Publications
4. Phillips & Drew London, England 01-628-4444	Dr. Paul Neild	Yes	No	No	
5. Institute of Economics Taipei, Taiwan Republic of China 115 7822019	Dr. Paul K. C. Liu	No	Yes	Yes	
6. Centre D'Observation Economique de la Chambre De Commerce et d'Industrie de Paris Paris, France 75008 561-99-00	Dr. Monsieru Devaud	Yes	Yes	No	
7. Gama 2 Rue De Rouen Nanterre, France 92001 (1) 725-92-34	Dr. R. Courbis	Yes	No	Yes	Publishes monthly & quarterly Global Forecasts. Annually Global Sectoral Forecasts

Frequency of Updating: The frequency of updating forecasts has a bearing on the quality of forecasts. Some bureaus update quarterly and others semi-annually or annually.

Use of company's input. Some bureaus have developed a formalized mechanism for incorporating the client's input for developing forecasts for its specific use. From the standpoint of a company, this may have some bearing on the quality of forecasts it receives ●

PART VIII

Regional Models

Chapter 28
Regional Forecasts—How Are They Prepared?

Leslie P. Singer
Indiana University Northwest

There appears to be a rising demand for regional forecasts. Executives are becoming increasingly more aware of divergent growth rates in submarkets served by their companies. The smallest regions for which forecasts are possible are MSA's (metropolitan statistical areas). Users include marketing executives and sales managers of national retail chains, utilities, automobile dealer associations, oil companies and beverage companies.

Many planning departments contemplating new sites for plants, as well as banks and financial institutions who supply capital funds, tend to rely on local forecasts.

In this paper we present a non-technical overview of methods of regional forecasting. We shall also report on the effectiveness of models used. We hope that forecasters of regional markets can benefit from our experience. Our experience applies to the region of Northwest Indiana.

Why Regional Forecasts?

Some users rely on the forecasting model to determine the outcome of different scenarios. These tend to be large firms with substantial capital investment, such as utilities, financial institutions, and insurance companies. One can estimate the effect on the local economy of different rates of growth of money supply; various levels of decline in local steel employment and payrolls; and the impact of public sector intervention. One can also estimate the probable effect on total employment and income resulting from entry of new firms into the local manufacturing sector.

Local Economy

Northwest Indiana's economy is typical of "rust belt" industrial regions. Steel and petroleum constitute the manufacturing core with six major companies. The secondary manufacturing sector comprises several hundred small to medium size fabricating and processing plants. All national retail chains and several local chains maintain outlets in the MSA. In the following section models that are used in these areas will be reviewed.

Models

The forecasting model incorporates elements of a structural economic model (SEM), a vector auto regressive model (VAR) and a Box-Jenkins integrated moving average and auto regressive model (ARIMA). The discussion on these models can be found in major publications. Therefore we are refraining from discussing the specific properties and shortcomings of each model.

MSA data on employment and payrolls are published monthly. Data on personal income, value added in manufacturing, retail sales, etc., are available with considerable lags and are of questionable reliability.

MSA is a small macroeconomy. There is an export sector, consisting of manufacturing firms and a limited number of service firms, such as national insurance companies.

The local economy derives its primary impetus from the manufacturing payroll, and fringe benefits such as pensions, supplemental unemployment benefits, payments for health care, and from wages earned from export of labor services (residents of the region who earn income outside the region). Public sector net transfers and state and federal grants are also external sources of income. Dividends, interest, and rental income are external money flows. However, such data are difficult to ascertain for MSA's. The domestic economy imports semi-finished and finished goods, services, and labor.

Conceivably if an up-to-date input-output model (IO) could be constructed, one might devise a satisfactory SEM forecasting system. This is rarely the case. Most IO based regional forecasting attempts have failed.

We have adopted a different approach to regional forecasting. We assume that the regional economy is embedded in the national economy. Putting it simply, the domestic sector is driven by the export sector and both sectors react to the national and Midwestern economic environment.

Model Structure

Investment, interest rates, money, etc., predict GNP, and GNP logically drives demand for local manufacturing output. However, in order to avoid compounding error terms, we regress the predictors on local manufacturing and other series.

We have no information nor a prior knowledge of specific structural relationships; however, we can search statistically for national and Midwestern series which tend to predict the economic environment within which it unfolds the local economic scenario.

Thus, the Northwest Indiana MSA forecasting model consists of three vector equations:

i. Domestic private establishment employment and payroll as a function of lagged export payroll plus lagged private sector nonwage income (including estimates of income from fixed and liquid assets), public sector nonwage income, national and Midwest time series and lagged values of the dependent variables.

ii. Public sector nonwage income and public sector employment as a function of lagged export payroll plus lagged private nonwage income, lagged national time series and lagged values of the dependent variables.

iii. Export payroll and export sector employment as a function of lagged national and Midwestern time series and lagged values of the dependent variables.

Each of the foregoing vectors, i. to iii., is disaggregated. Forecasts are made of eight employment series as presented in Table 1 and four payroll series. The categories roughly correspond to the reporting system adopted by state employment securities divisions.

(The detailed structure of these equations can be obtained by writing to the author — Division of Business and Economics, Indiana University Northwest, 3400 Broadway, Gary, Indiana 46408.)

Leading Indicators

Our experience shows that the regional cycle is out of sync with the national business cycle. If the index of twelve leading indicators constructed by the Department of Commerce correctly predicts the timing of national downturns or upturns, the same index would do poorly in predicting regional turning points. Leading indicators are economic time series which tend to turn down eight to nine months prior to a recession.

Local downturns lead the nation, whereas recoveries lag. The amplitude of the regional cycle significantly exceeds that of the national cycle. (For more details, see Table 2).

Moreover, the Fed and the government read the signals given by leading indicators and undertake corrective action. False signals given by leading indicators in 1962 and again in 1966 were probably the result of monetary and fiscal countermeasures. The private sector also reacts to fiscal and monetary policy. In order to account for this sequence of actions and reactions we specify:

1. Long series (which measure the path of the business cycle in the absence of countermeasurses) with a 9 months lead

2. Intermediate series (which tend to measure induced corrective actions taken by fiscal and monetary authorities) with a 6 months lead

3. Short series (which incorporate probable adaptive behavior by the private sector) with a 3 months lead

Computer Search

A computer search selects from each group, namely, short, medium and long series, a combination of 3 to 5 predictor series which are highly correlated with each other. The selected series produce a weighted sum which yields the lowest forecast error over its forecast range: namely, three, six or nine months into the future. We call these weighted sums "composite" predictors.

The search takes all possible combinations of three, followed by all combinations of four, and then all combinations of five indicator series. The lowest forecast error determines the number of series to be included in a composite.

Leading indicators often become coincident indicators during the course of a business cycle. That is, the series turn around in roughly the same period as the general economy. Leading indicators, if properly selected, can be used as independent variables in the expansion phase of the business cycle as one approaches the upper turning point. To forecast recoveries one must select series which drive the economy out of a slump. We call such series drivers.

TABLE 1
EMPLOYMENT IN NORTHWEST INDIANA ESTABLISHMENTS
(In Thousands of Employees)

	1984	1985	1985	1985	Projected 1985
	4Q	1Q	2Q	3Q	4Q
Total Employment	211.0(208.1)	210.6(207.4)	210.9(207.0)	213.0(212.6)	215.27(212.6)
Mfg. Employment	60.6(61.4)	60.8(60.09)	61.1(60.8)	60.2(61.1)	59.87(61.2)
Steel Employment	38.9(39.1)	39.2(39.1)	38.9(40.1)	38.3(38.3)	37.21(38.3)
Steel-related Mfg. Employment	18.6(19.0)	19.0(19.4)	19.7(19.7)	20.6(20.8)	20.6 (20.8)
Non-mfg. Employment	150.4(149.0)	149.8(148.5)	149.8(149.8)	151.8(151.4)	152.22(151.4)
Non-mfg. Industrial (Const. & util.)	22.4(22.7)	22.7(22.5)	22.5(23.1)	22.6(21.7)	23.0 (21.7)
Private Serv. Indus. (Incl. Retail, Insur., Fin., Banks	98.3(97.4)	97.4(99.0)	99.0(99.6)	100.9(100.6)	102.56(100.6)
Public Sector (Incl. Education)	29.7(29.8)	29.7(29.6)	28.3(29.3)	30.0(29.1)	29.24(29.1)

Note: (i)The values in parentheses next to the actual data were our predictions (see **Indiana Business Review**, May-June, 1985 and November-December, 1985, Table 1, pages 10 and 13.) The 4Q figures give one set of the revised projections. Previous projections are in parentheses. Projections for 4 quarters are revised every 6 months.
(ii) Quarterly rates are adjusted.

Drivers

The following is a list of important drivers which performed well in our model, though different selections may apply to other regions. Change in manufactures unfilled orders (BCD 25), change in real GNP (BCD 50c), personal consumption expenditures (BCD 55), index of consumer sentiment (BCD 58), new private housing units authorized (BCD 29), ratio of implicit price deflators to unit labor costs (BCD 26), compensation of employees as percent of national income (BCD 64), durable goods orders (BCD 232), defense department gross obligations (BCD 517).

In addition, we selected local drivers such as "value added over payroll" for local manufacturing, orders for local manufacturing output, and ratios of Midwest series over corresponding national series, such as auto sales, industrial production, durable goods manufacturing, retail sales, and construction contracts. The Midwest series are published by the Federal Reserve Bank of Chicago.

Drivers have cumulative impact. Certain elements such as the ratio of imports over domestic auto sales are specified as an exponentially weighted sum of past values. Some drivers are defined as 1 if the differenced index moves up 3 consecutive periods and −1 if the index declines 3 periods: 0 otherwise.

The weights are determined by an algorithm which maximizes the signal to noise ratio. The signal measures the principal phase of the business cycle such as recovery or recession. The noise component measures random deviations from the signal. If the signal is strong, the impact of the more recent observations will be greater. If the signal is weak relative to the noise, the weights will be more evenly distributed.

Indicators and drivers are combined in a single forecast equation. Drivers which do not lead, such as percent of change in GNP or net capital formation, are currently obtained from the consensus forecasts published in the Journal of Business Forecasting.

Nine to Eighteen Months Forecasts

The nine month associative forecast is subsequently fed into an univariate Box-Jenkins extrapolation. The predicted values are absorbed by Box-Jenkins as though the data were actually realized observations.

Censoring the Data

Unlike the national economy, entry or exit of large firms induces changes in the statistical regime. In other words, there is a statistically significant change in the economy's response over the entire business cycle. Consequently, the data file has to be truncated at the point where the change of regime has occurred. Previous observations, if included, may yield biased parameter estimates.

The statistical regime may shift because of an accumulation of structural changes, each of which individually might not have changed the regime. Consequently the program performs statistical tests capable of locating points at which the series must be truncated.

Estimation of Parameters

The model is constructed in a manner which allows for simultaneous estimating procedures. However, reduced form forecasts tended to perform less satisfactorily than ordinary least squares forecasts. Estimation of parameters is done by constraining aggregates. For example, non manufacturing employment plus manufacturing employment must equal total employment.

Var Method

Over periods of prolonged expansion or contractions, when the null hypothesis of constancy of coefficients is accepted, the VAR method tends to be most efficient. VAR is an extension of univariate autocorrelation. In a set of variables each variable depends on its own past values and on the past values of other variables.

The basis for the choice of driving variables for VAR is the small SEM model described in the foregoing. Unfortunately, there are serious data limitations in a small region model. Thus VAR may have limited possibilities. However, some new approaches, such as Bayesian forecasting models, are currently under review.

Accuracy

Forecasting is an art and not an exact science. Once the computer printouts are produced, one must use one's judgement and experience in formulating the final projection. Nevertheless, in our experience, whenever we made manual adjustments believing that the model's predictions were exaggerated, the model tended to be closer to subsequent realized values. We questioned the steep decline in local steel and manufacturing employement predicted by the model. Our upward manual revisions in the past were in error. The model correctly forecast a long shallow recovery in 1983-1985. Our intuition had expected a more pronounced re-

TABLE 2
CIVILIAN EMPLOYMENT FOR U.S. VS. NORTHWEST INDIANA MSA
DURING FOUR BUSINESS CYCLES
(December 1969-November 1982)

Average Lead to Peak of Northwest Indiana Cycle	Average % Gain in Employment from Trough to Peak	
	U.S.	Indiana
4.16 months	+7.645%	+10.3075%
Average Lag to Trough of Northwest Indiana Cycle	Average % Loss of Employment from Peak to Trough	
	U.S.	Indiana
11.7 months	−1.532%	−12.027%

116

bound following the 1982 recession. (For accuracy in employment establishments, see Table 1).

Software

The methods discussed in this paper have their justification in econometric theory. It is not our purpose to delve into these matters.

The model can be set up in combination with standard SPSS or SAS software. Data modifications can be carried out by "Do-repeat," "Compute," "IF," "Lag," "Weight," and "Test" commands.

The entire forecasts (except for VAR) along with most of the tests (except for truncation tests, which require a modest amount of additional pro

gramming) can be carried out in one afternoon on a terminal by an operator with only limited knowledge of programming ●

References

Brown, R.L., Durbin, J., Evans, J.M. "Techniques for Testing the Constancy of Regression Relationships Over Time." **Journal of the Royal Statistical Society.** Vol. 37, 1975, pp. 149-163.

Klein, R.L. "The Specification of Regional Econometric Models." Papers of the Regional Science Association. No. 23, 1968, pp. 105-115.

Lantham, W.R., Lewis, K.A. and Landon, J.H. "Regional Econometric Models: Specifications and Simulations of a Quarterly Alternative for Small Regions." **Journal of Regional Science.** Vol. 19, 1979, pp. 1-13.

Litterman, R.B. **Techniques of Forecasting. User Vector Auto Regression.** Minneapolis: Federal Reserve Bank of Minneapolis, 1979.

Schacmurove, Y. "Changes in the Dependence of State Employment on National Employment in the Last Decade: Some Evidence." **Indiana Business Review.** Vol. 60, March/April 1985, pp. 3-13.

Sims, C.A. "Macroeconomics and Reality." **Econometrica.** Vol. 48, 1980, pp. 1-48.

Singer, L.P. **Optimum Information Predictors: A Study In Econometric Forecasting.** Chicago: Illinois Bell Telephone Co., 1969, pp. 77-79.

Singer, L.P. "Steel and the Regional Economy." **Indiana Business Review.** Vol. 57, April 1982, pp. 10-12.

Zarnowitz, V., and Boschan, C. "Cyclical Indicators: An Evaluation and New Leading Indexes." **Business Conditions Digest.** May 1975, pp. VI-VIII.

Chapter 29
Determining The Impact of New Business on Local Economy

Dean G. Smith
University of Michigan

John R.C. Wheeler
University of Michigan

How a new business establishment would impact on the local economy is of interest to state and local governments, chambers of commerce, and private concerns. State and local governments are interested in such information because they want to know how much their community would benefit if such a business is brought into their area. Companies do such an analysis to secure a favorable tax treatment from state and local governments in exchange for locating in that area. This paper presents a method for estimating the economic impact of a new business or of a major investment by an existing company on the local economy.

Economic Impact Analysis

An economic impact analysis usually starts with an estimation of cash flowing to local economic entities—businesses and people—as a result of new business investment. If the analysis is at all complete, the cash flowing from a local entity to the new business activity has to be subtracted to arrive at the net impact.

The initial impact represents the first cash injection into the local economy due to the new investment. The cash injection flows to individuals, who use the money for consumption and savings purposes, and to business, which uses it to pay workers and purchase other production inputs. The new investment also has subsequent effects on the economy. Those who recieve income as a result of this investment save a portion of it and spend the rest, thereby generating addi-

tional income. The expenditure of one is an income of another. Thus, a given increase in new investment generates income by a multiplied effect. The total impact of an investment in a given community can be determined by the multiplier. If the multiplier is 4, it means that one dollar of increase in new investment will generate a total income of four dollars. The formula for the multiplier is:

$$\text{Multipler} = \frac{1}{1 - c(1-t)}$$

Where:
c = Marginal propensity to consume
t = Effective tax rate

The effective tax rate (t) is the sumtotal of effective federal income tax rate, average FICA rate, effective state income tax rate and average sales tax rate. The marginal propensity to consume (c) is the amount spent from the additional income of one dollar. The total impact of a given investment on the local economy depends upon the value of multiplier.

Mutliplier

To compute the multiplier, we need to know the marginal propensity to consume and effective tax rate. Spending can be divided into two parts: one which goes for durable goods and one which goes for other consumer goods and services. Expenditures on durables including shelter, which total 37 percent of consumption expenditures nationally, mainly occur within a local economy. Expenditures on food and drugs account for 20.6 percent of consumption expenditures. These items are also purchased pretty much locally. The remaining 42.4 percent (100.0 − 37.0 − 20.6) of expenditures are spent partly within the region of residence and partly in other regions. To

determine the percentage of these expenditures spent locally, additional information is necessary. In the absence of such informtion, because the majority of such expenditures occur locally, it is suggested that the analyst should assume that 60 percent of these expenditures take place locally.

Based on the numbers presented above, an estimated 83.2 percent of consumption expenditures [(37.0 + 20.6) + (60% of 42.4)] are made within a local economy. Using the national average propensity to consume of approximately 81 percent adjusted for the local expenditures, local marginal propensity to consume comes to 67.4 percent (81% of 83.2).

The next step is to estimate the effective tax rate (t). This can be accomplished by using readily available data on federal and state tax rates and income levels. For the United States, the average effective federal income rate is 13 percent, and the average FICA rate is 5.3 percent. For Michigan, as an example, the average effective state income tax rate is 3.5 pecent, and the average sales tax rate is 1.6 percent. Thus, the total effective tax rate is 23.4 percent (13.0 + 5.3 + 3.5 + 1.6).

Once estimates of local marginal propensity to consume and local effective tax rates are made, calculation of the total area multiplier becomes simple. It can be computed by substituting values in the above equation:

$$\text{Mutliplier} = \frac{1}{1 - 0.674(1-0.234)}$$
$$= 2.06$$

The multiplier shows that, for a given increase in investment, the final impact on the local economy will be 2.06 times the investment. If investment increased by one million dollars, the increase in the local income would be 2.06 million dollars.

Some Cautions

Since the multiplier for a local economic impact analysis depends on its local marginal propensity to consume and effective tax rate. the multiplier differs from one local area to the other. Each local area has a different marginal propensity to consume and a different effective tax rate.

The method discussed above assumes that the income flow, resulting from an investment, comes from individuals, rather than from businesses. To the extent that this assumption is not valid and to the extent that the local marginal propensity to consume of businesses differs from that of individuals, the method can

produce inaccurate multiplier estimate. In a situation where much of the initial income flow goes to businesses, the analyst may need to estimate separately the local marginal propensity to consume of businesses. The method can be adapted to estimate statewide impact as well. The statewide marginal propensity to consume will generally be higher than the local marginal propensity to consume. Expenditures within a local economy will usually be within the state as well, while expenditures made within the state may not be within a defined local market. Regarding the effective tax rate of a state, it will be lower than that of a local economy because of exclusion of much of state and sales taxes. Because of higher

marginal propensity to consume and lower effective tax rate, the state economy will tend to have a large multiplier. Local economies, which are very near other centers of commerce, will tend to have smaller local multipliers as people cross the boundaries to shop ●

References

United States Department of Commerce, Bureau of the Census. Statistical Abstract of the United States. Washington, D.C.: U.S. Government Printing Office, 1985.

United States Department of Commerce, Bureau of the Census. After-Tax Money Income Estimates of Households. Washington, D.C.: U.S. Government Printing Office, 1983.

PART IX

Leading Economic Indicators

Chapter 30
Leading Indicators Can Be Misleading

Howard Keen, Jr.
Conrail Corp.

I f you assume that a decline of any size in the Composite Index of Leading Indicators in any one month or even two or three months in a row is a signal that an economic recovery is at an end and recession is in the offing, there's a good chance you'll be wrong.

You can improve your chances of being right by assuming that the peak of the recovery is at hand when the Index experiences two consecutive months of *negative and decelerating* growth. Moreover, this criterion, or filter, gives you more time in which to adjust plans than any of the others.

A word of caution: There is no evidence that the opposite of this assumption—i.e., that two consecutive months of positive and accelerating growth—is a predictor of expansion.

These conclusions are based on an examination of the 11 recessions and recoveries since the end of World War II in 1945.

To facilitate discussion we will refer to each filter by number as follows:

1. A decline of any size from the previous month (technically this is not a filter).
2. Declines of any size two months in a row.
3. Declines of any size three months in a row.
4. Two consecutive months of negative and decelerating growth.

Application of filter No. 1 to the indices of the 11 postwar recoveries shows that it gave a false signal in each case, and that, on average, it produced 3.2 false signals per downturn. Criterion No. 2 produced false signals in 7 cases, and an average of 1.1 false signals per recession. The same figures for Criterion No. 3 were 4 and 0.4.

The major weakness of No. 2 and No. 3 is the average lag between the signal and the actual beginning of the recessions, only 1.5 and 1.9 months respectively.

The best of the four filters on the basis of calling the right turn most frequently (64 percent of the time) and the longest lag time (2.8 months) is No. 4.

Filter No. 4 is not commonly used by analysts; No. 2 and No. 3 are frequently cited in press reports and discussions of the Index.

Any sequence of two or three months in a row with negative changes in the Index constitutes a signal of recession under filters 2 and 3. Filter 4, however, requires a particular pattern in the rate of change in the Index. A three-month series of changes such as (−1%, −1%, − 2%), for example, would not constitute a signal of recession under this filter since the change in the middle month, although negative, is not decelerating from the change in the prior month. Examples of monthly rates that represent a signal of recession under filter No. 4 are (−1%, −1.5%, −2%), (−0.5%, −1%, −2%), and (+2%, −2%, −4%). In every one of these examples, growth in each of the last two months is *negative and algebraically lower* than in the previous month, satisfying the filter of two consecutive months of negative and decelerating growth.

The rationale behind filters 2, 3, and 4 is that as forces of expansion are dissipated, and elements of recession gather steam, the Index will reflect this transformation with *sustained* monthly declines. Additionally, filter No. 4 requires a pattern of *progressive* decline in the Index.

The historical performance of the filters is presented in Table 1.

The record covers the 11 postwar business cycle peaks—eight identified as such by the National Bureau of Economic Research (unofficial but authoritative arbiter) and three that were considered "growth recessions" (periods during which growth continued but at lower than the trend rate).

Past performance is summarized by the number of expansions in which the signal occurred by the peak month, the number of peaks that were not preceded by the signal, the lag between signal and peak, and the number of false signals. A signal is considered false when the Index subsequently increases, and then repeats the same signal before a recession begins.

One clear message from the record is the need for, and benefit of, applying some type of filter to the monthly movements of the Index. While filter 1 (which is not truly a filter) stacks up quite well with the alternative filtered signals in most categories, its usefulness as a reliable precursor of recession is severely limited by its tendency to give off false signals. In particular, false alarms occurred in each of the 11 expansions and with an average of 3.2 times in each one. This tendency can be drastically reduced through the application of even a simple filter. The average number of false signals per expansion is 66 percent lower for the signals given by filter No. 2, and about 86 percent lower with the other two filters.

Another clear message from the data is that the filter with the best historical record is not one of the two popularly-cited ones, 2 and 3, but filter No. 4, two consecutive months of negative and decelerating growth. This filtered signal occurred in each and every one of the 11 postwar expansions; it had the longest average lead time of any of the alternatives, and it displayed the fewest false signals per expansion. In short, it has the best record of the three simple filters in precisely those categories that are important in a leading indicator ●

FOOTNOTES

1. Examples of more complicated filtering rules for the Indexes of Leading as well as Coincident In-

THE LEADING INDICATORS

The Index of Leading Indicators, published monthly by the U.S. Dept. of Commerce, currently comprises the items listed below. The Composite Index represents a weighted average of the indicators.

1. Avg. work week, production workers, mfg.
2. Avg. weekly initial unemployment claims, state unemployment insurance.
3. New orders, mfg., consumer goods and materials.
4. Vendor performances, companies receiving slower deliveries from vendors.
5. Net business formation.
6. Contracts and orders for plant and equipment.
7. Building permits.
8. Change in inventories on hand and on order.
9. Change in sensitive materials prices.
10. Stock prices, 500 common stocks.
11. Money supply, M2.
12. Change in credit—business and consumer borrowing.

TABLE 1
PEFORMANCE OF ALTERNATIVE SIGNALS OF RECESSION FROM INDEX OF LEADING INDICATORS*
(Eleven Postwar Expansions)

Item	Filter**			
	1	2	3	4
No. of recessions for which signals given	11	11	10	11
Recessions for which signal not given	0	0	1	0
No. of recessions preceded by false signals	11	7	4	4
Avg. No. of false signals per recession	3.2	1.1	0.4	0.5
Lag between signal and recession onset (No. of months)				
Average	2.4	1.5	1.9	2.8
Minimum	1.0	0.0	0.0	0.0
Maximum	5.0	4.0	6.0	7.0

*Revised version of Index released March 1983.
**See definitions in text.
Excludes false signals.

dicators can be found in Victor Zarnowitz and Geoffrey H. Moore, "Sequential Signals of Recession and Recovery," **Journal of Business,** University of Chicago, 35:1, 1982 and Michael P. Neimera, "Sequential Signals of Regression and Recovery; Revisited," **Business economics,** (January 1983), pp. 51-53.

2. For a discussion of an earlier version of the Index of Leading Indicators in relation to filters 2 and 3 and others , see Beatrice N. Vaccara and Victor Zarnowitz, "How Good Are The Leading Indicators?" **American Statistical Association 1977 Proceedings of the Business and Economic Statistics Section,** Part 1, pp. 41-50.

Chapter 31
Are The Leading Economic Indicators Really Leading?

James Cicarelli
SUNY-Fredonia

U Jin Jhun
SUNY-Oswego

In the Winter 1983/84 issue of the Journal, Howard Keen raised some doubts about the reliability of the leading economic indicators. Since then those same reservations have been expressed in the popular business press by a number of prominent forecasters, among them Michael Evans, head of Evans Econometrics in Washington, D.C., Edward Guay, chief economist for Cigna Corp., a Philadelphia-based insurance and financial services firm, and Charles Lieberman, senior economist for Shearson Lehman Bros. Given that several leading forecasters have come to the same conclusion, one is tempted to question the validity of one of the most trusted and widely reported barometers of the future of the economy. Specifically, are the leading economic indicators really leading?

Rather than proceeding like a whodunit, we shall report straight away that the answer is yes. Using a modern test of causality, we conclude that the leading economic indicators are what they purport to be. What follows is a narrative explaining how we came to that conclusion. Before getting into that analysis, however, we would like to preface our remarks with a brief review of how indicator forecasting came to be.

Development of Indicators

Essentially an outgrowth of the statistical analysis of the U.S. business cycle, the leading economic indicators are measures of the aggregate economy or specific parts thereof. The earliest known set of widely used cyclical in-

dicators in the U.S. was devised in the 1920's by Warren M. Person who studied many economic time series over the period 1875-1913 and grouped them according to their characteristic timing. From Person's studies emerged the Harvard Index Chart which focused on three series—stock prices, commodity prices, and interest rates—as leading, coincident, and lagging indicators, respectively.

Today, references to leading indicators are usually references to the work of the National Bureau of Economic Research (NBER). The NBER published its first list of business cycle indicators in 1938. Compiled by Wesley Clair Mitchell and Arthur F. Burns, that list was based on a study of nearly 500 monthly or quarterly time series covering a variety of historical periods through the 1933 trough of the Great Depression. Mitchell and Burns selected the 21 most trustworthy indicators of cyclical revival, and presented a fuller list of 71 series that have been tolerably consistent in their time in relation to business cycle revivals.

In 1950, a new, more comprehensive study based on nearly 800 series and utilizing measures of cyclical behavior through 1938 was published. This study went beyond the earlier one in several ways: indicators of recession as well as revival were covered; probability standards against which the historical records of timing and conformity could be judged were introduced; a comprehensive analysis of 800 series was done in making the final selection of indicators; and the 21 series selected—8 leading indicators, 8 roughly coincident, and 5 lagging—were classified into the three categories reflecting their time at business cycle peaks and troughs. In 1960, this list was again

revised, resulting in the designation of 26 cyclical indicators—12 leading, 9 coincident, and 5 lagging.

In the fall of 1957, at the request of Raymond J. Saulnier, chairman of the Council of Economic Advisers, the Bureau of the Census started a research program to develop monthly indicators that would take advantage of the new findings about the relations between selected time series and the future state of the economy. Using sophisticated, large-scale electronic computing facilities, the Bureau of the Census experimented with a large number of economic and non-economic time series. In October 1961, after four years of testing, the Bureau began to publish its findings in a monthly publication *Business Cycle Developments*. The title of this publication was soon changed to *Business Conditions Digest* (BCD), and during the 1972-75 period, another comprehensive review of the 12 leading, 5 coincident, and 6 lagging indicators was carried out by the Bureau of Economic Analysis with the cooperation of the NBER research staff.

Today, *Business Conditions Digest* is probably the single most important, authoritative source of information on cyclical indicators and related data. *BCD* gives composite indexes for the leading, coincident, and lagging indicators; time series data for each individual cyclical indicator; cyclical indicators by economic process such as "Prices, Wages, and Productivity" and "Labor Force, Employment, and Unemployment;" and numerous constant and current dollar series dealing with virtually every aspect of National Income and Product.

Causality and Leading Indicators

A time series is said to be a leading indicator if its turning points corresponding to the ups and downs of the business cycle occur before those of the series that are considered coincident with the business cycle. In other words, the peaks and troughs of a leading indicator precede those of the economy as a whole in much the same way that cause precedes effect in any cause-and-effect relationship. The present set of leading indicators are so designated because past experience, based largely on judgmental methods of evaluation, indicate that swings in these Twelve Time series and their composite Index anticipate cyclical movements in the economy as measured by the Index of Industrial Production.

What would happen to the whole notion of indicator forecasting if the twelve designated series and the composite index were subjected to a statistically objective, uniform criteria of evaluation? For instance, can the leading indicators pass modern causality tests as readily as they do the historical and seemingly subjective tests of evaluation currently in use? In applying modern causality test, we are not trying to prove that variations in the indicators cause swings in the business cycle. Rather, we are merely trying to determine whether or not turning points in the indicators precede those of the entire economy. In short, we are attempting to verify the presence of temporal ordering, that is, priority in time, not pure cause-and-effect.

By its very nature, causality in economics is rooted more in the laws of probability than in the realm of exact relationship usually found in the physical sciences. Such causality is, therefore, measurable in a statistical sense. The first person to develop a modern empirical-based measure of causality was N. Wiener who sought to apply his results in the area of communication engineering. In 1969, C.W.J. Granger expanded upon the work of Wiener, investigating causal relationships using econometric models and cross spectral methods. Granger's basic purpose was to develop a statistical test or measure of causality that was particularly appropriate for the analysis of time series data. While Granger's analysis has come to be regarded as the seminal work in economic causality, it is safe to say that the combined efforts of Wiener and Granger form the foundation of contemporary, statistical-based, causality theory.

According to the Wiener-Granger concept of causality, a time series X is said to cause (lead) another time series Y if the past values of X contribute to the predictability of Y after the contributions of the past values of Y have been accounted for. If this is not the case, that is, if the past values of X do not improve the ability to predict Y after the contributions of the past values of Y have been considered, then unidirectional causality does not exist, or X does not cause (lead) Y.

Analytical Framework

In this study, a statistical procedure developed by C. Sims is used to test for unidirectional causality from the leading economic indicators to the Index of Industrial Production. A number of factors influenced this choice. First, the Sims approach has been shown to be statistically equivalent to the Granger test for causality. Second, the Sims test is the most widely known and best understood measure of Granger causality within the areas of business and economics. Third, the sheer simplicity of the Sims test relative to other empirical methods of measuring causality recommends it. Monthly data for the period 1975-1981 were used in this study.

The Results

The numerical results, which we will gladly share with any interested reader upon request, showed that the future values of the leading indicators do not improve appreciably the ability to predict the Index of Industrial Production. Thus, causality from the twelve leading indicators and the composite index to the Index of Industrial Production is unidirectional; in short, the leading indicators are indeed leading. (The detailed information on the methodology and results can be obtained by writing to: Dr. James Cicarelli, Chair and Professor, Dept. of Business Administration, SUNY-Fredonia, Fredonia, NY 14063.)

Of course, no forecasting instrument is perfect, and despite these results, leading indicator forecasting still has its drawbacks. Principal among these are the tendency to signal turning points and lead times falsely. Nevertheless, over the long haul, leading indicator forecasting consistently predict swings in the business cycle and so justifies the confidence economists, politicians, and business professionals have placed in this barometer of the future ●

References

Chamberlain, G. "The General Equivalence of Granger and Sims Causality." **Econometrica.** 50(2), May, 1982, pp. 569-581.

Granger, C.W.J. "Investigating Causal Relations by Econometric Models and Cross-Spectral Methods." **Econometrica.** 37(3), July, 1969, pp. 424-438.

Gorton, G. "Forecasting with the Index of Leading Indicators." **Business Review: Federal Reserve Bank of Philadelphia.** Nov./Dec., 1982, pp. 24-27.

Hicks, J.R. **Causality in Economics.** New York: Basic Books, 1979.

Keen, Jr., H. "Leading Economic Indicators Can Be Misleading, Study Shows." **Journal of Business Forecasting.** 2(4), Winter, 1983-84, pp. 13-14.

Kelegian, H.H. and Oates, W.E. **Introduction to Econometrics** (Second Edition), New York: Harper and Row, 1981.

Lempert, L.H. "Leading Indicators" in W.F. Butler and R.A. Kavesh, editors. **How Business Economists Forecast.** Englewood Cliffs, N.J.: Prentice Hall, 1966.

Moore, G.H. (editor). **Business Cycle Indicators.** Princeton University Press for the National Bureau of Economic Research, 1961.

————, and Shiskin, J. **Indicators of Business Expansions and Contractions.** New York: NBER and Columbia Univ. Press, 1967.

Sims, C.A. "Money, Income, and Causality." **American Economic Review.** 62(4), Sept. 1971, pp. 540-552.

PART X

The Long Wave

Chapter 32
The Long Wave

Alan K. Graham
Mass. Institute of Technology

Econometric models and short-term business and political thinking are hiding the real causes and depth of the current worldwide economic downturn. The fact is that the economies of the world's industrialized nations are in the most precarious position since the depression of the '30s.

The Main Street-Wall Street reward system (MS-WS) that rewards politicians for short-term "quick fixes" (MS) and professional business managers for short-term profit optimization (WS), is diverting the debate over remedies away from the real issues.

The situation is not likely to be reversed by the reward-system strategies, because it is not just another business cycle downturn; it is the final phase of a "long-wave" cycle similar to those that preceded the great worldwide depressions of history. But it also marks the early stages of the next cycle, a period of great technological innovation and opportunity for bold investors and innovative managements who know how to pick the right technologies of the future. Historical evidence indicates that each long-wave cycle lasts 50 to 60 years, and that the period of transition that is marked by turbulence and depression lasts about 10 years.

The corporate strategies adopted during the transition usually determine who survives to reap the benefits of the next long wave and who perishes.

Those are the major conclusions drawn from an interview with Dr. Alan K. Graham, director of research, System Dynamics National Model group, of the Mass. Institute of Technology (MIT), and from selected papers written by him and other members of the group, including the developer of System Dynamics, Dr. Jay W. Forrester who heads the group.

Following is a partial text of a recent talk by Dr. Graham in which he expands on the major concepts of the long-wave, and provides some insights on how to survive. (A.M)

men and the elephant: each man, with his own area of expertise, accurately reporting the facts and doing his best to draw conclusions. But none of them has arrived at the unifying concept of "elephant" that would both explain the facts and lead to new insights on how to deal with elephants.

My colleagues at M.I.T. are developing a working hypothesis to explain many of the present cross-currents. As a working hypothesis, it is not unequivocally proven true, but is nonetheless useful both in explaining circumstances and producing useful insights about how to deal with them. At first blush, the hypothesis might appear unlikely: that industrialized economies do not develop smoothly, but rather in waves of economic development interspersed with depressions about fifty years apart.

The theory of the economic long wave provides a novel and potentailly important perspective on economic change . . . it identifies a 40- to 60-year cycle in economic growth. Sources of the cycle appear to lie in overexpansion of capacity to produce physical capital, and overcommitment to particular mixes of technologies which eventually reach diminishing returns. The long wave seems especially important for understanding the shifting economic conditions of the 1970s and the prospects for renewed economic growth in the 1980s. The theory suggests that low rates of capital investment, lagging productivity growth and innovation, and rising unemployment, particularly in traditional capital industries, are characteristic of the latter phases of a long-wave expansion.

There is widespread evidence that the decade of the eighties will be a time of transition. Economic growth is grinding to a standstill, even as social and political change accelerate. Long-term productivity growth has ceased, even though technology daily reveals new miracles. A transition, perhaps, but from what and to what?

Alvin Toffler has suggested that an epic technological transition is upon us, comparable in magnitude only to the industrial revolution. Economic forecasters ascribe the tumult to OPEC and Federal Reserve policy, as well as to a host of lesser factors. Politicians and others have spoken of outdated social institutions and the need to "reindustrialize." Financiers bemoan overextended credit, and demographers blame the entry of the unskilled into the workforce. The situation is reminiscent of the parable of the blind

Transition Period

From this viewpoint, the 1980s appear as a period of fundamental transition. Industries that served as the backbone of economic growth in the 1950s and 1960s, and which began to stagnate in the 1970s, will decline, eventually releasing productive and financial resources for the growth in new industries. Debt accumulated during the expansion of the past thirty years will be liquidated. Forces underlying inflation will conflict with deflationary pressures that traditionally arise during a long-wave transition. Failure to understand this shifting context for national and corporate policy can lead to inappropriate actions that can exacerbate the dislocation and suffering of the transition.

The long-wave hypothesis has been taken seriously even before theories to explain it existed. The first person to discover statistical evidence of long waves was Nikolai Kondratiev, a Russian social scientist working in the 1920s. When the Great Depression occurred, his long-wave statistics implied a recovery from the Depression in the late '30s. Unfortunately, his findings clashed with the Soviet orthodoxy of the time, which interpreted the Depression as the death throes of capitalism. The conflict was resolved when Kondratiev was exiled to Siberia.

Since Kondratiev's time, a body of evidence has accumulated that supports the idea of a long wave. What is particularly impressive about this body of evidence is not the persuasiveness of any one piece, but rather the extraordinary diversity of the evidence.

The Evidence:

Materials production. Kondratiev discovered 50-year cycles in long time series for such quantities as iron and steel production, coke production, and coal usage.

Prices and interest rates. Although it might surprise those of us who have become accustomed to decades of inflation, Kondratiev also discovered that historically there has been about as much deflation as there has been inflation, alternating in 50-year waves; there are corresponding movements in long-term interest rates.

Descriptive histories. Beyond Kondratiev's statistical work, there are descriptive histories that recount events that seem to move in 50-year cycles—the character of wars, politics, the incidences of social reform such as women's liberation, financial panics, and inventions.

Unemployment. Figure 1 shows unemployment data for the United States, starting from 1890. When we start to consider such specific economic data, the long-wave hypothesis gains in importance; if we add fifty years to a 1933 peak in unemployment we infer that another surge of unemployment could be due any year now. Indeed, the recent unemployment above 9 percent is the highest since the depression and the end of a fairly clear uptrend that began back in 1944.

Capital/labor mix—how much physical capital is used per person—showed a distinctive pattern during the entire long wave from 1890 to 1940, and this pattern seems to be repeating.

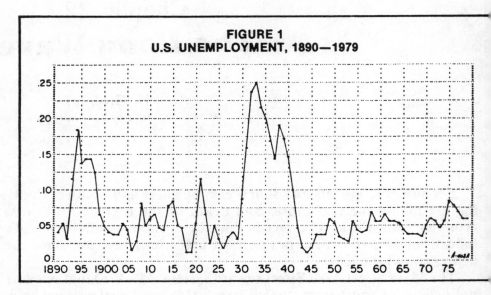

FIGURE 1
U.S. UNEMPLOYMENT, 1890—1979

Political attitudes. Political attitudes and values turn out to be quite measurable and show distinct 50-year cycles. A computer can be used to analyze the attitudinal connotations of words in American party platforms and other political documents. Whole clusters of separately measured attitudes correlate quite closely with the phases of economic development. For example, there have now been four shifts to political conservatism at the end of a long period of economic expansion. The previous peaks in conservative attitudes were in 1933, 1881, and 1829.

Technological Innovation. This also turns out to be quite measurable far back in history. Basic innovation—innovations that are commercially or widely available and that create new industries or transform existing ones—were measured by Gerhard Mensch. He assembled several histories of technological innovation and tallied the dates when they first became widely available. Figure 2 from Mensch's book, "Stalemate in Technology," shows the frequency

of basic innovations per decade, from 1740 through 1960. The most striking feature of this graph, of course, is that the frequency of basic innovations is not at all smooth—surges tend to occur about fifty years apart. The last such surge was in the 1930s and early 1940s, which saw the introduction of radio, television, penicillin, nylon, jet airplanes, and radar, to name a few.

If there is a 50-year cycle, where are we on it? Closer examination of the evidence points to the '80s and early '90s as being years of transition—out of a period of slowed economic growth, through a period of actual economic depression coupled with a surge in basic innovation, and toward a new growth period in the late '90s and beyond. To capture the full implications of this transition, we must first know more about the underlying causes.

There is an hypothesis on the mechanisms that create long waves; it was discovered quite unintentionally. I am working with a group of researchers at M.I.T. to develop the System Dynamics National

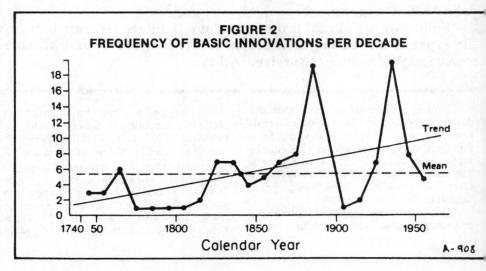

FIGURE 2
FREQUENCY OF BASIC INNOVATIONS PER DECADE

Calendar Year

Model, a computer simulation model intended to perform 200-year simulations of economic behavior, encompassing business cycles, inflation, energy transition, and economic development. Long waves were not originally part of the project's purpose. But one day model simulations began to show a pronounced 50-year cycle, and the more we examined its causes, the more plausible they became. Only afterwards did we discover that there was in fact a body of statistical and descriptive evidence on long waves.

Figure 3 shows three variables out of the several hundred variables in our computer model. The figure shows one typical cycle out of a much longer computer run. There are random inputs to the model which are deactivated in this particular simulation, which suppresses the short-term fluctuations we usually see in real economic time series. The model's long-term behavior arises roughly as follows: a depression inhibits investment and construction. But after several years of depression, the capital plant and equipment have deteriorated to the point where replacement investment is needed. Enough of this activity finally stimulates the economy and the rebuilding begins. In the last Great Depression, that rebuilding had started shortly before World War II.

As the demand grows for physical capital (that is, plant and equipment), the sector of the economy that supplies these must expand much faster than the economy as a whole. And rebuilding virtually from scratch, firms are able to draw on several years of technology that had not been used due to the Depression. There are numerous incentives to draw technologies out of the laboratory and into commercial innova-tions. This accounts for the surges in innovation.

The rebuilding initiates a long wave of economic development lasting about three decades. We could characterize the 1940s through the 1960s as the decades of rebuilding. As the wave progresses, a variety of mechanisms intensify the expansion of the capital-producing sector of the economy. For example, the capital sector must rebuild its own plant and equipment; this "bootstrapping" adds to the demand for physical capital. The capital-producing sector attempts to produce by drawing labor away from other sectors; this bids up wages and motivates producers throughout the economy to use less labor and more plant and equipment, which again increases the demand for physical capital.

Eventually the economy runs out of the ability to absorb still more plant and equipment. It becomes increasingly expensive to hire still more workers. Sufficient factories, a highway system, and an air transport system are already built. Although the economy has reached a new peak in material wealth, it is increasingly difficult to go further. Productivity and standard of living level off or decline. Capacity utilization declines. New construction falls off, and investments become decreasingly productive and increasingly speculative. Demand for new plant and equipment falls. Business mergers and business failures both rise. Business-cycle recessions become deeper, and the recoveries become weaker. This should sound very much like the current situation, as it unfolded during the 1970s and delivered us into the 1980s.

So this is a sketch of the theory and evidence that lies behind the working hypothe-sis of 50-year long waves. More evidence will be introduced below, but in the context of looking at the implications for business and a technological strategy.

Business Strategy

The good news about the coming long-wave transition is technological innovation. The bad news is overcapacity, slackening demand, and rising unemployment. The business press identifies overcapacity in a variety of industries—chemicals, textiles, steel, shipbuilding, automobiles, to name a few. The long-wave transition is a time of great opportunity and great stress. The business history of the '30s offers insight into what business strategies will be successful during the transition. In brief, the "success factors" are the same as for the expansion period; the difference is the amount of slack available after mistakes. More specifically, the factors involved have been:

Demand for product. Will the demand for a given product shrink, grow, or stay the same? The long-wave transition has both technological and economic effects. In the '30s, autos and trucks were supplanting railroads. In the steel industry, profitability was strongly influenced by the balance of the product line between railroad rails (declining) versus high-quality, flat-rolled sheet steel. Demand for this product grew rapidly due to the new popularity of automobiles and electric appliances. In fact, one steel company launched a major capacity expansion in 1931, when the bottom had come out from under the economy, and no one knew how far it would drop. But the expansion was quite profitable, because it was in sheet steel, then a growing market. So the technological shift in modes of transportation affected the growth of product lines.

Naturally, the state of the economy affects demand for product. The long-wave transition of the 1870s to 1890s manifested itself as three severe depressions, as opposed to the one very severe depression of 1929-33. During the three depressions, both the New York Central and the Pennsylvania railroads became major systems by acquiring branches whose volume would not be much affected by economic fluctuations. So haulers of foodstuffs or coal, for example, were much better acquisitions than haulers of lumber, furniture, or wood.

Economic difficulties actually cause some products to flourish. In the '30s, people were less able to afford vacations and luxuries, so they turned in increasing numbers to moving pictures. The '30s became "the Golden Age of Hollywood." The same process can be observed today, for example, when liquor buyers eschew more expensive brands for the less expensive. Economists call this the "substitution effect;" marketing people call it "trading down," and it will be widespread during the long-wave transi-tion.

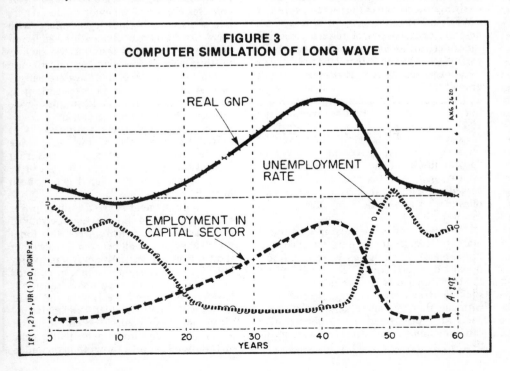

**FIGURE 3
COMPUTER SIMULATION OF LONG WAVE**

REAL GNP

UNEMPLOYMENT RATE

EMPLOYMENT IN CAPITAL SECTOR

YEARS

Market enterability. The history of technological innovation tells time and again of inventors who market a new product, only to have a new competitor improve on it and capture the market. When the depression of the 1930s began, there were many car companies. The small ones tried to gain customers with new innovations. But whenever a gimmick began to be popular, the major producers would incorporate it. Eventually, many small producers became subsidiaries of GM, Ford, and Chrysler.

By contrast, the aircraft industry was considerably more diversified and technologically sophisticated. Market niches were more specialized, and it was harder for large companies to displace small companies. Several companies were founded in the '30s that lasted to the present day: Republic Aviation, Bell Aircraft, Beech and Piper, and Sikorsky, to name a few.

Production costs in an era of capacity excess will determine which companies will be able to price to capture market share and which won't. Japanese autos and steel capture market share through lower production costs. Dow Chemical is expanding in Europe in products where there is already overcapacity, because Dow plans to be the low-cost producer, with more energy-efficient production than competitors. More specifically, low variable costs (labor, materials, energy) will allow continued operation even when every producer in a market is unprofitable. Those with higher variable costs will be the first to have cash-flow problems, unless the debt loads are different.

Debt burden. During the long-wave transition, the economic climate is much less forgiving than in previous phases of the wave. Larger business risks make banks less willing to loan, and profit margins are much lower. In addition, inflation can no longer be counted on to nibble away at debt burdens. Figure 4 shows the producer's price index from 1800-1973, with a consistent pattern of irregular inflation up to a peak, followed by deflation. Recent decades show an inflation continuing longer than previous long waves, due to monetization of government deficits. With the tightening of Federal Reserve policy and slowdown of inflation in the recent few years, the business press is now discussing deflation as a possibility.

The long wave produces widespread overcapacity, which is deflationary. But long-wave movements are amplified by events in the financial markets also. The 1960s and 1970s have seen debt increase and inflation linked in a vicious cycle: inflation raises asset values, allowing borrowing, creating money, raising prices and asset values. This same process does work and has worked in reverse to produce deflation. The popular economic press sometimes describes the deflation of the '30s as caused by the Federal Reserve. In fact, the reduction in money supply was initiated when

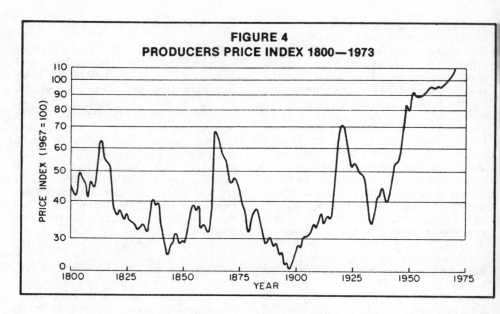

FIGURE 4
PRODUCERS PRICE INDEX 1800—1973

deteriorating business conditions made commercial banks unwilling to lend, which collapsed the money supply. At most, the Fed was guilty of failing to stem the tide of private liquidation of debt and money. The result was a debt-deflation spiral. The threat posed by large debts increases dramatically during the long-wave transition. Low profits squeeze cash flow, deflation increases the burden of existing debt, and higher risks make banks less willing to lend to troubled companies.

Treacherous Propositions

So far, it appears that the best way to survive a depression is to be the largest, lowest-cost producer in a non-enterable, growing market and have no debt. Obviously. But to complete the picture, consider several business propositions whose riskiness has risen relative to rewards, because the underlying assumptions about economic performance are no longer valid:

"Forget technology; that market won't grow." This proposition confuses devices and technologies; devices stay as they are, but technologies can be improved. In the 1940s, most people assumed that straightforward carbon paper could never be replaced by an expensive, dirty, unreliable copying machine. But carbon paper didn't improve, and copying machines did. They carved out a major share of the office supplies market and made many Xerox investors wealthy.

"Be safe and stick to our traditional markets." The assumption is that the traditional markets will in fact be safe. "Traditional" does not equal "conservative;" if the traditional markets are declining, then sticking to them is equivalent to going down with the ship. As manufacturers of autoparts have discovered, being conservative can sometimes mean breaking with tradition.

"It's a safe investment—there's a price subsidy/oil glut/tax loophole/war/high-margin industry." History is replete with examples of heavy, long-term investments in situations that, at least in retrospect, were clearly temporary. One of the reasons that the agricultural sector was hit so hard during the 1930s is that, even after a decade of hard times, it was still overinvested from World War I. (The war crippled European agriculture, and both high prices and the U.S. government encouraged farmers to buy "lots of" land and equipment. They did.) To paraphrase the Bible: He who lives by the price umbrella shall die by the price umbrella.

"When business picks up, we can be profitable/repay the loan/do R&D." This confuses economic behavior modes. There is a short-term business-cycle mode, with three- to seven-year fluctuations superimposed over the longer-term modes, such as the long wave. Business-cycle recoveries are of limited magnitude, and they are temporary. And in the long-wave transition, as economic activity peaks out, business-cycle recessions become more severe, and recoveries become weaker. There is also the risk of major disasters such as the 1929 stock market crash. So business tactics that depend on business-cycle recovery will be much riskier in the '80s than they have been in earlier decades.

"The investment is safe, because prices will rise." Figure 4 shows several periods of price decline, all synchronized with long-wave behavior and all being initiated rather suddenly. With a restrictive monetary policy in force, prices certainly cannot be counted on to rise during a long-wave transition. Historically, prices have fallen, and companies with high debt loads and deflating income have suffered. Especially hard-hit are the speculative investments that depend on inflation for profit rather than on underlying productive value. In the '30s, stocks, but also real estate, crashed. Now, real estate—especially farmland and some types of housing—seems inflated far beyond productive value.

Coming Innovations

If one extrapolates the surges in innovation, it would appear that the next surge is due to begin in the mid-'80s and peak in the early '90s. To get some guidance about what will occur, consider the past transition periods and surges of innovation. Figure 5 shows selected innovations from the surge of 1930-40 and the surge of 1870-90. There are two numbers shown for each technology: the first is the date of *innovation,* which marks the time when the technology first entered widespread or commercial use. The second is the number of years it took to get to the innovation stage from the *invention* stage, where the technology first functions in a laboratory setting. Given such information, one can begin to abstract the characteristics of the new technologies of the next wave, as they exist now before the surge starts:

Major economic benefit. Radically new technologies are very difficult to implement. The first (and often overlooked) characteristic of successful basic innovations is that they offer the potential for major economic benefit. Many of the technologies in Figure 5, for example, eventually yielded tenfold increases in capability over earlier technologies. And each technology related to a large commercial or military market. By contrast, radical new technologies seem

doomed to failure if they are sharply limited with respect to size of markets or to available increase in performance.

Resisted by infrastructure. One reason that basic innovations do not appear until the beginning of the long-wave upturn is that at the long-wave peak, when a capital infrastructure has been built up based on previous technologies, basic innovations are often incompatible with the existing infrastructure. For example, the petroleum economy that exists now is working very well. The highways, the auto dealerships, the service stations, and even the location of cities and housing are all in place to make oil-based transportation very efficient. When so much transportation capacity is already in place, it is hardly economical to build additional infrastructure based on some completely different type of transportation. Before a surge of innovation and capital investment can occur, the old capital base must wear out.

Shift from improvement to basic innovation. Improvement innovations make an existing technology more efficient without founding or transforming new industries. After the surge of basic innovation in the 1930s and 1940s, most of the technological activity involved improving automobiles, computers, consumer electronics, and so on. However, by the end of a long-wave expansion, the opportunities for further improvement innovations have diminished. This condition has been called a "technological stalemate". Simultaneously, research and development have become highly organized to perform the improvement innovations. This means that basic innovations can often appear to be "crackpot ideas" to a research establishment. They can almost literally fall between organizational cracks.

Prototypes being developed and sorted out. For the technologies of the 1930-1940 surge listed in Figure 5, the inventions (working prototypes) preceded innovations by over three decades on average. This pattern implies that the new technologies that will underlie the economic expansion of the next long wave exist now, but as laboratory prototypes or as limited-application devices. The current press identifies a whole host of technologies as technologies of the future. A few will be, but many will not. The time of economic malaise and low capital investment is a time when inventions are being sorted out, nonviable versus viable. We can look back to the '30s to see the competition among airplanes, dirigibles, helicopters, and autogyros. Only airplanes went on to become a major economic force.

It seems unlikely that the sorting-out process can be done quickly. The technological "winners" are good ideas that turn out to be very improvable. But no one can really know which technologies are very improvable without actually producing the device, making it work, and improving it. Turning

out several generations of a basic innovation can require a decade easily.

Cross-fertilization creates ensembles of technologies. The shift from improvement to basic innovation also implies a qualitative change in the direction of technological progress. While improvement innovations can be created and implemented merely by doing "more of the same," but better basic innovations often involve cross-fertilization from widely-separated technologies, and sharp alterations of trends. Basic innovations cause an "avalanche effect," where one innovation may make several others possible and may create the need (commercial market) for still other innovations. The surge in basic innovations becomes self-reinforcing (just as the surge in capital investment is self-reinforcing within the capital-goods-producing sector). In the 1920s, the vacuum-tube technology of telephone amplifiers spread rapidly to radio, then television, radar, and computers, each building rapidly on its predecessor. These applications in turn created advances in vacuum-tube technology and, finally, solid-state electronics. Similarly, advances in automobiles motivated, and then were stimulated by, the innovation of catalytic petroleum refining in 1935.

Along with a technological stalemate at the peak of the long wave, and with depressed capital investment during the downturn, the avalanche effect shapes basic innovation into surges at the beginning of the upturn. That surge creates the ensemble of technologies that are built into the ensuing wave of capital accumulation.

Figure 6 shows distinct long waves in energy technology or, more specifically, the fraction of total energy use supplied by each of several fuels. To illustrate the timing of these waves, Figure 6 has superimposed a portion of Figure 3, the frequency of basic innovations per decade. For the wave beginning at the innovation surge of the 1930s

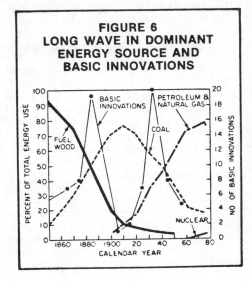

FIGURE 6
LONG WAVE IN DOMINANT ENERGY SOURCE AND BASIC INNOVATIONS

through 1940s, petroleum is the dominant fuel source. After the surge of the 1880s, coal dominated energy use. And in the prior wave, fuel wood was preponderant. During each energy-source transition, basic innovations peaked; changing from one ensemble of technologies to another creates a need for many individual basic innovations causing more of the avalanche effect.

Technologies other than energy show ensembles coincident with long waves. In communication, the telegraph dominated in the wave of the 1830s to the 1880s. Then advances in electrical technology created short-distance telephony and transcontinental telegraphy in the next wave. And in the present wave (1930s on), electronic amplification allows telephone, radio, and television of unlimited range. In transportation the wave of the 1830s-1880s had wood-fired locomotives; the 1880s-1930s had electric trolleys for intra-city use and much more sophisticated, coal-fired locomotives. This was the "Great Ages of Steam," which ended when the present wave began with diesel-electric locomotives, trucks, and airplanes.

The outstanding example of cross-fertilization in the present long-wave transition is the computer. It has made possible an increasingly interrelated ensemble of information-processing technologies that automate a plethora of tasks, from engineering to line management to drug development.

Many doublings. An industry created or spurred on by basic innovations will double in size many times before it reaches economic maturity. A small industry growing for a long time offers tremendous profit potential. But selecting the *right* small industry must be done on a technological basis, rather than on analyses of market potential given present technologies. The progress of a technologically-driven industry is predictable, given a willingness to predict the kinds of innovations that will be needed to allow further market growth. (Such an exercise has been done for the economics and technology of computer software.)

Avoiding Basic Innovation

There is a widely distributed poster that gives fifteen ways to kill a good idea; such negative propositions can be more useful than their positive counterparts. In that same spirit, here are several ways to avoid basic innovations:

"That technology is only used in the X business." This assumes that technology will not improve, will not cross-fertilize with other new technologies, and thus will not expand to wider applications. The assumption of static technology and continuing trends is more likely to be wrong during the long-wave transition than during any other period.

"The technology isn't practical, because there's no infrastructure." A basic innovation that offers major economic benefits will call up infrastructure investment over a period of years, or find a way to go piggy-back on existing infrastructure. Currently, data communication networks use existing phone lines first, before graduating into dedicated facilities. In the '30s, scheduled airlines expanded one route and one airport at a time, often starting with government-backed facilities for airmail. For an innovation whose time is coming, lack of infrastructure means expansion will be stretched out over several years.

"We just want a little improvement in our present technology." This proposition confuses two very separate missions of R&D; improvement innovation (small investment, limited payoff) versus basic innovation (large investment, major economic benefit). In major technology-based companies like Bell and GE, these two functions are served by entirely separate organizations, for much the same reason that the Federal Reserve Board is separated from the executive branch: avoidance of cross-interference. If the two research missions are not separated, short-term tactical pressures often cause companies to cling to attempts to improve older technologies. RCA, for example, eventually lost its dominance of the electronics industry by devoting its R&D to improving vacuum tubes in the face of competition from transistors.

"This is a mature industry—we don't need to worry about technology." This assumes future technological change will be like the past—for mature industries, slow, small, and unnoteworthy. Even without specifying the mature industry, the assumption seems most unlikely; given the advances in electronic communications, there are innovations seemingly capable of transforming the management, if not the products, of almost any industry.

"But the payback is so long." How should R&D investments be evaluated? It may be adequate for tactical considerations

to judge on the basis of payback period how long it takes a project to repay its own costs. But for long-term strategy making, payback period is a deceptive measure, because it totally ignores what happens after the initial investment has been paid back. In the '40s, was it a better investment to improve carbon paper or to develop xerography? The answer, measured by payback period, would have been to stick to carbon paper. But it was investment in xerography that made people wealthy.

Crosscurrents To Riptides

The 1970s saw many puzzling departures from the standard economic behavior of earlier times. Diverse crosscurrents appeared in inflation, unemployment, growth, productivity, and innovation. The long-wave hypothesis suggests that during the '80s these crosscurrents will shift into riptides: a time of economic depression matched with technological and managerial resurgence. Even though the long-wave hypothesis is supported by evidence both consistent and diverse, it is not necessary to believe in the long wave to deal with the shifts; but it is necessary to recognize that longer-term forces are shifting the economic and technological climate and that the shifts are accelerating.

A shift in the economic climate implies a shift in the workability of various strategies. At all times, there is an appropriate balancing point: between traditional markets and prospective markets; between financial risk taking and financial conservatism; between improvement and basic innovations. In the '80s and '90s, the balance will shift strongly toward technological and managerial innovativeness, financial conservatism, and new markets. As an example of a strategy whose time has passed, observers ascribe ITT's current difficulties to the long-standing (and hopefully former) strategy of aggressive business activity (acquisitions) coupled with conservative technological investment (especially neglecting new communications technology).

The strategies that work best flow with economic and technological tides. If the metaphor for the '70s is crosscurrents, then the metaphor of the '80s is riptides. One can of course survive riptides by knowing why and when they occur; the long-wave idea provides some of the knowledge needed to navigate the travails of the 1980s. ●

PART XI

System Dynamics

Chapter 33
System Dynamics vs. Econometric Models

Jay W. Forrester
Mass. Institute of Technology

(The following is a partial text of a recent talk by Dr. Forrester, director of the System Dynamics National Model group, Alfred P. Sloan School of Management, Mass. Institute of Technology (MIT). In it Dr. Forrester, the developer of System Dynamics, describes the method, and provides some insights on its use in developing national and corporate strategies. Ed.)

Effectiveness of an economic model is largely determined by how it uses the wide range of information arising from the real system. The inadequacies of economic analysis can be substantially attributed to inappropriate and biased use of available information. By inappropriate use of information, I refer to overemphasis on finding statistical relationships between economic variables, and underemphasis on the internal causal mechanisms that produce economic behavior. By biased use of information, I refer to overdependence on numerical data, and underutilization of information available from written and mental sources.

In creating a system dynamics model, information is used in a substantially different way from the use of information in regression analysis and econometrics. The different uses of information arise from a difference in structure between a system dynamics model and an econometric model, from a broader range of information sources used for creating a system dynamics model, from a different way of arriving at parameter values, from a different use of historical time-series data, and from a different purpose for which a system dynamics model is intended.

Information is available from . . . three kinds of data bases—mental, written, and numerical . . . the amount of available information declines, perhaps by a factor of a million, in going from mental to written information, and again by another factor of a million in going from written to numerical information. Furthermore, the character of information content changes as one moves from mental to written to numerical information. Each kind of information can fill a different role in modeling a national economy. (At this point in his talk Dr. Forrester describes each type of data base. We will delay that discussion to a later point in the article, and present Dr. Forrester's description of System Dynamics first. Ed.)

System dynamics is less related to the methodologies of the social sciences than to the methodologies of practicing management and engineering. In the system dynamics approach, the methods of management have been extended and improved by methodologies developed in engineering. System dynamics can be described as a substantial extension of the case-study approach, as that term is used in management education.

System dynamics grows out of three prior activities—traditional management, feedback systems (cybernetics), and computer simulation. By traditional management, I mean the way people have managed families, businesses, and nations since the beginning of human society. The great strength of traditional management lies in the tremendous data base to which it has access. Most of that data base exists in people's heads. The data base records experience, observation, and participation in life. The mental data base is rich in knowledge about structure, that is, how the system is organized and how it is connected. The mental data base contains the most directly accessible information about polices that govern decisions. But traditional management suffers from three weaknesses:

First, traditional management is overwhelmed by too much information. As one of its contributions, feedback theory provides principles for choosing relevant information and rejecting the preponderance of information that would be useless for constructing a dynamic model.

As the second weakness, traditional management lacks organizing principles (as a guide on how to assemble information into an effective framework). That is, traditional management has no theory for assembling an appropriate model. As a second contribution, feedback theory supplies principles about structure to guide the organization of information into a model.

As the third weakness, traditional management has had no way to manipulate its mental models except by intuition. There

has been no reliable way to determine the behavior implied by the available knowledge about structure and policies. Probably no mathematician would presume to solve by inspection even a simple fourth-order linear differential equation. By contrast, the working environment of a manager or politician is far more complex; he is undertaking to solve, by discussion and compromise, systems that are highly nonlinear and of at least hundredth order. The task is nearly impossible. But now, computer simulation can do perfectly the formerly impossible task of revealing the dynamic behavior implicit in a complex model.

The modeling process starts with the purpose of a model. The motivation usually arises from troublesome behavior of the real system. In a corporation, perhaps market share has been falling, or employment has been fluctuating more widely than for other companies in the industry. For a national economy, the motivation could come from controversies over inflation or a steadily increasing amplitude of the business cycle as has occurred during the last fifteen years. Such a model of the national economy would be expected to explain troublesome behavior, not merely in the sense of correlations between historical variables, but instead by actually generating the troublesome symptoms from the same underlying structural and policy mechanisms that generate the real-life symptoms.

During model construction, the central focus is on information available from mental and written sources and numerical information other than time-series data. Such other numerical data includes, for example, average delays in filling orders, typical ratios of inventory to sales rate, relative costs of production inputs, and lead times for ordering factors of production.

The full range of information and the purpose, along with appropriate modeling concepts, are interpreted through principles from feedback-loop theory to yield a model structure.

Parameters are also usually derived directly and individually from the mental, written, and numerical data bases. (Dr. Forrester gives the terms "variables," "parameters," and "constant" meanings that are different from those used in econometric modeling. The differences are clear from the context of the example. Ed.) I believe that in

135

the social sciences too sharp a distinction is drawn between structure and parameters. The distinction is fluid. For a simple model to be used over a short time span, certain quantities can be considered constants that for a model dealing with a longer time horizon should be converted into variables. Those new variables would, in turn, depend on more enduring parameters. For example, a policy for reordering goods for inventory might in the short run suffice, if it sought to maintain a specified number of units in inventory. But for a model that is intended to be valid over a longer run, sales might change substantially, and a constant inventory would no longer be appropriate. The policy for managing inventory might instead be cast in terms of a variable target inventory that would try to maintain inventory equal to a specified number of weeks of average sales. Weeks of sales covered by inventory is a more enduring parameter than an absolute level of desired inventory. In creating a structure of variables and the associated parameters, one must continuously decide what will be considered a variable and what a parameter.

In a system dynamics model, every parameter should have meaning in the real-life setting. Its numerical value should be discussable with operating people in that part of the real system where the parameter is relevant. A plausible range for each parameter can be initially estimated from field information. Then, simulation tests can help to refine a parameter value within its plausible range. A particular parameter is likely to influence primarily a single dynamic mode of the system and some specific behavior within that mode. Because two parameters seldom have the same effect on system behavior, a change in one parameter will not often substitute for a change in another parameter. Sensitivity testing, with results interpreted against a wide array of real-life data, tend to converge toward a rather well-defined set of parameters. Further sensitivity testing will usually show that a choice between policy alternatives is not likely to be affected by reasonable changes in parameters.

A preliminary determination of structure and parameters yields a model. But an initial model formulation is only the beginning of the system dynamics process. Model behavior is generated in the form of time-series data for as many of the model variables as one chooses to plot. The diversity of variables makes possible a multitude of comparisons between the model and the real system.

Model behavior can be compared with the many kinds of behavioral information from real life. Available information will include knowledge of logical possibilities. For example, real inventories do not go negative even though model inventories often

do in dynamic models with inadequate shipping functions. When such a finding is traced back to its cause in the model, a weakness is revealed, or an intended shortcut in model construction is shown to be unacceptable.

Time series data is used primarily in comparing the time-series output of a model with the time-series output of real life. Because of the way randomness in decision-making influences both the real world and a model of that real world, one does not expect model output and historical data to match on a point-by-point basis. Instead, one looks at the behavioral characteristics of the time-series data stream from the model and compares them with the corresponding characteristics of the real data. For example, what are the typical time lags in the business-cycle mode between variables and what is the statistical dispersion in those lags, or what are the relative amplitudes of fluctuation of different variables?

The comparison of real-world behavior with model behavior will reveal discrepancies. Each discrepancy must be evaluated to judge whether or not it justifies the time and effort to make a correction. Discrepancies become the sign posts that lead back through the prior stages of model formulation. The discrepancies create a new perspective from which to reevaluate the mental, written, and numerical data bases, to test parameters for their effect on behavior, and to modify structure so its behavior aligns better with the real system.

When a model has been judged satisfactory for its particular purpose, it can be used for policy analysis. A policy change, which is usually a parameter change in a policy statement, is made, and a new simulation run obtained. Behavior from the new policy is compared with behavior from the old policy to evaluate relative desirabilities of the policies.

When the model is put on a computer, the simulation results show that the model itself generates the same difficulty that prompted the modeling. In other words, the very policies people are intentionally following in the hope of solving the problem are sufficient, when interconnected, to cause the problem. The situation is deceptive. People believe they know the solution and act accordingly. They do not perceive that their actions are causing the problem. As the situation becomes worse, they apply more of the assumed solution, which makes matters still worse. A downward spiral can develop. Application of the policies worsens the situation, which in turn is taken as need for more vigorous application of the policies.

But no one perceives that the unfavorable consequences are being created by the ensemble of known and intended policies.

We embarked on the National Model expecting that well-known policies and

structures in industry and government would be found to create the observed economic difficulties. Such seems to be true. Quite ordinary managerial policies in industry can create business cycles and longer disturbances. National policies for perpetuating prosperity can accentuate major depressions . . . Inflation is being increased by policies intended to reduce inflation.

The National Model brings the structure and policies of the national economy into the laboratory where controlled experiments can be performed. As a replica of the economy, the National Model generates the broad range of behavior seen in the real economy. The model exhibits such realistic behavior without depending on exogenous inputs. By generating macroeconomic behavior from internal microstructure, the National Model shows how the many policies in industry, banking, and government interact to create troublesome behavior of the total socioeconomic system.

(We now proceed to Dr. Forrester's description of the three types of information—mental, written, and numerical-mentioned at the outset. Ed.)

Human affairs are conducted primarily from the mental data base. The mental data base is far more extensive than the other stores of information . . . If the mental data base is so important to the conduct of human systems, then I believe a model of such systems must reflect knowledge of policies and structure that resides only in the mental data. (For modeling purposes, mental information can be classified three ways: 1. Observations about structure and policy, 2. Expectations about system behavior, and 3. Actual observed system behavior.) The categories differ in reliability, and in their role in modeling.

The first category deals with why people act as they do, and how the parts of a social system are interconnected. The mental data base contains extensive information about policies and structures, the very things one wants to know to build a system dynamics model. The mental data base is rich in structural detail; in its knowledge of what information is available at various decision-making points, where people and goods move, and what decisions are made. The mental data base is especially concerned with policy, that is, why people respond as they do, what each decision-making center is trying to accomplish, what the perceived penalties and rewards of the specific social system are, and where self-interest clashes with institutional objectives.

The . . . mental information . . . about policy and structure is directly tapped for transfer into a system dynamics model. In general, the mental data base relating to policy and structure is reliable . . . The second category—the expectations about behavior—are intuitive solutions to the nonlinear, high-order systems of integral equations that reflect the structure and policies of real systems. Such intuitive solutions to complicated dynamic systems are usually wrong . . . the expectation arises from a judgmental simulation of a complex socioeconomic system. The third category of mental information is useful. It is about past experience with the actual system. From past behavior come the symptoms of difficulty that provide the motivation for a dynamic study, and for a model. After a model is operating, behavior of the model can be partially evaluated against knowledge of past episodes and behavioral characteristics of the real system.

The written data base contributes to a dynamic model at several stages. Part of the written store of information is simply a recording of information from the mental store. Another part of the written record contains concepts and abstractions that interpret other information sources . . . In its totality, the written record is an excellent source of information about system structure and the reasons for decisions . . . The temporal nature of a decision sharply restricts the kind of literature in which actual operating policy will be revealed. Decisions control action. Decisions are fleeting. There is only a single instant in time when one can act. That time is now.

As a consequence of the short life of a decision, it is primarily the literature of the present in which decisions are discussed in terms of goals, threats, limited information, and restraints on action . . . The professional literature emphasizes how decisions should be made rather than how they are made, how equilibrium is determined rather than how dynamic behavior arises, and how macroeconomic theory might apply rather than how the micro-structure creates the macrobehavior.

But the current business literature is not easy to use for model building. No single issue of a publication is meaningful by itself. The economic world keeps changing. At any one time, only a subset of possible inputs are important to a particular decision point. At one time, it may be high and rising inventories, at another time falling liquidity, and at still another time the need for more production capacity. Comprehensive policies, suitable for a model that will operate properly over a wide range of conditions, must embody all the considerations that can occur. To be useful, the literature must be pieced together, decisions must be interpreted into policies, and policies and structure must be perceived as causing modes of behavior that may extend over years or decades. One must read between the lines, and round out each picture with information from other times and places. It may be that such interpretation of the current business literature cannot be effectively done without first-hand knowledge of the mental data

base used by operators in business and politics. Such first-hand knowledge can be obtained only by living and working where the decisions are made, and by watching and talking with those who run the economic system.

The written record has two major shortcomings compared to the mental data from which the written data were taken: 1. Since it usually cannot be queried, it is not responsive to probing by the analyst as he searches for a fit between structure, policy, and behavior . . . 2. the information has been filtered through the perspective and purposes of the writer. His purpose may have been very different from that of a person seeking the internal causes of a particular dynamic behavior.

Part of the written data base deals with abstractions about structure. An example is the Cobb-Douglas production function. Closely related is the concept of marginal productivity of the factors of production. Such concepts are seldom explicitly recognized by practicing management, and would not emerge from discussions with those who make economic decisions. The fact that such important concepts are hidden from the practitioner leads to a fundamental issue in designing a system dynamics model.

There are processes that one believes important in real life but that do not enter explicitly into practical decision-making. Such processes play a role that is not directly visible. How are such hidden concepts to be handled in a dynamic model? The answer is that they should be included in the structure because they are believed to be real, but should be veiled from the decision points of the model as they are obscured in real life. Management does not know with assurance whether money would be spent most effectively for a production worker, a lathe, more raw inventory, a vice president, advertising, or another pilot for the executive jet. Yet, if marginal productivities are seriously out of balance, the underlying truth will gradually be perceived. It emerges from conflicting pleas, from crises, and from repetition of minor bits of evidence.

. . . the modeler must play a dual role in dealing with underlying fundamental concepts in the context of practical decision-making. On the one hand the model builder must act as an omniscient observer who puts into the model what must exist in real life. But on the other hand, he must degrade information about "true" conditions within the model before it is used in decision-making by the model, so as to approximate the distortion that occurs in the actual system.

The numerical data base is of narrower scope than the written and mental data bases. Missing from numerical data is direct evidence of the structure and policies that created the data. The numerical data does not reveal the cause-to-effect direction

between variables. From numerical data one can make statistical analyses to determine which time-series data streams correlate with one another, but that still leaves unanswered the question *of internal causality.* The numerical data base contains at least three bodies of information that are useful in modeling a national economy.

First, specific numerical information is available on some parameter values. For example, average delivery delay for filling orders exists in corporate records and summaries of business information. Typical ratios of factor inventories to production output can be found. Many normal values, around which variation occurs, are available, such as money balances, inventory coverage, and time to fill job vacancies.

Second, numerical information has been collected by many authors in the economics literature to summarize typical characteristics of economic behavior such as periodicities, and average phase relationships and their dispersions between variables in an economy.

Third, numerical information contains time-series data. In system dynamics modeling, time-series data is used much less as the basis for parameter values than in econometric models. But in system dynamics, the simulation model itself generates synthetic output time-series data that can be compared in a variety of ways with the real time-series data. . . . this independent use of time-series data for validating model behavior is less vulnerable to errors in the data than is the econometric use of data for trying to derive meaningful parameters ●

INDEX

142

NOTES

NOTES

NOTES

NOTES

NOTES

NOTES